ADVENTURES OF A
BALLAD HUNTER

FOCUS ON AMERICAN HISTORY SERIES

The Dolph Briscoe Center for American History

University of Texas at Austin
Don Carleton, Editor

BRISCOE CENTER

ADVENTURES
OF A
BALLAD
HUNTER

JOHN A. LOMAX

UNIVERSITY OF TEXAS PRESS

AUSTIN

Requests for permission to reproduce material
from this work should be sent to:
    Permissions
    University of Texas Press
    P.O. Box 7819
    Austin, TX 78713-7819
    utpress.utexas.edu/rp-form

The paper used in this book meets the minimum requirements of
ANSI/NISO Z39.48-1992 (R1997) (Permanence of Paper). ∞

Library of Congress Cataloging-in-Publication Data

Names: Lomax, John A. (John Avery), 1867–1948, author.
Title: Adventures of a ballad hunter / John A. Lomax.
Description: First University of Texas Press edition. |
    Austin : University of Texas Press, 2017. | Series: Focus
    on American history series | "Originally published in 1947
    by the Macmillan Company." | Includes index.
Identifiers: LCCN 2017010489
    ISBN 978-1-4773-1371-8 (pbk. : alk. paper)
    ISBN 978-1-4773-1372-5 (library e-book)
    ISBN 978-1-4773-1373-2 (non-library e-book)
Subjects: LCSH: Lomax, John A. (John Avery), 1867–1948. |
    Ethnomusicologists—United States—Biography. | Ballads,
    English—United States—History and criticism.
Classification: LCC ML429.L68 A3 2017 | DDC 781.62/130092
    [B] —dc23
LC record available at https://lccn.loc.gov/2017010489

doi:10.7560/313718

In Grateful and Affectionate Memory of
Professor Barrett Wendell
of Harvard University
Gallant Gentleman
Inspiring Teacher and Loyal Friend

CONTENTS

FOREWORD

John A. Lomax III, Anna Lomax Wood, and John Nova Lomax

One for the blackbird, one for the crow,
One for the cutworm, and two to grow.

This brief corn planting song, one of the first John Avery Lomax learned, also begins the original preface to *Adventures of a Ballad Hunter*. Published in 1947, the book has been out of print for decades. It vividly chronicles a toilsome Texas childhood, a marriage and family life filled with love, hilarity and tragedy, and John's collecting days, and includes portrayals of singers, lyrics of their songs, and the songs' context. John breezily touches the milestones of his fourscore years in an engaging, episodic style, with humility, wit, and not a few self-deprecatory jabs.

He takes us with him as he travels on foot, horseback, by wagon, boat, train, and in early automobiles down every dusty, teeth-rattling or mud-encrusted road, all for the sake of the songs and songsters he hoped to find and preserve.

He devotes abundant space to source singers and characters—to cowboys like Silver Jack and Big Jim Swanson, railroad workers like Henry Truvillion, and many prison inmates and officials. He relates his visits with Father Finnegan, who walked the last mile with 133 prisoners condemned to die in the electric chair. He introduces us to the "blind" man and his "gypsy" fortune-telling wife, Rose, who sang "Git Along Little Dogies."

John tells us about his longtime friend and folk-song lover Carl Sandburg, who played a key role during John's Chicago years, and about a meeting with rough-riding Teddy Roosevelt, who penned the foreword to *Cowboy Songs and Other Frontier Ballads*. This, John's first music book, was published in 1910 and later reprinted as *Cowboy Songs*.

John was expansive, entertaining, and greatly sentimental, with a wealth of amusing stories that were enriched by his varied experiences during his collecting years. Not all of his anecdotes made it into the pages of *Adventures of a Ballad Hunter*, including the time he stopped off to record a distant relation by marriage, Herman Weaver, singing "The Buffalo Skinners." Herman operated a lumber mill in Big Thicket, northwest of Beaumont, Texas. "The Buffalo Skinners," which now resides in the Library of Congress, was Herman's specialty. When John played it back, Herman was delighted and called for it over and over. By the time they had eaten supper and imbibed from a flask, and it was time for John to leave, Herman would have none of it. Suddenly, in the dim light John saw the gleam of shotguns as Herman, backed by old Littleton Weaver and Herman's ten-year-old son, barred his path. "No, John, you ain't leavin' till I give you the go ahead," said Herman. "I ain't done listening to my song!" John remained as a guest for four days.

John was born on September 23, 1867, near Goodman, in rural north-central Mississippi, but he grew up on the Texas frontier along a branch of the Chisholm Trail. The family set out by oxcart from Holmes County, Mississippi, before John's second birthday. They settled outside Meridian, in a part of Texas still subject to Comanche raids, close by the Brazos River, where the cotton-rich blackland prairies meet the western cedar-studded crags of the Hill Country.

It was there that his love of American folk song—as sung by both blacks and whites—took root. His interest was nurtured by the songs of passing cowboys and by his closest friend, Nat Blythe, an eighteen-year-old former slave his father had hired as a farmhand. Blythe quickly became a surrogate brother to nine-year-old John and his siblings.

John describes much of his childhood as one of grueling labor in the fields. His father James Avery Lomax made shoes for the Confederate army during the Civil War and established a small farm after they arrived in Texas. James was illiterate, fathered twenty-one children by two wives, and was given to frequent bouts of hellfire Methodism. James's second wife and John's mother, Susan Cooper Lomax, homeschooled her children and read to them from the Bible and John Bunyan's *Pilgrim's Progress*, the first book John said he read in its entirety. But John's "Boyhood in Bosque," a 1944 remembrance that dwells on aspects of his early years, seemingly borrowed from *The Adventures of Huckleberry Finn*, in which Blythe, for three formative years, played no small part.

To the children's delight it was Blythe who devised a method of extorting a little sugar for his butter-biscuits at dinnertime from their petty, tyrannical, older brother Richard; Blythe who was the lynchpin in the human pyramid that was the pièce de résistance of the "Lomax Circus Extraordinary." And it was Blythe who was the star pupil of "Mulberry Academy," an ad hoc school the children created under a mulberry tree.

Under the shade of that tree John taught Blythe to read and write, and he passed along what basic math, history, and geography he himself possessed. Blythe taught John to sing field hollers and play Juba, or "Hambone," a shouting, thigh-slapping, arm-patting dance originally from West Africa and known throughout the Caribbean and the American South. "From Nat I learned my sense of rhythm," John wrote. "He danced rather than walked. When he slapped his big friendly hands against his thighs they almost sang a tune. If he stopped chanting:

Oh, rabbit skipped and rabbit hopped,
Oh, rabbit eat my turnip top,
Oh, rabbit, rabbity hash—

and kept on patting, you forgot the song and listened absorbed to the speaking rhythm of his hands. . . . He taught me many jig tunes, like

> Big yam potatoes in sandy land,
> Sandy bottom, sandy land,

. . . I came to love Nat with the fierce strength and loyalty of youth."

Imagine thirteen-year-old John Avery in 1881, easing out of the family homestead as the rest of the Lomaxes slept, lured from his bed by the voices of unseen cowboys, singing their songs in the flickering firelight of the central Texas night. He wanted to get closer to the cowboys, the better to hear their songs. Sometimes they sang to soothe their herds as they traveled up a nearby fork of the Chisholm Trail. During cowboy "office hours" young John might hear a "crooning yodel" ripple through the stillness of the night, "most like the coyote; only restful and not wild." It might have been followed by lullabies like this verse from "Night-Herding Song":

> O, say, little dogies, when you goin' to lay down
> And quit this forever a-siftin' around?
> My legs are weary, my seat is sore;
> O, lay down dogies, like you've laid down before—
> Lay down, little dogies, lay down.

Other times the cowboys came roaring out of Meridian's Road to Ruin saloon, "a-howlin', loose at both ends and goin' somewhere," and bellowing drunken declarations you might expect to hear from modern-day outlaw bikers, songs like the lesser-known:

> We're the children of the open and we hate the haunts of men,
> But we had to come to town to get the mail;
> And we're ridin' home at daybreak, 'cause the air is cooler then,
> All 'cept one of us who stopped behind in jail.

Shorty's nose won't bear paradin', Bill's off eye is darkly fadin'
And our toilets show a touch of disarray;
For we found that city life is a constant round of strife
And we ain't the breed for shyin' from a fray.

Chant your war whoop, pardners dear, while the east turns pale
    with fear
And the chaparral is tremblin' all around
We're the sons of desolation, we're the outlaws of creation,
A-ridin' up the rocky road from town.

At home, and up one such rocky road, John began writing down the words to the songs he heard. Lacking musical training and books to guide him, he created his own system for remembering their melodies.

John began his advanced education in 1887. In a heart-wrenching moment he describes selling his favorite pony, Selim, to finance his first courses at Granbury College, the closest institution of higher education. After a few years of study and teaching in rural schools, he entered the University of Texas in 1895. Compensating for his late start in academia, he took a double course load, including Greek, Latin, and Anglo-Saxon. The Victorian poets and novelists, Tennyson and Browning, first encountered at Granbury, made an indelible impression on him. In them he found a reflection of his own love of language coupled with the vagaries of the human character.

Looking back, the turning point of his life came not from his UT colleagues but when he obtained a grant to attend Harvard as a graduate student in English literature in 1906. He studied with Barrett Wendell and world-renowned scholar George Lyman Kittredge, who encouraged students to get out into the field. For Kittredge the cowboy songs John had been transcribing opened a door into an unknown America. "Go and get this material while it can be found," he told the young Texan. "Preserve the words and music. That's your job."

Preserve them he did, in "Arkansas mountain cabins, Mississippi prison farms, New Orleans saloons, Minnesota lumber camps and

Texas cattle camps," as the original press release noted. *Adventures of a Ballad Hunter* describes how he first discovered and recorded the Western classics "Home on the Range," "Git Along Little Dogies," and the ballads of the outlaws Sam Bass and Jesse James.

It also details the second phase of his collecting career, featuring his discovery of the songs of black convicts such as Lead Belly, James "Iron Head" Baker, and "Clear Rock." (Readers interested in John Avery Lomax's relationship with Lead Belly and others are encouraged to read Nolan Porterfield's *Last Cavalier* as well as *Negro Folk Songs as Sung by Lead Belly*, John and Alan Lomax's 1936 chronicle.)

John's recordings, however, were hardly limited to cowboy songs and Southern prison laments. He found and presented Appalachian ballads, banjo and fiddle tunes, fife and drum selections, country blues, sea chanteys, field hollers, spirituals, children's game and play songs, toasts, stories, tall tales, lullabies, and interviews. He recorded the bargemen of the Erie Canal and the Hispanics of the Southwest. The 1930s recordings he and his son Alan made in Louisiana gave impetus to the Cajun revival of the 1970s. All of these widely varying narratives provided vital glimpses of the times and the people living in them, creating a cultural mosaic for others to study.

John provides fascinating accounts of his fieldwork technique and enlivens his narrative with verses from the songs and dialogue with his sources as often as not in the vernacular. His explorations took him to thirty-three states, down hundreds of roads on which he sometimes returned to visit those who had become friends. He takes us with him on these travels, describing in elegant and charming detail a cast of song-contributing originals and their surroundings— characters like Richard Amerson who swears he always tells the truth "except when I'm alone or with other people." We meet "Iron Head" Baker who, like Lead Belly, traveled with John for two months. Iron Head lived most of his life behind bars and was destined to die there following his seventh conviction for theft as he just couldn't resist "a little mo' porch-climbin'."

Adventures of a Ballad Hunter is not a travel book by any means though John certainly does some hard travelling. Like Paul Theroux, he also displays an interest in conversing with those he encounters, leaving us to enjoy those exchanges. He listens, really *listens* to what people say and displays the same warmth and civility to the convicts as he does to the wardens. His enthusiasm to hear the songs, his excitement, are apparent on every page. Just imagine the effect he had on everyone he met. Once he became officially connected to the Library of Congress and its Archive of American Folk Song he became known as "the man from Washington."

Anyone reading his account will be amazed by John's determination to accomplish the tasks he set for himself and the effort required to do so. For example, his 1933 trip with eighteen-year-old son Alan to gather material for *American Ballads and Folk Songs* encompassed four months, during which they drove 16,000 miles. John was sixty-five then, had recently lost his wife as well as his job at the Republic Bank, and was battling health problems.

They set out in a Ford Model A with a near quarter-ton recording machine built into the trunk, a piece of gear whose batteries weighed seventy-five pounds. That vehicle also carried the aluminum discs they used to record the music, their cots and other camping and cooking gear, their clothes, maps, and the equipment needed to repair the recording machine and their vehicle.

They suffered automobile breakdowns, recording machine malfunctions, and illnesses, including malaria with fevers of up to 104.5 degrees. Father and son slept under the stars many nights, sometimes in the yards of those they were recording, other times by the roadside, there being few "tourist courts" then.

The journey in Texas traveling the many farm-to-market roads and dirt byways often limited them to today's school zone speeds. That alone would be remarkable if they simply *drove* those many thousands of miles. But the two Lomaxes stopped often in their work to find the singers, explain their mission, and socialize, while unpacking and setting up the recording equipment; then they had to conduct the session, disassemble, and repack everything. It was all done in health and in sickness, throughout the heat of the summer, eighteen-hour day succeeding eighteen-hour day.

During his many travels John was accompanied variously by Alan, for a short spell by Lead Belly, and for many years by his second wife and resourceful field assistant, Ruby "Deanie" Terrill, who, enlightened as she was, never ceased to be mortified when he bellowed "Miss Terrill!" in hotel lobbies and other public places.

John was named National Advisor on Folklore and Folkways for the Federal Writers Project in 1936. His interviews helped to motivate the collection of former slave narratives for the FWP (1936–1938). "The WPA project to interview former slaves assumed a form and a scope that bore John's imprint and reflected his experience and zeal as a collector of folklore," wrote sociologist Norman R. Yetman, in *Voices From Slavery: 100 Authentic Slave Narratives*.

John coauthored *Our Singing Country* with Alan Lomax and Ruth Crawford Seeger in 1941, an innovative compendium of folk music containing precise transcriptions of the recorded performances by Seeger. In all, John wrote or coauthored five books on American folk songs.

He lived the last two decades of his life in "the house in the woods," on San Benito Way near White Rock Lake in the Forest Hills section of Dallas. The four-bedroom, L-shaped ranch house was built around a patio with a backyard that fell off into dense woods and the Union Pacific railroad tracks. He kept the front yard au naturel, what might be called xeriscaping today: riot-run with oak, elm, and pecan trees, bushes, ivy, and ferns. A gravel driveway wound through the trees for about a hundred feet before reaching the street. He called it his "anchorage."

Family lore has it that famed naturalist and longtime friend Roy Bedichek came to visit for a few days. The two men solemnly agreed that they would not discuss politics during the visit, as Roy was a New Deal Democrat and John, despite his musical populism, a rock-ribbed Republican. The men stuck to their pact until Roy began backing out of the narrow, twisty driveway. His erstwhile host walked beside the car, cursing Roosevelt every foot of the way.

Just a year following this book's original publication in 1947, John suffered a massive heart attack while at a press conference/

"come-all-ye" gathering in Greenville, Mississippi, the night before "John Lomax Day." He was recently reunited with Alan (they had been out of touch for many months), and was in full celebratory mode when he suddenly collapsed into a coma. He lived long enough for Deanie and oldest son John Jr. to be with him when he died on January 26, 1948.

John was a bridge between the oral tradition of passing songs from person to person in real time, to a new era in which musical and poetic moments are preserved forever by technology. Each new generation can rediscover the songs and stories that John and his fellow folklorists collected in those early days—snapshots of a time beyond our remembrance.

Without John we may have lost forever "Goodbye, Old Paint," "The Old Chisholm Trail," "Rock Island Line," and "In the Pines," which he introduced to Lead Belly, as well as Vera Hall's "Boll Weevil Blues" and "Another Man Done Gone." They and many others became part of our culture and thus live on. Without these songs and the past we can visualize and intuit through them, our sense of who we are as Americans would be impoverished.

Setting forth on horseback in 1908 with his Edison phonograph and wax cylinders, John was one of the very first to travel about the nation making field recordings of the songs and stories of America. Though he is long gone, the folk songs he recorded live on, many of their singers celebrated today. We are thankful for his perseverance, his commitment to the cowboys, farmhands, jokers, card sharks, hustlers, levee workers, stevedores, lonesome riders, and the men and women who lived out their days on state-run plantations and county farms. For him, these were the bards who sang the many stories of America.

PREFACE

One for the blackbird, one for the crow,
One for the cutworm, and two to grow.

Years ago I used to chant this rhyme as I dropped seed corn into a freshly turned furrow. I followed close behind a scooter, pulled by two sturdy mules that ripped open a trench in the warm earth. Even in the early morning the soft, moist loam felt friendly to my bare feet.

One plowboy and team opened a furrow, another plowboy and team followed to cover up the corn, while I, younger and smaller than the other field hands, walking between the two teams, dropped the seed corn close behind the plow that opened the land. A tin bucket full of grains swung from my left hand, holding every color—white and yellow and speckled and red. We picked the longest ears and planted only the fully-grown kernels. Plant full-grown seed from big ears, and you'll reap big ears, said my wise old father.

With my free right hand I would reach for a handful of corn from the bucket; then, as I walked along the furrow, I would let the grains slip through my fingers down alongside my bare leg, a steady trickle of color, one and one, and one and two: two kernels for the fowls of the air, one for the burrowing worm, two to fill wagonloads of corn for our log cribs. Backward and forward across the broad field went this group—two teams, two plows, and one chanting barefoot boy:

Whistle and hoe,
Sing as you go;
Shorten the rows
By the songs you know.

All through the day, though my hands grew tired (I plunged them deep into the cool, shiny grains when we stopped for a moment at the turnrow), my legs ached and my feet grew heavy, I would bolster my courage with jingles, chanting the old rhymes. For long before sundown a six-year-old boy drooped from weariness. Scattered over the field were flocks of blackbirds and crows, a line of them almost filling the freshly opened furrows, scratching busily for worms and their share of the seed; while Brother Cutworm he "lay low," waiting for the corn to sprout, for tender shoots to push upward on which he could feast.

Just as I dropped corn when I was a six-year-old boy, blindly trusting the chance of wind and rain and sunshine, openly paying tribute to the known enemies of growing corn, the blackbird, the crow, the cutworm, so in some such way have I put together *The Adventures of a Ballad Hunter*. I kept few notes during the more than thirty years wherein I was on the lookout for folk songs. I write from memory, from letters and from some stories cut into records.

All my life I have been interested in the songs of the people—the intimate poetic and musical expression of unlettered people, from which group I am directly sprung. In my boyhood we sang songs around our fireside on winter evenings in a home where the library consisted of *Pilgrim's Progress* and the Bible. At work and at play folk songs were my mental food. I began early to set down the words; later the music also. And now the Library of Congress houses records of more than ten thousand tunes placed there by my son, Alan, and myself.

In 1934 at the close of the annual meeting of the Modern Language Association in Philadelphia, Professor S. B. Hustvedt of the University of California at Los Angeles urged me to set down the story of my experiences as a ballad collector. A day or so previously

I had appeared before the Division of Popular Literature with the Negro, Lead Belly, a paroled convict from the Louisiana penitentiary. I translated the words of the Negro's songs each time before he sang. His dramatic rendition of raw folk songs shocked his hearers into attention.

Professor Hustvedt, perhaps, thought that more of my encounters had been as romantic as the finding of Lead Belly when a convict. He declared that my experiences had been unique, that the detailed story of my search might prove helpful to other collectors. He set me to thinking about what I should tell and what I should omit in case I did attempt to relive ballad-collecting journeys, half a million miles or so, that I have taken into all the states except North Dakota. The tale has turned out to be tortuous and long, quite enough to fill half a dozen volumes.

Choosing the incidents reminded me of my corn-planting days. Some of the seed that looked most promising turned out to be fit only for blackbirds, crows and cutworms. Moreover, I have lost some of the confident hope of the barefoot boy who trusted two kernels would grow into kingly stalks burdened with hanging ears of corn.

A ballad collector meets many people, the real people, the plain people, devoid of tinsel and glamour, some base, a few suspicious and surly, many beautifully kind. And many are the stories they tell. From the thousands I may choose only a few. The reader will find herein no theories about ballad origins or parallels. That task is for others. I have merely taken some pictures from my files and rearranged them in story form. I have made another book; though not the book my friend, Professor Hustvedt, had in mind.

In Texas we call land, grubbed of stumps, freshly broken and cultivated for the first time, "new ground." On such virgin land the first crop is usually bountiful. There have been many ballad hunters. I have heard of no one who has attempted to fill a book with stories of his search. My trail has been longer than most, both in miles and in years. In so far, then, I cultivate new ground.

ADVENTURES OF A
BALLAD HUNTER

1

BOYHOOD IN BOSQUE

My family belonged to the upper crust of the "po' white trash," traditionally held in contempt by the aristocracy of the Old South and by their Negro slaves. Father always owned a few acres of land, which kept him from being at the bottom of the social scale. However, his brother, whose wife inherited a large cotton plantation and a swarm of slaves, lived close enough so that Father's family was sneered at as poor kinfolk.

During the Civil War this brother organized and became captain of a Home Guard Company in which my father was a fifty-year-old private. Later the Confederate Government detailed Father, his rheumatic eldest son, and a group of Negro slaves to tan leather and make shoes for Southern soldiers. My uncle resented this action. Recently, it has been found that the Confederate records on file in Washington show that opposite Father's name on the roster of the "Guards," my uncle wrote in his final report, "Deserter." Both my father and his brother had been dead fifty years when this record was uncovered, though, happily, it was not too late to find abundant evidence to prove that the charge was utterly false. This strange, unbrotherly stab in the back remains a mystery. The unfriendly attitude of his brother may help explain why Father soon after the Civil War determined to come to Texas, although he always said it was "to give my boys room to expand."

From the Black River country of Mississippi, a hundred miles north of Jackson, to our home on the Bosque river in Texas, we moved a distance of five hundred miles. We started west in August, 1869, when I was only two years old, one of our covered wagons dragged by two mules, Jack and Fan, the other by two oxen, Bright and Berry, and it was near Christmas when we saw the cedar-covered hills of Bosque County. When past eighty my mother (who lived to be ninety-four) wrote the story of the trip:

We wanted to come to a new place so our children could grow up with the country. I came willing (my husband said he could live ten years longer in Texas); and I have never regretted it one moment, but oh, how sorry I was to leave our Mississippi home where six of my children were born; four came with us, two were left back in Shady Grove graveyard . . . I have never been back to see the first home I ever had. . . .

There was a line of wagons before us, I think a mile long, waiting to be put across the Mississippi River by ferry. All these folks were coming to Texas. . . . Through the swamps there was bad muddy places, the kind that stick like tar. One evening we came to the worst place we had struck. . . . The mules pulled, pulled, surged, struggled, almost pulling their shoes off. Their feet would pop as loud as a pistol. . . . They unhitched the oxen, drove them in and hitched them to the wagon. They just walked out easy with the wagon because they had cloven feet and the mud does not stick to their feet. . . .

The men and boys had guns and dogs and would go hunting and never failed to bring in some kind of game. Once they dressed a coon. Some ate it, not I though. . . .

When we sold out our household things, cows, horses, mules, with our land, we had about four thousand dollars in gold. It was given to me to take care of. I made a broad belt, sewed in two rows of twenty-dollar gold pieces. I was to wear it around my waist. I found I could not do it, for it was too heavy. We had a willow basket that held a half-bushel. I tied the belt to one handle, laid it down on the bottom, and tied the other end to the other handle. I never felt so uneasy. It was put right beside me at night. I have waked up many times and felt for the basket. Sometimes when I felt uneasy I would raise the cover and put it under close by my side. . . .

We finally got to a place in Texas now called Morgan. It was then the Nichols place. Then on to Dr. Russell's on Steel's Creek. I remember well what a dinner we had. There was a large dish filled with turnips and the greens cooked together with a large square of beef that looked exactly like streaked bacon. I thought it was the best thing I had ever tasted, so I handed my plate for a second helping. When we went to leave, Dr. Russell went out, climbed up a live-oak tree, took down a shoulder of meat and put it in the wagon. . . .

Dr. Russell killed a wild turkey soon after we got here that weighed twenty pounds dressed. We could hear the turkeys gobble every morning just before day. We bought a beef weighing 800 pounds for seven dollars. We had pork but no dainties. I made all my own soap. I did all my own washing, made all the clothes for the family. Kept them clean. They never went with holes in their clothes or stockings. . . . Women, they stayed at home and did the work. I would work hours at night after I had put my little children to bed. Sometimes I could do more at night than I could in daytime.

At the time we moved to Texas the rich black lands of Navarro and Hill counties were selling at fifty cents an acre. My father, reared on a creek where water and timber were plentiful, preferred to pay six dollars an acre for bottom land which had to be grubbed of thick trees before a plow could turn the soil. But his boys were numerous, and they did the job during a long period of back-breaking years. We went down into the soil around the trees with mattock and grubbing hoe, and cut the taproots, sometimes two feet below the surface.

Our home was on the big road north of Meridian, a sort of Broadway, leading from Waco up the Bosque valley to the vast northwest section of Texas. Along this road traveled settlers in covered wagons, herds of horses, cattle, sheep (in later years), and many men on horseback. Buggies and carriages were seldom seen. Frequently travelers spent the night in our home. I can still feel the thrill at hearing some belated person, late at night, down at the big front gate, shouting amid the barking of dogs, "Hello! Hello!" The big, outside world was knocking at our door.

I hunted and fished, went in swimming, and lived with my kind—Frank and Tom Gandy, Joe and Harvey Francis, Billy Dysart, Sherman Graves, John Hornsby. John Cochran, a relative by marriage, was the only "town boy" I was comfortable with.

Frank Gandy lived on a high bluff on the opposite side of the Bosque from our farm. He and I developed a long-distance speaking code or call of recognition, which we shouted, to each other back and forth across the river. At dawn or dusk we could make the call carry clearly a mile or more:

Whoo—ee, whoo—ee-e, whoo-oo-oo
Whoo—ee, whoo—ee-e, whoo-oo-oo
Whoo-oo-oo

For us it meant, "Good morning, Johnny" or "Good night, Frank."

Before the soil from cultivated fields sealed up the wayside springs, stopped the flow of small creeks running from the hills to the river, covered with mud the gleaming white shoals scattered along the river bed, and turned the water from glistening silver to brackish brown, the Bosque river was a beautiful stream. In those days it ran clear and clean down a valley screened in by chains of cedar-clad hills. Along its banks grew overhanging willows, sycamores, cottonwoods, elm, hackberry and other trees. From some high point a traveler, seeing the ribbon of green that fringed the stream, named it Bosque, which means wooded. And as I galloped my pony, Selim, over unfenced meadows, carpeted with wild flowers, the beauty of the region grew into my soul.

In July and August, when it was hot and the crops were laid by, the churches, especially the Methodist Church, would hold "camp meetings," open-air services under brush arbors. Zealous Methodists would grudgingly admit that a person could get to Heaven without joining that church, but it was mighty risky. Our campgrounds were located on Spring Creek, ten miles over the mountain from where we lived. The permanent improvements for a place of worship consisted of forked posts set into the ground with connecting crisscross poles over the top, on which each year were spread freshly cut branches. The seats were puncheons (split logs resting on long pegs) or planks laid across logs. A dry goods box often served as a pulpit, surrounded by the mourners' benches where the penitents came at the urging of the preacher to be prayed and sung over as their friends whispered words of instruction and advice.

The campers—often entire families, with their dogs, horses, mules, and chickens—drove in from many miles around, and camped in open clearings or under live-oaks. Usually a camp meeting lasted eight or ten days, through two consecutive Sundays. During this time the women cooked over campfires and served meals on makeshift tables. Darkness provided the only privacy. Late to bed and early to rise was the rule. "Camp meetings," the men used to say, "are hell on women but paradise for children and dogs."

We were earnest folk and we worked hard at our religion, particularly at camp meetings. Besides the three regular services each day, we had sunset or "grove meetings" where the men and women in separate groups held prayer and song services. Often we added an "experience" meeting where each person told publicly how the Lord had helped him amid the trials and tribulations of frontier life. When Uncle Ben Cooper got "happy" and shouted at the top of his voice, "Whoopee! Hurrah for Jesus! Bully for Christ! Whoopee!" no one was shocked.

The singing played a tremendous part. The preacher thundered his Sam Jones plea to "quit your meanness"; then, generally underscored by an "exhorter," he invited mourners to come to the altar. The congregation sang:

I am bound for the Promised Land,
I am bound for the Promised Land,
Oh, who will come and go with me?
I am bound for the Promised Land!

Alas, and did my Savior bleed
And did my Sovereign die?
Did he devote that Sacred Head
For such a worm as I?

Brother Levi Harris, not much of a preacher, though he could "sing religion into a Comanche Indian," usually led the singing. Between songs the most devout among the laymen were invited to pray for the mourners, that their hard hearts be touched so that their sins might be forgiven. Frank's father was "powerful in prayer" and was often called on to pray at climactic moments when a little extra urging was needed. I remember one striking statement: "Oh, Lord," he would plead, "finger around their heartstrings with the finger of Thy love."

One camp meeting time Frank and I were left at home to care for the chickens and stock, milk the cows night and morning, and every couple of days ride horseback across the mountains to carry food to our families. One night we got within hearing of the campgrounds when the meeting had reached its high pitch. Our horses were loaded down with sacks of roasting ears, buckets of butter and eggs, bunches of chickens tied together by the legs and swung behind our saddles, and other provisions. The preacher and the exhorter had both spoken, the invitation to the mourners' bench had been given, the singing was in full swing. We stopped our horses and listened. Down the hollow, high above the sweep of the song, came the cries of one of the mourners, deeply convicted of sin, shouting his woes to heaven.

"Oh, Lord," he cried over and over again, "I never told a lie, I can prove it by Joe and Bill Thompson." (Joe and Bill Thompson were highly respected and well-to-do churchmen and farmers who lived in the Spring Creek community.)

"Oh, Lord, I never swore an oath, I can prove it by Joe and Bill Thompson; oh, Lord, I never stole a cow, I can prove it by Joe and Bill Thompson . . ."

On and on went the category of denials: he had never cut a barbed wire fence, he had never shot a man, he had never stolen his neighbor's wife, and he had the Thompson brothers as witnesses to prove it.

Frank and I sat quietly in the darkness and listened to the wailings of this stricken soul. We couldn't see the torch lamps about the brush arbor; we couldn't see the faces of the passionately earnest souls who wanted to help him unload his weighting sins. But we respected the sincerity of the mourner just as we respected the honest zeal of the earnest helpers who knelt around him and tried to point out the safe road that leads "way over to the Promised Land." Yes, these people really meant it when they sang:

Brother, will you meet me in the Promised Land?
Oh, Brother, will you meet me in the Promised Land?
I hope one day we'll all get there,
'Way over in the Promised Land.

⚶

Come, butter, come; come, butter, quick;
For old Aunt Kate's a-waitin' at the gate
For a piece of Johnny cake.
Come, butter, come!

So I once chanted as I pulled the dasher up and down inside the tall wooden churn. The flub-flub as the dasher hit bottom, the raucous whir of the coffee mill, the shriek for grease of the wooden axle of the ox-wagon, and the whine of the homemade grindstone are among the almost forgotten sounds of frontier life. I was already tired one morning when the sound of the grindstone reached me. I rushed to the back yard where, under a mulberry tree by the smokehouse, a handsome black boy was turning the sandstone slab as my father pressed down an axe on its whirling surface.

"You've lost your job," said my father. The Negro smiled at me.

So I met Nat Blythe, and a three-year friendship began. He was eighteen, I nine. Nat was an infant when his mother died. She left him a bond servant to Colonel Blythe until he was twenty-one. That same day at noon, I found Nat resting under the mulberry tree studying a Webster's blue-backed spelling book. He was as far as "Ba-be-bi-bo."

He became my first pupil. During the long hot summer our midday sessions lasted three or four hours under the shade of the mulberry tree. Several neighbor children joined the Mulberry Academy, but Nat was my star pupil. At the end of the final term of the three-year course he was through the fifth reader, he had studied history and geography and arithmetic, and he could write a good letter.

Whenever we came in from the field for water from the well we next went to the kitchen for sandwiches of cold biscuits and butter, Occasionally Richard, the oldest boy, would dare to get a bit of sweetening from the wooden sugar bucket.

"Mr. Richard, please give me some sugar," Nat would whisper.

"No."

"Please, Mr. Richard."

"Shut up. No."

"Mr. Richard, if you don't give me some sugar, I'm goin' to tell Miss Susan." ("Miss Susan" was my mother.)

No sugar.

"Miss Susan!" Softly, then louder and louder Nat would call until catastrophe was averted by a generous helping of the forbidden sugar.

A circus caravan passed along the Big Road, a single elephant and several camels plodding among the wagons, a calliope bringing up the rear. Tremendous excitement among the five Lomax boys and Nat, at work in the adjoining field! When we got back from the circus the next day, up went an acting pole in the back yard, a trapeze in a near-by giant live-oak tree; the piles of bagasse from our cane mill served as landing place for daring somersaults. We formed living pyramids, three stories high, with the youngest, Robert, at the peak, giant Nat as the key man in the center, all five boys festooned around him. In time we could reproduce nearly every feat we had seen at the circus. We organized the *Lomax Circus Extraordinary*. Nat was our star. As he ran to the field he would turn handsprings and flips along the path. He learned to do the giant swing on the acting pole; his feats on the flying trapeze were the talk of the countryside. One day I saw him driving a fence-breaking cow from the field, standing erect and barefooted on his bareback horse, yelling at the top of his voice. He held the long bridle reins in his teeth and used his arms for balancing.

From Nat I learned my sense of rhythm. He danced rather than walked. When he slapped his big friendly hands against his thighs they almost sang a tune. If he stopped chanting

Oh, rabbit skipped and rabbit hopped,
Oh, rabbit eat my turnip top,
Oh, rabbit, rabbity hash—

and kept on patting, you forgot the song and listened absorbed to the speaking rhythm of his hands. Sometimes he dropped into the quicker movement of

Juba dis and Juba dat,
Oh, Juba killed a yaller cat,
Oh, Juba! Juba! Juba!

and his feet would back-step or double-shuffle in time with his hands in such enthusiastic abandon that all of us would join in the patting and dancing. He taught me many jig tunes, like

Big yam potatoes in sandy land,
Sandy bottom, sandy land,

or another with a more graceful swing:

Up Red Oak and down Salt Water,
Some old man gonna lose his daughter.
Oh, my pretty little black-eyed Susan.
Oh, my pretty little black-eyed Susan.

I came to love Nat with the fierce strength and loyalty of youth. The day he was twenty-one Colonel Blythe handed him his savings of more than a thousand dollars, and Nat took me to town and had two pictures of me made, one for himself. I still have mine.

I have never since seen or heard of him. His Negro friends think he was murdered for his money, and his body, bound with baling wire and weighted down with scrap iron, thrown into the Bosque River. As I have traveled up and down the South these recent years, I find myself always looking for Nat, the dear friend and companion of long ago. I loved him as I have loved few people.

At thirteen I was "converted" under a brush arbor built back of the one-room Grapevine schoolhouse, three miles north of Meridian. Under the camp meeting code my age and experience entitled me to sit on a back seat where the lights were dim. One night Danna Moore, several years older than I, came and sat down close by me during the mourning period and rubbed her cheek against mine. I found the sensation pleasant. Up to that time I cannot recall any other sin I had committed, nor do I think that experience influenced my con-version. Perhaps my mother led me to make my first and only trip to the mourners' bench, together with the emotional appeal of Brother Levi Harris' singing. Anyhow, I remember that between stanzas he kept urging all the unsaved to come up and have their sins forgiven. Somehow, I got up to the altar. When I knelt in the straw and pushed my doubled-up fists into my eyes I felt no twinges of conscience for the sins that were supposed to rest heavily on me. I did not cry or pray, I only felt sorry for myself. When one of the helpers whispered to me to "trust in the Lord, give yourself wholly into His keeping," I was not helped a bit. I simply did not know what she meant. But I did know that I was embarrassed and anxious to put an end to the ordeal. Near me I could hear my mother praying as if she were in deep trou-ble. I had never heard her pray before, and it hurt me to know that I was the source of her grief. End it I must as soon as I could.

Presently Brother Harris asked all who felt that they had been saved to stand up. Instantly, I rose to my feet. Brother Harris shook my hand; my mother seemed happy. I was greatly relieved that I could get out of such a public place, that I never would have to go to the mourners' bench again. Soon afterward I joined the church and "renounced the vain pomp and glory of the world, and the carnal desires of the flesh, so that I would not follow or be led by them." Again, in an agony of self-consciousness, I had to be the center of many eyes. The strange experience left me in a mental daze. When this ceremony was over and I was at home again, I went out to the lot where my pony was sunning himself, put Selim's head over my shoulder, leaned against him and promised that, since I was a Christian and belonged to the church, I would never again ride him with a curb bit or strike him with a quirt. And that night I fed my favorite pet chicken an extra big supper.

Life in Bosque was hard—both in work and in play. Religion was of the hellfire and damnation brand. "Lost! Lost! Lost!" was the cry that filled hearts and souls with terror.

> There is a fountain filled with blood,
> Drawn from Immanuel's veins,
> And sinners plunged beneath that flood
> Lose all their guilty stains,

sang loud and lusty voices. To me it was a gory picture. Often I awoke at night from a nightmare, dreaming that I myself was immersed in a pool of blood, oceans of blood. Against this background of ideas my father and mother must have worked out the rigid rules of conduct they imposed on their children. I cannot remember, however, that I ever felt rebellious. I never flatly disobeyed them on any important issue. We children never played games on Sunday, not even marbles, frog-in-the-middle, mumble peg, roley-holey, antny-over, one-eyed cat, town ball, stink base or bull pen. We could pick up pecans that had fallen to the ground, but we could not climb trees and shake more down. We couldn't pull out a catfish from a set hook that happened to be left out over Sunday, nor could we swim in the silvery Bosque.

Throughout the week we were busy at work on the farm; so our free time for recreation was scant. Sometimes we got Saturday afternoon off for swimming or pecan gathering. But the winter nights were long and on week-ends our friends often came to stay all night, and we could return such visits. The three or four winter months that we went to school gave us our real playtime for outdoor games. But this lack of freedom aroused our inventiveness for indoor amusements. Each family had its stock of riddles and rhymes. Groups musically inclined sang songs and swapped stories with each other.

About the only common meeting place for the country and town folks (and this was only for the men) was the saloon. These "poor man's clubs" were about as numerous in Bosque County as filling stations are today. One of them that I remember bore the brutally frank name of "The Road to Ruin." Over at Eulogy (some of its citizens say it should, be called Apology) a saloon had this sign on the wall: "Spit on the ceiling. Anybody can spit on the floor." Through the winters on Saturday the saloons did a big business. Someone said that bartenders were as thick in Bosque County as the proverbial fiddlers in purgatory. The gang of wild buckaroos from the country, led by Bob Hanna, who had been up the trail, habitually rode into town to tighten their belts with a few good drinks. Throughout the day and far into the night they played pool, rattled dice, drank and fought. I used to lie awake as they came past our house, "a-howlin', loose at both ends and goin' somewhere." Bob Hanna and his merry crew, soused to the gills, were riding out of town:

> We're the children of the open and we hate the haunts of men,
> But we had to come to town to get the mail;
> We're the sons of desolation, we're the outlaws of creation,
> A-ridin' up the rocky road from town.

The tournaments (everybody called them toonaments) of the Texas cowboys helped crystallize my interest in their songs. The six-foot lances, carried by the riders at top speed, were not pointed at an enemy, but at five small rings hanging from the arms of upright posts strung fifty yards apart along a track two hundred yards in length. Each "knight" rode down the track three times, and a perfect score meant that the rider must thread on his lance all fifteen rings, and take no more than twelve seconds for each ride. The prizes were three wreaths of prairie flowers, which would be worn proudly by the chosen ladies. I remember one tournament as if it were yesterday.

At the end of a large glade stood the judges' platform where later in the evening the dance would be held. The rough uprights were wrapped in gayly colored bunting, and flags fluttered overhead. Men and women—the women on sidesaddles with long riding skirts of flashing colors nearly sweeping the ground—rode singly or in pairs across the field. Scattered among them were the contending knights, broad ribbon sashes over one shoulder, fastened with a rosette on the opposite side at the point of the hip, just below the waist-line. There the two bands of ribbon crossed, each one ending in streamers tipped with gold or silver fringe. Feather plumes were arched along their hat brims, plumes either snatched from protesting white ganders or peafowls or borrowed from girls. The crowd converged at the grandstand near where the track began.

The ten contestants on their gayly decorated and prancing horses filed singly before the judges' stand and were introduced by the master of ceremonies, Judge James Gillette, who stood by the Queen of the Jousts and her ladies-in-waiting:

Ladies and gentlemen, I present ten brave and gallant knights who will tilt today each for the favor of a fair lady, not in bloody conflict but with peaceful lances at golden rings in this lovely valley of Bosque County. May the best man win and may the favor of his lady be granted him.

I present to you Ed Nichols, the Knight of the Silver Cross.

Ed touched his pony's rein. The horse rose on its hind legs, stood for a moment almost perpendicular, dropped to its feet, plunged forward for several bounds, whirled and faced the announcer, then lowered its nose slowly to the ground in a bow as gracefully as Emma Abbott when she took the call after singing "The Last Rose of Summer." Ed rode his horse as if "growed" there.

Each knight as his name was called curvetted his horse or executed some caracole, no two alike, and rode into line with Ed Nichols. They were:

Asa Gary, The Knight of Bosque County
George Scrutchfield, The Knight of the Golden Spur
Johnny Rundell, The Knight of the Lost Cause
Sam Russell, The Knight of the Southern Cross
Jeff Hanna, The Knight of the Lone Star
Ed McCurry, The Knight of the Morning Star
Otto Nelson, The Knight of Green Valley
Frank Hornbuckle, The Knight of Double Mountain
Bob Hanna, The Knight of the Slim Chance

As the last name was called, Ed Nichols swung his horse to the end
of the track, leveled his lance, leaned over as he touched his plunging
horse with his spurs. He darted forward. By the time he reached the
first overhanging ring the lance point was steady and the first ring
clicked as it was strung on the lance and struck against the guard just
in front of where Ed's hand clasped the shaft.

Click—click—click—click!

In twice as many seconds the five rings were on Ed's lance, now
held proudly erect. As he galloped to the judges' stand to have his
successful run verified, he shouted to Bob Hanna:

"Oh, you Knight of the Slim Chance, you ain't got no chance
against me!"

The crowd clapped approval, the next knight took the rings from
Ed's lance and hung them up carefully for his run. The tournament
was really under way. Rider followed rider, none getting all five rings,
until it was Bob's turn. He strung all five. On Ed's second try his horse
"flew the track" and he had no chance at the last two rings. Bob took
all five rings again, and repeated on the last run. He was cheered as
the champion. Frank Hornbuckle was next, with Ed Nichols having
made the best time. When Bob had crowned his lady love he led the
dance that started at once on the platform back of the judges' stand.
Early the next morning he started out on horseback for the range just
south of Abilene.

But Ed Nichols stayed in Morgan, and there are few more interesting men in the world than he. Ed could ride the hardest pitching

horse so that daylight couldn't ever be seen between him and his saddle. He made a beautiful figure astride a horse. He never pulled leather; "I never was throwed," he claims. I believe he tells the truth. He once told me about riding a vicious, man-killer horse for two miles with the horse pitching a "fence row high, wide and handsome" and landing stiff-legged at every jump.

"I thought I was a goner," he said. "But at last the horse dropped his head between his legs, his feet spraddled out, and he bawled like a yearling. He was give out and so was I. When I got off, blood was dripping from my nose and ears. Another time, another horse pitched a mile and a half with me and then fell dead."

Ed was full of stories: "Frank Hornbuckle"—the man who won second place in the tournament—"would ride 'em for a drink of whiskey. Harry White had a pretty gray mare that had never been rode. One morning Frank roped her out, put his saddle on her and told Harry to bring him the jug of whiskey and he'd ride her. Harry went to the wagon and found that the jug was empty. He told Frank to pull off his saddle, that the whiskey was all gone. Frank said, 'Bring me the jug.' He took it, pulled out the stopper and smelled. 'Turn her loose,' he said. He rode that mare for a smell of whiskey."

Like many another bullwhacker, muleskinner and cowpuncher, who had little opportunity to read, Ed carried in his memory reams of songs, verses and old ballads. He promised his mother never to drink. But he did not promise her that he would not play cards. In describing one game he told me, "I was so lucky, I could draw to a cow chip and catch a pair of oxen." In describing a room he slept in over in the Cross Timbers, he said it was "so small I had to jump up to get out of my britches."

Tom McCullough over at Kimball's Bend told me this story to show how tender-hearted Ed was: "One night he was riding horseback alone between Hico and Iredell. Passing through a thick wood he heard an old cow mooing. A cow in trouble can sound mighty pitiful. Ed got down, hitched his horse and began to look for her. At last he found her at the bottom of an abandoned windlass well, six feet or more in diameter at the top. The old cow heard Ed and mooed and mooed. Ed had a hard job ahead, but he was full of resources. He looked around until he found a running spring, took off his big, wide-brimmed Stetson, filled it with water, carried it to the old well and poured it in. Again and again he emptied hatfuls of water until finally he filled the well up to the top and the struggling cow swam out."

Men like Bob Hanna and Ed Nichols deepened my love for cowboy songs. I couldn't have been more than four years old when I first heard a cowboy sing and yodel to his cattle. I was sleeping in my father's two-room house in Texas beside a branch of the old Chisholm Trail—twelve of us sometimes in two rooms. Suddenly a cowboy's singing waked me as I slept on my trundle bed. A slow rain fell in the darkness outside. I listened to the patter on the pine shingles above me, and through the open window I could hear the soft musical tinkle of water pouring from the eaves and striking the gravelly earth beneath. These sounds come back to me faintly through the years, a foggy maze of recollections; and my heart leapt even then to the cries of the cowboy trying to quiet, in the deep darkness and sifting rain, a trail herd of restless cattle:

Whoo—oo-oo-ee-oo-oo, Whoo-oo Whoo-whoo-oo

O, slow up, dogies, quit your roving around,
You have wandered and tramped all over the ground;
O graze along, dogies, and feed kinda slow,
And don't forever be on the go—
O move slow, dogies, move slow.

O, say, little dogies, when you goin' to lay down
And quit this forever a-siftin' around?
My legs are weary, my seat is sore;
O, lay down, dogies, like you've laid down before—
Lay down, little dogies, lay down.

Whoo-oo-oo-ee-oo-oo, Whoo-ee-whoo-whoo-whoo-oo

Again came the crooning yodel, most like the wail of the coyote; only restful and not wild. Over and over and over the fresh young voice of the cowboy rang out in the long watches of the night, pleading with the cattle to lie down and sleep and not to worry:

It's your misfortune and none of my own,
For you know Wyoming will be your new home.

There was a stream near our house, a good place to rest the cattle before they plodded up the trail through the Indian Territory, across Kansas, Nebraska, and then, finally, sometimes to Montana and Wyoming. During a period of twenty years ten million cattle and a million horses were driven northward from Texas on the Chisholm Trail and other cattle trails. As the cowboys drove the cattle along they called and sang and yodeled to them, they made up songs about trail life. I began to write down these songs when I was a small boy.

Perhaps my interest in the outside world began when travelers spent the night at my home; certainly it was awakened when at the age of ten I saw my first railroad train. When it puffed into Morgan, from Waco, with several coaches filled to the doors with visitors to a Bosque County barbecue, it was a fearful sight. The black panting engine, the trembling ground, filled me with awe. I could hardly keep from running. Then the old Negro hotel runner, who met every train, cried out, "Come right over to the Morgan House, the best second-class hotel in the city. There ain't no fust class!"

I have found few people who have ever read *The Wandering Jew*. How or whence the book came into my hands when I was about sixteen I cannot remember. I had never before read a historical romance—in fact I had read no novel whatever except a Sunday school story about a prig named Cyril, whom I despised.

I had my precious book in the attic bedroom. After the household was asleep I would slip out of bed and light the little brass lamp. It burned a round wick not much larger than a lead pencil. The lamp held about a pint of kerosene. I would bend over the table and hold

the feeble flame of the lamp close to the line of print that I was reading. I had to sleep some, for I must drive a double team to a turning
plow the next day. But I didn't sleep much.

I remember vividly the picture on the first page (the book cover
was gone) that showed a Cross stamped into the earth by the feet of
the Wandering Jew as he walked round and round the world. I don't
recall how many times he had already made the circuit. The Jew had
to keep moving because he had refused to let Jesus bearing his Cross
rest on his doorstep. Then the Master had looked at him and said,
"Verily, thou shalt go on forever." It took me a month to finish the
book. Throughout the days I was reliving the stirring story. I went to
my farm work in a daze. I had no wish to talk to anyone. Meanwhile
my father discovered what I had been doing. He didn't reproach me
or punish me.

"One more *Wandering Jew* for you," he said grimly, "and we'll be
sending you wandering off to the Austin Insane Asylum." Since then
I have found that the book was an attack against the power of the Jesu-
its. To me it was only a moving drama, which came into my life with
the help of a little brass lamp in a corner of the attic.

When I was nearly twenty years old my father allowed me to sow
eleven acres of wheat for myself. The rule of the family was that each
child should "go off to school" for one year; that year would complete
his twenty-one years of service for the common good of the family. My
wheat flourished mightily, growing higher than my head. Neighbors
said it would make forty bushels to the acre. Just when the grain was
"in the milk," rains came, it seemed to me for forty days and nights.
One morning I looked and could not see a single stalk of wheat. The
Bosque River was out of its banks and stood in some places ten feet
deep over the field. When the flood went down my wheat lay washed
flat on the ground, so encrusted with silt that it withered and died.
I cut the dead stalks with a mower when the ground dried. People
laughed at the curious, tall shocks. It took Pink Parks and his thresher
crew two entire days to thresh the wheat. The weather was hot and
stifling, and the dust billowed up about the men and machine so that
they couldn't be seen from a hundred yards away. The wheat flowed

out of the spout in little sickly grains mixed with small chunks of mud—half and half, I should say. When Pink took out his toll, I had one hundred and sixty bushels of mixed mud and wheat.

I had arranged to swap flour for part of my board at Granbury College. My brother Jess and I loaded a lot of the wheat on two wagons to have it ground into flour, and set out. When we were about twenty miles from home rain began to fall. We carried the two-bushel sacks of grain to an abandoned house. During the night the Bosque got on a rise and threatened to drown us and our mules. Shortly after midnight we reloaded the wheat and drove out of danger; then we waited in Clifton two days for the road to harden. We double-teamed nearly all the way to Valley Mills, where my wheat was "tolled" again for the grinding. When Jess and I got back home with my flour, we had been away more than a week, having traveled a distance of not more than eighty miles.

Granbury College was thirty miles away. My flour and I had another trip to make. But first I discovered that I must sell my beloved pony, Selim, for money to supplement the returns from my unlucky wheat crop. I delivered him to Dallas for sixty dollars. For me the ride was a ninety-mile funeral journey; for every footfall of Selim sounded like the clods on the coffin of a friend. As I walked away from a horse-lot in East Dallas, Selim put his head far over the fence and watched me. Just as I turned the corner he neighed anxiously. I went on down the street sobbing to myself.

One morning in September, 1887, Jess and I loaded my flour into a wagon, placed my trunk on top, and headed for Granbury. Two mules, Jack and Fan, Junior, drew the wagon. When we crossed the Bosque County line, between Walnut Springs and Glen Rose, my physical connection was severed forever with the region where I first realized that dawn has beauty of its own, matched only by the peace and quiet of twilight. The days and nights, the sights and sounds of my childhood were shoved behind me. No longer was Bosque County my home. But it would always be a part of me, for, hidden at the bottom of my trunk, I carried in secret, tied up with a cotton string, a small roll of cowboy songs.

2

COLLEGE

During the one year I spent in Granbury College (my first entire year in any school), I soaked up information like a sponge. The scant equipment, bare library shelves, teachers without much training or background (except David S. Switzer, Master of Arts, University of Mississippi); a narrow, small-town atmosphere; discipline smacking of the Hoosier Schoolmaster days; general supervision under the Methodist Church—I then felt none of these manifest shortcomings. The teachers heard lessons from morning till night. They had no time for study themselves. A half-dozen instructors must look after two or three hundred boys and girls from the primary grade up through college seniors. These seniors and other upperclassmen sat all day in rows of desks, supervised by a monitor, just as if they were first graders.

Sitting still at a desk didn't bother me, for I recited every hour of the day. In mathematics I studied "complete" arithmetic, two years of algebra in one, geometry, trigonometry; Steele's *Fourteen Weeks in Physiology*; spelling, in which I won a five-dollar medal; formal grammar, in which I was taught to diagram sentences; first year Latin. For decorative purposes a lot of the students took elocution. I learned to recite "Lasca," and made a ponderous final oration (which won no prize), similar in style and content to one I had heard on "The Past and the Present and Their Relation to the Future." English literature, history, and civics were not taught in Granbury College.

However lacking in breadth of culture, the teachers were earnest and kind. I do not think I was ever so happy. I was like a fish that had escaped from a shoally stream into a pool of clear, sunshiny water. I reveled in "book learning," and across the fifty-odd years I look back with affection to this frontier college. Today not a stone of the college buildings remains.

With this slender equipment I taught for one year in the public school at Clifton, Texas, and for six years, part of the time in the preparatory department, at Weatherford College, where Professor Switzer and his faculty of seven persons struggled to instruct two hundred to four hundred students from their a-b-c's until they "finished" fifteen years later. Again no library, no laboratories worthy of the name, more teachers with meager training. Perhaps the luckless boys and girls got some profit—I do not know.

Although I had been promised time for my own studies, the drudgery of twelve or fifteen classes a day shriveled my brain and corroded my spirit. In order to broaden the curriculum, perhaps, I was encouraged to spend a summer at Eastman Business College in Poughkeepsie, New York, where I was graduated with distinction in bookkeeping and penmanship and given a heavy gold medal studded with seventeen diamonds. At once I was placed in charge of the "business department" of Weatherford College (instruction in plain and fancy penmanship, which I also taught, was extra), with no let-up in my duties as principal of the preparatory department. I was the entire faculty for two departments. Someone once said I ran the Business Department with my left hind foot. Too true, too true, I sadly recall.

This period of teaching in Weatherford College, when I felt so utterly incompetent (as in reality I was), seems to blight a portion of my past. My face flushes with shame as I recall what I did not have to offer those eager boys and girls. That one is now an economics professor, another in Congress, and many others fine citizens, brings me no comfort. I helped them none at all. I knew this even then, and I cast about for some means to improve myself.

I resented the unreasonable discipline I was called on to help enforce. I was supposed to report any boy noticed walking with his sweetheart up a shady lane (I never saw them, thank goodness!). It was against the rules to smoke a cigar (I often wanted to and sometimes did!). The college was almost a part of the local Methodist Church. If one of the "professors" was too often away from his pew, eyebrows were raised and inquiries were made. I fell easily into this church regime, for life on a small farm had given scant chance for any social life. A group of blooming sixteen-year-old girls chose me for their Sunday school teacher. Even today I do not know which girl I loved the best; I only know that I loved them all. But I reached the depth of mortification when I faced the fact that in my position in the church I was assuming that I was somehow different, that I was better than others on the "outside." And in my heart I knew that not to be true.

For three summers I traveled north to the six-week summer school at Chautauqua, New York, to study Latin, mathematics and English. There, for the first time, I heard of Tennyson and Browning. I listened to some good music in the amphitheater and to occasional lectures. One—"The Miseries of a Half-trained Mind"—sent me away almost in terror, for the lecturer seemed to be reading my thoughts. Through the following years I attempted the Chautauqua reading course. I would fall asleep over the books. Perhaps one reason was, as I later found out, that at that time all the textbooks were written especially for the Chautauqua people—hastily thrown together treatises, stiff, stupid and insipid. Once I undertook a regular correspondence course in higher mathematics under a competent teacher. The going was hard. When some problem floored me I had no one to turn to for discussion or help. Gradually I became discouraged, failed to send in my lessons on time and forfeited my registration.

I became desperately aware of my lack of any substantial education. The years were passing, and I saw no way out of the coil of circumstance that surrounded me. At first my salary had been forty dollars a month. Now it was seventy-five, but I had spent all my savings in abortive, futile efforts to educate myself. Moreover, I had assumed a security debt that, at the end of fifteen years of paying, cost me four thousand dollars. I was terribly unhappy, in a frenzy of apprehension as if some awful calamity was about to swallow me, as desperate and undecided as when making up my mind to sell my pony, Selim. For years I had read a catalog of Vanderbilt University, thumbed it until the pages were frazzled at the edges. The specimen entrance examinations printed on the last pages were beyond my ken. I couldn't solve the mathematics problems. Even with a pony the Latin passages were beyond me. I didn't have the heart to write and ask if the officials would relent for a Texan. Too late I was told they sometimes did. One day, in the Fort Worth Union Depot, I met Joe Etter of Sherman, Texas, then a student at the state university. "The University of Texas is the only place for you," he said. Instantly my mind was clear. To "Texas" I would go. All doubt was gone. Since that day I've stubbed my toe against many, many flinty rocks; I've blundered into frequent bypasses, but the main road over the horizon has always been plain if only I shifted my eyes and looked ahead. For many years thereafter, the University of Texas was the core of my life.

One glad June day in 1895, when the afternoon Santa Fe train took me south from Weatherford, away from all this pretense, another chapter of my life was closed for good and all.

In Austin Miss Mignonette Carrington (afterward Mrs. J. E. Pearce), brilliant and fun-loving, taught me enough grammar to get me over the stile past Dr. Morgan Callaway, Jr., head of the English Department. How she managed the other subjects I can't imagine. I only know I took no entrance examinations. During the summer I had met President Leslie Waggener at evening gatherings of a group studying Shakespeare, my first introduction to the dramatist. President Waggener afterward suggested that I enter his senior class in Shakespeare during the regular session. Soon he asked each member of the class to prepare an essay on *Richard II*. I had never in my life written an essay, not even a one-page theme. When I set myself to the task of tearing apart the machinery of Shakespeare's play, after the plan of Dr. Waggener (attempting to see the parts and how they fitted together, what made the whole thing tick), I got so excited that I forgot to sleep. I wrote on and on, into the dawn, twenty-five closely packed pages or more. One other time only—and years afterward—did I study all night.

Dr. Waggener did not return my paper when he handed the marked essays back to my classmates. Instead, he asked me to come to his office. I felt that the end had come, that I was to leave his class or to resign from the University. He asked me to sit down, and then looked at me gravely. I remember how dry my mouth felt, that my hands were shaking. "I called you in to tell you," he said, "that I have credited you with three full courses in English. Look at the corner of your essay," he added, smiling.

When I could see, there shone in red ink, written in his small copperplate handwriting, an E. Afterward, when I had stumbled speechless from the room, a friend told me that E meant "excellent," the highest mark. Those few minutes in Dr. Waggener's office were the high-water mark in my entire college career.

Dr. Waggener was a Kentuckian, Harvard '61, a gifted teacher. He was also a bred-in-the-bone Southerner, who had been shot down and left for dead on the field of battle in the Civil War. To me he had seemed like a god, far removed, reserved, stately. But now he had bent down and pinned an accolade on me. His large gray eyes had softened in kindness. I knew now how a serf felt when the lord of the manor called him from the ranks and knighted him. With credits also in mathematics, I had really started on my way, more than a fifth the distance to the magical AB degree dangling down the road ahead of me.

An AB degree! Never before would I allow myself to dream that I could earn such golden acclaim. I didn't want a PhB or a BS or any other chaffy group of letters. I wanted only the majestic AB, Artium Baccalaureus. To me the words brought visions of philosophers strolling among Grecian pillars, of senators discussing grave matters of state in the Roman Forum. So, in addition to English and mathematics in my freshman year, I plunged into beginners' Greek and Freshman Latin—I had had little Latin and no Greek at all, not even one letter of the alphabet. To these four subjects I added chemistry, history and Anglo-Saxon—twenty-three recitations a week when the normal number was twelve. Never was there such a hopeless hodge-podge. There I was, a Chautauqua-educated country boy who couldn't conjugate an English verb or decline a pronoun, attempting to master three other languages at the same time—Anglo-Saxon, Latin, Greek!

But I plunged on through the year, for, since I was older than the average freshman, I must hurry, hurry. I don't think I ever stopped to think how foolish it all was. Through the following summer I only increased the tempo of my haste. I went for the three summer months to the University of Chicago, doubling in Latin and Greek, and tackling French for good measure. I got a bit of pleasure from a class sight-reading Plato's Dialogues. Otherwise, for sixteen hours a day, I grubbed doggedly at the roots of three languages the same way I had grubbed at the pecan stumps in the Bosque County river bottom.

The beginning of the second year in the University of Texas found me over the hump in the number of credits. Still ahead of me was more Greek and Latin and French, more government and history and philosophy. But I had got my second wind and could swing along steadily and surely. I felt many "rosy-fingered" dawns in Homer and and found satisfying beauty in the lyrics of Horace and Catullus. Dr. Waggener taught me to appreciate Browning, even "Sordello" and "The Ring and the Book." Otherwise, the maze of this jam-packed two years of ill-advised and fruitless hurry seemed only dust and ashes. When the diploma was handed to me the luster of the golden AB had faded to dull lead. I had won a coveted bauble, but there had been little joy in the working. I had given myself no time to look around me or to plan for the future. I had been blindly rushing somewhere, I didn't know where.

But in the University of Texas I had come in contact with a few genuine scholars, somewhat fewer who could really teach what they knew. For my blunder in tearing through my undergraduate years I could blame only myself. No longer was I forced to live in a world of make-believe. In some degree I had acquired intellectual independence. The little I knew, I knew that I knew. I was no longer ashamed.

The day after I was graduated I went to work for the University of Texas as secretary to the president, as registrar in charge of all admission correspondence, and as steward of the men's dormitory, etc., etc., all for $75 a month. On the side I was supposed to take enough studies to complete a Master of Arts degree within two years.

In 1903, when my education was at a standstill, for at night I was too tired for study, I was rescued from this coil by David F. Houston, who thought I could teach English to the freshmen boys at the Texas Agricultural and Mechanical College. As I struggled along on a salary of twelve hundred dollars a year, President Houston, himself a Harvard man, proposed a year for me at Harvard (I had never in my wildest moments dared to dream of Harvard!). One-third of my salary was to go on. An Austin Scholarship from Harvard solved the remaining difficulty, and I was off on my final academic adventure with a wife and baby Shirley.

When I first went to the University of Texas in 1895, I had carried in my trunk the tightly rolled batch of manuscript of cowboy songs. They were written out on scratch pads and on pieces of cardboard. I had not included certain songs that Bob Hanna was fond of singing to groups of workers resting in the shade of a threshing machine while repairs went on. I had listened intently, but I never dared to write out the words of "The Keyhole in the Door," "Winding Up Her Little Ball of Yarn," "The Oaks of Jim Darling," "The Transom over the Door," "Her Apron So Neat," and other favorite songs current in Dodge City, the end of the cattle trail. Nor can I recall any plan or purpose in making my collection of cowboy songs, or why I should wish to show them to Dr. Leslie Waggener, who was then teaching me Shakespeare. But one day I did take my roll of songs to his office. Never before had I shown them to anyone.

Dr. Waggener referred me to Dr. Morgan Callaway, Jr., a Johns Hopkins University Doctor of Philosophy, whose scholarship is reflected in three studies, "The Absolute Participle in Anglo-Saxon," 1889; "The Appositive Participle in Anglo-Saxon," 1901; and "The Infinitive in Anglo-Saxon," 1913. Timidly I handed Dr. Callaway my roll of dingy manuscript written out in lead pencil and tied together with a cotton string. Courteous and kindly gentleman that he was, he thanked me and promised a report the next day. Alas, the following morning Dr. Callaway told me that my samples of frontier literature were tawdry, cheap and unworthy. I had better give my attention to the great movements of writing that had come sounding down the ages. There was no possible connection, he said, between the tall tales of Texas and the tall tales of Beowulf. His decision, exquisitely considerate, was final, absolute. No single crumb of comfort was left for me. I was unwilling to have anyone else see the examples of my folly, or know of my disappointment. So that night in the dark, out behind Brackenridge Hall, the men's dormitory where I lodged, I made a small bonfire of every scrap of my cowboy songs.

Years afterward an associate of Dr. Callaway in the English faculty, Dr. R. H. Griffith, asked to examine a first copy of *Cowboy Songs and Other Frontier Ballads.* The following morning he brought the book to my desk, thanked me for the loan, turned on his heel and went away with no word of comment about my first venture in the field of folksongs. The disfavor of my Cowboy Song project still survived.

I chose American Literature among my English courses at Harvard in 1906. At the beginning of the second term the instructor, Professor Barrett Wendell, asked each man to select examples of regional literature for study until the end of the session, and to prepare a thesis to be read in class. "I am worn to a frazzle," Professor Wendell declared, "with reading, year in and year out, dissertations on Emerson, Hawthorne, Thoreau, Holmes and Poe. You fellows come from every section of the country. Tell us something interesting about your regional literary productions."

We were to call later with our subjects for his approval at his office in Gray's Hall. I can still feel the cheer of the big open fireplace piled with burning logs, just to the left of his desk, as he greeted me one snowy February morning in 1907. With him at the time was an editor of *Scribner's Magazine* arranging for publishing Mr. Wendell's Sorbonne lectures. I told him that I could write a paper on Negro songs or the songs of the cowboy. He instantly preferred cowboy songs. When I said that the cowboys themselves had made up songs describing the life on the round-up and trail, Professor Wendell sprang from his chair, and, in his enthusiasm, came around the table to shake my hand.

"Do you know Kittredge? I'll arrange a meeting."

A day or two afterward while I was chatting with a group of classmates in the Yard, they suddenly froze into silence. I looked up to see a tall, gray-clad, alert man with eyes fixed on me. He shot me with his vocal forty-five: "Is your name Lomax? Can you come to my house for dinner next Tuesday? I'll be looking for you."

He was gone. Thus the Phoenix from the ashes of my bundle of cowboy songs began to rise and shine again in Cambridge at the behest of these two men, Barrett Wendell and George L. Kittredge. That moment was the real beginning of my connection with the Archive of American Folk Song, established many years later in the Library of Congress. I began immediately to plan the best means of increasing my stock of ballads. At once the idea of eventually issuing a book of these songs occurred to me. I therefore prepared the letter which follows, secured the endorsement of Professors Wendell and Kittredge, and mailed it to the editors of a thousand newspapers in the West:

67 Oxford Street, Cambridge, Mass.
April 12, 1907

To the Editor: I am a member of the English faculty of the Texas Agricultural and Mechanical College on leave of absence for a year, which I am spending in the Graduate School of Harvard University. As a part of my work I am endeavoring to make a complete collection of the native ballads and songs of the West. It will hardly be possible to secure such a collection without the aid of the Press; for many of these songs have never been in print, but, like the Masonic ritual, are handed down from one generation to another by "word of mouth." They deal mainly with frontier experiences: the deeds of desperadoes like Jesse James and Sam Bass; the life of the ranger and the cowboy; the trials of the Forty-niners, buffalo hunters, stage drivers, and freighters going up the trail—in short, they are attempts, often crude and sometimes vulgar, to epitomize and particularize the life of the pioneers who peopled the vast region west of the Mississippi River.

Such early pioneer ballads *do* exist. Already I have collected nearly a hundred from one state—Texas. I wish to solicit your aid in preserving from extinction this expression of American literature. Eventually it is expected that the ballads will be published in book form. An editorial request from you to your readers for copies of frontier songs will doubtless result in valuable material. I shall greatly appreciate your help to this extent, and your further favor in forwarding to me whatever material may come into your hands.

May I add that ballads and the like which, because of crudity, incompleteness, coarseness, or for any other reason are unavailable for publication, will be as interesting and as useful for my purposes as others of more merit. It is my desire to collect the songs and ballads now or lately in actual existence, and in the precise form which they have popularly assumed.

Yours very respectfully,

(Signed) JOHN A. LOMAX

The endorsement ran as follows:

Harvard University,
April 12, 1907.

Mr. Lomax's plan has our hearty approval. The materials which he collects are to be preserved in the Harvard College Library, where they will always be accessible to investigators.

(signed) BARRETT WENDELL,
Professor of English
G. L. KITTREDGE,
Professor of English

There came an immediate and surprising response to this appeal. First widely printed by newspapers receiving it, it was reprinted in summary by Eastern newspapers and magazines. Special news stories appeared about the project, and, finally, the small weeklies, even in thinly populated sections rich in folk stuff, found room in their columns to run the story. Letters poured in to my Cambridge address and for a long time followed me on to Texas. Even twenty years afterward a few still trickled in. Perhaps it is true that the thinner the population is, the kinder the people.

One correspondent wrote:

I got the eleven cowboy songs I am sending you while working on the range out on the Pecos (Texas) River.

Mrs. M. B. Wight of Fort Thomas, Arizona, who gave me many songs, wrote:

> I am an old white-haired woman, sixty years old, weigh 215 pounds, seldom leave the ranch. If you come into this part of the country, come to see us. You will be welcome. You will find all classes of people, cowboys, freighters, ex-rangers, and old frontier scouts in the big ranches and mining towns. Ask for Bud Snow, a saloon-keeper at Wilcox. I think he can put you on to the best places in that part of the country to get songs.

From Mrs. Wight came the long freighting ballad, beginning:

> Come all you jolly freighters that has freighted on the road,
> That has hauled a load of freight from Wilcox to Globe;
>
> And it's home, dearest home, and it's home you ought to be,
> Over on the Gila in the white man's country;
> Where the poplar and the ash and mesquite will ever be,
> Growing green on the Gila, there's a home for you and me.

Said a correspondent from Howell, Michigan:

> I am going to North Michigan to hunt deer. Think I can find some old lumber-jack songs up there. I can sing the tones of the ones I am sending just as they were sung to me. But I do not know how I could send you the tone by mail!

From many widely separated places testimony on a hotly disputed theory concerning the origin of ballads came in. From Lawrence, Kansas:

> I have one song in my collection which I prize very highly. It was first drafted by a cowboy by the name of Wilson and as it was read to different groups of cowboys changes of words and of phraseology were offered by different members of the groups before it

received its final setting. That word, phrase, or sentence or new idea was finally retained which to the greatest number seemed to be the most agreeable and which expressed the original idea, whether it was in the original draft or suggested afterward. I was at the camp on several occasions when this building-up process was going on, and believe it a fairly correct specimen how all folk songs are built up and receive their final setting. So that, as a rule, they are the product of many minds rather than the finished product of one mind, while the original draft is probably the product of one mind.

Another early correspondent wrote:

> I notice an article in the Houston *Chronicle* that you are collecting the old Negro songs. I enclose herewith the words to some old nigger songs which may be of interest to you. If you wish to learn more about them you should visit the niggers in the Brazos bottom around Richmond, that's where I learned them. Most of those old backwoods niggers are still singing the old songs they sang fifty years ago. A good many of their songs are too smutty to send through the mail. I left off several verses from the songs I enclosed on that account. Then there are such songs as: "Uncle Ned went out to—, but the hogs et him up." Which wouldn't do at all!

A sample stanza from one of his songs:

> Soon as I gits my new boots on,
> I'm gwine to wade all 'round this crawfish pond:
> Gwine to go to shootin' my forty-fo',
> An' there won't be a nigger in a mile or mo'.
> I'm a rowdy soul, I'm a rowdy soul;
> I don't give a damn if I work or no.

J. M. Monteith of the Provincial Police Office, Ducks, British Columbia, sent this letter:

I see that you are collecting old sea chanteys. Here is one that you may not have. I am quoting the words from memory and I had quite a job recalling the words. I may state that I served my time as apprentice in a British Four Masted Barque of some 3,000 tons register and learned a lot of chanteys. I heard this one while we were running our easting down bound from New York to Melbourne, Australia. We had just come through a bad blow in which we lost one of the boys from the Mizzen upper top-gallant yard. We had all canvas off for forty-eight hours but the fore topmast Staysail Goosewing Main lower Topsail and Jigger Staysail. It was a bright moonlight night and I was sitting on the Main Topsail Yard overhauling the Buntlines as the yard was being hoisted. There was a heavy swell running and sometimes the men would be up to their waists in water as a green one come over the rail as they were tramping round the Capstan while the Palls* were ringing like Bells and keeping time to the chantey:

There's one thing more I'd like to say:
May that old duffer never have a grave,
May he be drowned in some dark watery hole,
May no candle never burn and no bell never toll,
May the sharks have his body and the devil have his soul.

With a riddle all day,
With a riddle all day,
That's a sailor's life at sea;
Look out, boys, here comes a squall,
Dowse your flying kites, haul, boys, haul;
Take a reef in your topsails, then stow them in,
And when you've done that, you can set them all again.

The first use I made of the contributions that flowed in, together with what I could recall of my early cowboy song collection, was to prepare a term paper for the class in American Literature. It required an hour for me to read it and sing sample songs to my somewhat startled classmates. From that incident I won the active interest and

*Pawls.

support of Professor Barrett Wendell. His unflagging enthusiasm for the importance of folk song literature remained constant until the day of his death. Without him I probably never would have gone forward. He wrote a gratifying introduction to *Cowboy Songs* in which he spoke of my reading "some of these ballads to one of my classes in Harvard, then engaged in studying the literary history of America. From that hour to the present, the men who heard these verses, during the cheerless progress of a course of study, have constantly spoken of them and written of them, as of something sure to linger happily in memory."

Following my return to Texas with a master's degree from Harvard, Professor Wendell's interest, supplemented by the backing of Professors George Lyman Kittredge, Fred Robinson and Dean Briggs, expressed itself in an offer of a thousand dollars a year from Harvard University, on condition that my college grant me a leave of absence from teaching. This condition the Directors of Texas A. and M. refused to meet. Later, however, there came along from Harvard three successive Sheldon Fellowships for the "investigation of American ballads." These fellowships were of five hundred dollars each, and I used the money for vacation travel in ballad collecting. *Cowboy Songs and Other Frontier Ballads*, published in 1910, was the first result of this work.

3

HUNTING COWBOY SONGS

When in 1908 a check for $500 came from Harvard University for my first year as a Sheldon Fellow, I was the happiest person in the world. Never before at one time had I owned so much money, money that brought me both honor and responsibility. I was entirely free to spend it in running down the words and music of cowboy songs. In a glow of anticipation I made plans to travel the following summer throughout the cattle country.

It proved a long and hard road that I started on, as I made my way, walking, on horseback, by buggy, by train and automobile, a tortuous journey that has since then wound a half-million miles into every part of the United States. Very few of my associates in the University of Texas expressed sympathy or took the project seriously. For them this crude product of the West had no interest, no value, no charm whatever. Governor Jim Ferguson quoted stanzas of my cowboy songs in political addresses to cheering crowds, and sneered at the University of Texas for having me on its faculty, just as he sneered at a teacher of zoology, asserting repeatedly that this professor was trying to make wool grow on the backs of armadillos and thus bring down the price of sheep! Both of us were sorry fools to him.

It was cowboy songs I most wished, in those early days, to round up and "close herd." These I jotted down on a table in a saloon back room, scrawled on an envelope while squatting about a campfire near a chuck wagon, or caught behind the scenes of a bronco-busting outfit or rodeo. To capture the cowboy music proved an almost impossible task. The cowboys would simply wave away the large horn I carried and refused to sing into it! Not one song did I ever get from them except through the influence of generous amounts of whiskey, raw and straight from the bottle or jug. Once I was invited to speak at the Texas Cattlemen's Convention in San Antonio. To advertise my undertaking, I attempted to sing some of the tunes I wished to record from the trail men. My poor efforts brought only derisive whoops. One belligerent cattleman arose and announced: "I have been singin' them songs ever since I was a kid. Everybody knows them. Only a damn fool would spend his time tryin' to set 'em down. I move we adjourn." And adjourn they did, to a convenient bar.

One night in the back room of the White Elephant Saloon in Fort Worth, where I had cornered a bunch of Edi-phone-shy cowboy singers, a cowboy said to the crowd: "I told the professor" (that's what they jokingly called me) "that the old Chisholm Trail Song was as long as the trail from Texas to Montana. I can sing eighty-nine verses myself. Some of the verses would burn up his old horn, and anyhow, I'm not goin' to poke my face up to his blamed old horn and sing. The tune ain't much nohow." The tune wasn't much—but it suited the cowboy's work. He could sing it when he went dashing out to turn a runaway steer back to the herd, singing:

Feet in the stirrups and seat in the saddle,
And I hung and rattled with them longhorn cattle,
Coma-ti-yi-yippee, yippee yea, yippee yea,
Coma-ti-yi-yippee, yippee yea.

And he could sing it with a roaring chorus as the men sat about the campfire during the long winter evenings.

"Back in the Seventies," said another cowboy in the crowd, "we sang 'The Old Chisholm Trail' all the way from San Antonio to Dodge City. There was never a day that some one did not build a new verse." There is another "Chisholm Trail" tune—a quiet, jig-joggy tune— when a fellow was riding alone, scouting for drifting cattle, riding the "line" through lonely stretches of country. I finally persuaded one of the boys to sing it. But not for my recording machine. I learned the tune and later recorded it myself for the Folk Song Archive.

Out on a busy corner near the cattle pens of the Fort Worth stockyards I had come upon a blind old man twanging his guitar while he sang doleful ditties and listened for the ring of quarters in his tin cup.

"I don't know any cowboy songs," he explained to me. "But lead me home to lunch; my wife can sing you a bookful."

The old man shuffled along beside me, clasping his guitar as I guided him over the rough places in our path. We were headed for the trees that fringed the West Fork of the Trinity River near Fort Worth. Often I stumbled, for I was carrying the heavy Edison machine.

We found the blind singer's wife out behind a covered truck, a forerunner of the trailer, seated in front of a gaily colored tent. She wore a gypsy costume, richly brocaded. She had used paint and powder with skillful discretion on a face naturally comely. While I chatted with her, the old man disappeared into the tent. In a few minutes out he came. Gone were the round, humped shoulders, the white hair, the shambling gait, the tottering figure—and the colored glasses! Before me stood a young, handsome, dark-eyed man, alert and athletic. He made no explanation. He was a perfect and fascinating faker.

"We do team work here. My wife shakes down the saps who like to hold her hand while she reads their fortunes in the stars. All the self-righteous fools go away from my tin cup happy, marking down one more good deed on their passports to Heaven. We aim to please our customers, and I think we do." Thus the faker rambled on while a smiling Negro man served delicious food and a bottle of wine. Later on through the long Texas afternoon, amid the cheerful talk, the fortune teller sang the songs of the road. She and her family for generations had lived as gypsies.

"This lady," said the faker, "who has joined her fortunes with mine, travels with me now from Miami, Florida, to San Diego, California. We belong to that fringe of society which takes life the easiest

way. We toil not, neither do we spin." Raising a tent flap he showed
me rich purple hangings, thick Persian rugs, a divan spread with soft
silken covers—amazing luxury.

"With our burros, Abednego and Sennacherib, to pull our covered wagon, we travel as we like. Our rackets roll in the money."

He lay flat on his back on the mesquite grass, puffing a cigar, as
he gazed at the white patches of clouds that swept across the deep
blue Texas sky. I glanced curiously at Abednego and Sennacherib as
they munched their alfalfa. They seemed as old as the pyramids and
as solemn as a pair of Aztec idols—which they, indeed, resembled.
They seemed to talk to each other with abundant, constantly moving
ears, fastened loosely to their great bony heads. And here, close by,
sat the fake gypsy lady, dressed like a princess, strumming her guitar
and singing the songs that she had picked up in her wanderings.

She scorned the clumsy horn fastened to my recording machine,
and I caught few of the tunes. I remember that she sang me the first
blues that I ever heard, moving me almost to tears, and a pathetic
ballad of a factory girl who got splinters in her toes. Many and many
another song she sang that unhappily are gone with the Texas wind.
Then came four stanzas and the refrain:

> As I was walkin' one mornin' for pleasure
> I met a young cowboy all ridin' along;
> His hat was throwed back and his spurs was a-jinglin',
> As he approached me a-singin' this song:

> Whoopee ti yi yo, git along, little dogies,
> It's your misfortune and none of my own.
> Whoopee ti yi yo, git along, little dogies,
> For you know Wyoming will be your new home.

"To me," she said, "that's the loveliest of all cowboy songs. Like others, its rhythm comes from the movement of a horse. It is not the rois-
terous, hell-for-leather, wild gallop of 'The Old Chisholm Trail,' nor
the slow easy canter of 'Goodbye, Old Paint.' You mustn't frighten

the dogies. They get nervous in crowds. Lope around them gently in the darkness as you sing about punching them along to their new home in Wyoming. They'll sleep the night through and never have a bad dream."

After the refrain she would give the night-herding yodel of the cowboy, born of the vast melancholy of the plains; a yodel to quiet a herd of restless cattle in the deep darkness of a rainy night, when far-off flashes of lightning and the rumble of distant thunder meant danger. While the cattle milled around and refused to lie down, close to the fringe of the circle of moving animals rode the cowboys giving this wordless cry to the cattle, like the plea of a lonesome lobo wolf calling for his mate, like the croon of a mother trying to quiet a restless babe in the long watches of the night, like the soft moo of a cow wooing her young offspring from its hiding place to come for its milk. "Quiet, cattle, quiet. Darkness is everywhere, but we, your friends, are near. Lie down, little dogies, lie down." The yodel was pervasive, far-reaching. Even in its high notes it was soothing and tender. It seemed to catch up in its lilt all the perils of the night and merge them into a paean of peace.

As the gypsy woman, swayed by the beauty of her notes, yodeled on, the leaves of the overhanging cottonwood trees fluttered noiselessly, the katydids in the branches stopped their song and seemed to listen. In all our world there was no other sound save that beautiful voice imploring all little dogies to "lay still, little dogies, lay still."

I visited many cattle ranches, among them the widely known King Ranch, the Swenson Ranch, both in Texas, and the New Mexico Hearst ranch before it was split up. Often the men would have none of the horn. With smaller groups on remote ranches I enjoyed better fortune. Two or three Negro cowboys sang lustily when I got them away from the crowd. Students from the cattle regions, attending colleges throughout the country, brought me a lot of material when I gave talks to them on folk songs.

I read through the files of Texas newspapers that printed columns of old songs, and I bedeviled librarians for possible buried treasures in frontier chronicles. In a second-hand bookstore in San Antonio I found a battered copy of *Johnson's New Comic Songs* with a San Francisco date line of 1863. Along with the old favorites, "Gentle Annie" and "Nellie Gray," I came on the words of "Poker Jim," "The Miner's Song," "The Dying Californian," and other song products of the days of Forty-nine.

Some months afterward I asked the Librarian of the University of California at Berkeley if he knew of other pamphlets of early frontier songs. He had none catalogued. He then took me to the Bancroft Library and left me to rummage in some habitually locked-up cases. I came on a stack of dog-eared, paper-backed pamphlets tied together with an ancient cotton string. Though I lifted out the pile with care, the cotton string crumbled in my fingers. There they were—not a complete file of the "20,000 song books" advertised by D. E. Appleton & Co., San Francisco, but a choice selection of early "California Songsters": *Ben Cotton's Songster, The Sally Come Up Songster, Put's Original California Songster, Put's Golden Songster,* and many another. I discovered that "Old Put" and a group of men singers went from gold camp to gold camp in the early Fifties and sang to the miners. When they ran out of songs Old Put and his like made up songs describing the life of a mining town, telling how the Forty-Niners got to California and sometimes how they got back East. They were rough and crude creations, but among them I turned up "Sweet Betsy from Pike" and the "Days of Forty-nine," and afterward also discovered the tunes to which they were sung:

> Did you ever hear tell of Sweet Betsy from Pike,
> Who crossed the wide prairies with her lover Ike,
> With two yokes of cattle and one spotted hog,
> A tall Shanghai rooster and an old yaller dog?

Betsy and her man lived—

> In the days of old when they dug out the gold,
> In the days of Forty-nine.

There's old "Lame Jess," that hard old cuss,
Who never would repent;
He never missed a single meal
Nor never paid a cent.
But old "Lame Jess," like all the rest,
At death he did resign,
And in his bloom went up the flume
In the days of Forty-nine.

Uncovering these two songs repaid me for the long trip from Texas. Old Put's Preface to his *Original Songster* was another find:

In dedicating this little Book of Songs to the Miners of California, those hardy builders of California's prosperity and greatness, the author deems it his duty to offer a prefatory remark in regard to the origin of the work and the motive of its publication.

Having been a miner himself for a number of years, he has had ample opportunity of observing, as he has equally shared, the many trials and hardships to which his brethren of the pick and shovel have been exposed, and to which in general they have so patiently, so cheerfully, and even heroically submitted. Hence, ever since the time of his crossing the plains, in the memorable year of '50, he has been in the habit of noting down a few of the leading items of his experience, and clothing them in the garb of humorous, though not irreverent verse.

Many of his songs may show some hard edges, and, he is free to confess, they may fail to please the more aristocratic portion of the community, who have but little sympathy with the details, hopes, trials or joys of the toiling miner's life; but he is confident that the class he addresses will not find them exaggerated, nothing extenuated, nor aught set down "in malice."

In conclusion he would state, that after having sung them himself at various times and places, and latterly with the assistance of a few gentlemen, known by the name of the Sierra Nevada Rangers, the songs have been published at the request

of a number of friends; and if the author should thereby suc-
ceed in contributing to the amusement of those he is anxious to
please, enliven the tedious hours of a miner's winter fireside, his
pains will not be unrewarded.

 —San Francisco, September, 1855.

Tom Hight and I spent two happy days together recording songs in
an Oklahoma City hotel. Tom was made happier, as I am sure I was,
by the added presence of two quart bottles of rye which he consulted
frequently between songs. Tom knew more cowboy melodies than
any other person I have ever found. He gave me fifty.

"Ever since I was a boy," said Tom, "I have been a singing fool.
I could sing down any man in our cow-camp in the Panhandle.
When the fellers backed me against the neighboring camp, I won.
They challenged the whole damn Panhandle. The champeens of each
camp met at a central point, and we lifted up our heads like a pack of
coyotes, only we lifted 'em one at a time. The rules was that each man
was to sing in turn, one after the other, round and round. The man
that sung the last song, he won the prize. It took us mighty near all
night to get sung out. The other feller couldn't sing no more, because
he didn't know no more songs. But I was ready with the last one and
had more roped and ready. Of course you couldn't use no books and
no writing. I was mighty proud of being the champeen singer of the
Texas Panhandle. My cowboy friends even gave me a pair of sil-
ver-mounted spurs for a prize with my name engraved on them."

Twenty-five years after the Oklahoma singing bee Tom Hight
wrote to me from California:

The first contest I can remember having was on a nice little
creek, near old Be[a]ver City (about five miles) in the old neutral
strip, or No Man's Land, just north of the Texas Panhandle. We
was holding 2,500 head of cattle there on good grass and water
and two men rode up and asked to stop overnight with us and in
those days everybody was welcome. So they stayed three nights
and two days until the horses rested up, for they was rode down

when they came and they had two sixshooters and Winchester each and wore good clothes, shop-made boots and Stetson hats and was 25 or 30 years old and never both slept at once. So the second evening while sitting around camp something was said about singing and one of them said he would sing song with any-one. So the boss said that he had a kid that he would sing against him. I was 20 years old.

So after supper we hooked up. The others stood my guard from 8 to 9 and we sang songs until about 10 P.M. Then he said, 'Kid, I have sang all I know.' Then the boys gave the cheers—there was no wager but I got a thrill out of it. So they saddled up the third morning and bid us the time of day, rode off. So in a few days we heard the Coffeyville Kansas Bank had been robbed and we all thought them a part of the ones. We never asked their names, as that wasn't often done those days. I can't remember any of the songs either he or I sang, as that was 50 years ago.

The name of the boys was Ralph Church (the boss), Jack Leonard and Shorty Allen, Les Laverty, Bell Fillops, Charley Straw, Billie Hill, and John Laverty, the cook.

I sang against a fellow in Weatherford, Texas, in a wagon yard. His name was Ben Green, his and my friends done the matching of it for a quart of whiskey. So we had quite a jolly time, about 30 men, and they sure got a kick out of it. I beet him in about 3 hours. He said he had never been beet before.

The last letter came from Tom Hight when he was more than eighty years old. He spoke of riding into the sunset, his closing words being: "Farewell, until we rattle our hocks on the other side."

Among my students in the A. & M. College of Texas was a young fel-low from Denison, Texas, by the name of Harry Stephens. Harry had worked cattle in New Mexico and Arizona for three or four years; and he brought with him to college a handsome saddle, saddle blan-ket, bridle, spurs and other equipment. His saddle was ornamented with silver. He used to wear his high-top boots and ten-gallon white hat to class, whenever he could. Harry didn't like the college uniform and he wasn't much interested in English literature, but he warmed up when I mentioned cowboy songs. He would stay after class and recite and sing songs to me. Now and then he would drift down to my home on Sunday and lean over the fence and sing a song to attract my attention. I never could get him further than the gate.

Early in the spring, when the world was turning green again, Harry called on me one morning just as the bugle was blowing for the first class period. I went out to the gate on which he leaned. "Well, Professor," he said, "grass is rising—and I got to move on. I'm lonesome. I want to hear the wolves howl and the owls hoot." Twenty years went by before I saw Harry again. Meanwhile, for years afterward, he sent me western songs. Some I'm sure he made up. Some he "doctored," some he had taken down from the singing of others. One day I received a letter from him. He was on a ranch in southern Idaho. Enclosed were the words of what I consider the most beautiful cowboy poem in the language. The opening stanza runs:

Oh, it was a long and a tiresome go,
Our herd rolled on to Mexico;
With music sweet of the cowboy song,
For New Mexico we rolled along.

Years afterward, a young woman at Flagstaff, Arizona, after one of my folksong talks, came up and said that she knew Harry Stephens who was then in a hospital some hundred miles away as a result of a serious accident bulldogging steers. But it was a long time before our paths crossed again. Meanwhile, I carefully filed away all his letters. From Grand Junction, Colorado, he wrote to me on July 11, 1909:

I have just read over a pretty good spiel put up by Panhandle Pete in Wyoming and decided to send it to you. Am sorry I haven't got more but lacked the pencil and papper to copy down what I had the chance to get. Worked on the XIT in the Panhandle a while but work was so long and the fellows so tuff that I couldn't get anything out of them. The old boss, who was a good fellow, got killed in a mixup with some cattle thieves and after a mixup with the straw boss I had to vamuse. Rode on the divide a while and liked it pretty well but it was mighty cold up in the snow in the mountains on the summer range. I got off with some pretty good prize money in the steer tyings through Oklahoma this spring. There will be some two or three hundred dollar prizes through Montana and Wyoming next month and I intend to take some of those tyings in. This is a pretty country through here and some big Live Stock companies. This is a peculiar country. It is full of greece weed, California thistle, peons, cedar stumps and cactas; and prairie dogs, badgers, rattle snakes, lizards, mountain boomers, owels and coyotes all live in one hole. The coyotes are keeping me good music while I write this letter. Am going to see Utah in a few days and then Idaho and on. The cattle and sheep men have been going it out here but Uncle Sam's soldiers put a warm stop to it. Every thing is swinging along pretty smoothly now after a very hard winter. The stock men lost heavy, and there are lots of bone piles where the cattle huddled in the snow and starved. Am enjoying this old happy go lucky roving life pretty well and don't think I can give it up again for college life. If I get anything will send it in.

P. S.—Met an old Pard from Colorado yesterday, a kid that I used to run with a good deal. He knew some songs but me and another fellow were pealing some bronks for hat collections and I did not have time to copy them. He told me he wanted me to go to Texline with him the first of next month and help drift his brother's cattle over toward Nevada. He also said they were going to have a squirrel-turner's reunion [dance] over a cross the river next week and be sure and come so if I see him I may have a chance to get the songs as they were pretty good ones. One of Booger Red's fellows sang a song that went something like this:

Oh, give me a job
With the 2-o's
And I'll spur great holes
In their wild broncos

If I could get these few songs that I have got—about 14—
copied down, in a pamphlet to give around to my friends and sell
to others at a dime to pay expenses and in it tell about your work
and a promise of a large book from you later on at a low price if
they will send in all they can get I believe it would take effect.

H. R. S.

Harry sent me from Yellowstone Park many years ago a song he had
made up while watching and herding a bunch of horses at night. The
song pictures the feeling of a tired night-herder alone with a bunch of
restless cattle in the night-time:

Oh, slow up, dogies, quit your roving round,
You have wandered and tramped all over the ground;
Oh, graze along, dogies, and feed kinda slow,
And don't forever be on the go—
Oh, move slow, dogies, move slow.
Hi-oo, oo-oo, oo-oo.

I have circle-herded, trail-herded, night-herded, too,
But to keep you together, that's what I can't do;
My horse is leg-weary and I'm awful tired,
But if I let you get away I'm sure to get fired—
Bunch up, little dogies, bunch up.
Hi-oo, oo-oo, oo-oo.

Oh, say, little dogies, when you goin' to lay down
And quit this forever a-siftin' around?
My limbs are weary, my seat is sore;
Oh, lay down, dogies, like you've laid down before—
Lay down, little dogies, lay down.
Hi-oo, oo-oo, oo-oo.

Oh, lay still, dogies, since you have laid down,
Stretch away out on the big open ground;

Snore loud, little dogies, and drown the wild sound
That will all go away when the day rolls round—
Lay still, little dogies, lay still.
Hi-oo, oo-oo, oo-oo.

One day out in Abilene, Texas, I met an old-time buffalo hunter and asked him to tell me some of his adventures. Back in the days just after the Civil War, these hunters used to go out on the plains in wagon trains and kill buffalo for their hides. The stark naked, ghastly looking bodies were left lying on the plains and down along the ravines to rot and to furnish food for wolves and buzzards. (My Uncle Charlie Cooper killed as many as seventy-five a day with his famous Needle gun.) The hides were hauled to the nearest railroad and from there shipped East where the skin side was tanned and softened, while the "warm side, fur side, outside," was left untouched. The fur was long, soft, shiny, of all shades from light brown to deep black. Big buffalo bull fur was often jet black at certain seasons of the year. The first hunters were glad to get a dollar for one undressed hide. Years later, a fine, dressed buffalo hide sold for one hundred dollars, buffalo overcoats up to $250. Buffalo hides, properly tanned, made beautiful rugs and were also often cut and fashioned into cloaks for fair ladies. The Indians likewise wore them thrown over their shoulders, and also sometimes used them as floor covering for their teepees.

The old man had been a sharpshooter in his younger days. He carried a Needle gun and killed the buffalo for the entire hunting party. The gun carried so far that the bullet "never landed till next day." While some of the gang skinned the dead animals and spread the skins out to dry, the others packed the hides and loaded them into the wagons. "Two to shoot, four to skin, one to cook," says an old chronicle.

The old hunter went on to tell the story of a group of buffalo hunters that he had led from Jacksboro, Texas, to that region of Texas far beyond the Pease River. The hunt lasted for several months. The plains were dry and parched. The party drank alkali water, "salty as hell-fire," so thick it had to be chewed; fought sandstorms, flies, mosquitoes, bedbugs, and wolves. The Indians watched to pick them off from near-by Mexico. At the close of the season the manager of the outfit, who had been hauling the hides to the nearest market, announced to the men as they broke camp for the trip home that he had lost money on the enterprise and could not pay them any wages. The men argued the question with the manager.

"So," the old man told me, "we shot down old Crego, the manager, and left his damn ol' bones to bleach where we had left many hundreds of stinking buffalo. It took us many days to get back to Jacksboro. As we sat around the campfire at night, some one of the boys started up a song about our hunt and the hard times and old Crego. And we all set in to help him. Before we got to Jacksboro we shaped it up and our whole crowd would sing it together."

And he sang to me in nasal, monotonous tones, "The Buffalo Skinners." Professor Kittredge called it his favorite American ballad. From twenty-one separate versions from all over the West, I put together the five stanzas quoted here and six others:

Come, all you jolly fellows and listen to my song,
There are not many verses, it will not detain you long;
It's concerning some young fellows who did agree to go
And spend one summer pleasantly on the range of the buffalo.

It happened in Jacksboro in the spring of '73,
A man by the name of Crego came stepping up to me,
Saying, "How do you do, young fellow, and how would you
    like to go,
And spend one summer pleasantly on the range of the buffalo?"

"It's me being out of employment," this to Crego did I say,
"This going out on the buffalo range depends upon the pay.
But if you will pay good wages, give transportation, too
I think, sir, I will go with you to the range of the buffalo."

The season being near over, old Crego he did say
The crowd had been extravagant, was in debt to him that day.
We coaxed him and we begged him, but still it was no go—
We left old Crego's bones to bleach on the range of the buffalo.

Oh, it's now we've crossed Pease River and homeward we are
    bound.
No more in that hell-fired country shall ever we be found.
Go home to our wives and sweethearts, tell others not to go,
For God's forsaken the buffalo range and the damned old buffalo.

The opening stanza of the ballad of Sam Bass, as first sung by Texas cowboys, authorship unknown, includes many of the material facts of the life of this famous outlaw. Frank Dobie calls it a model opening stanza for all ballads:

Sam Bass was born in Indiana, it was his native home,
And at the age of seventeen young Sam began to roam.
He first came out to Texas a cowboy for to be,
A kinder-hearted fellow you seldom ever see.

He left Indiana at the age of seventeen, in 1860, in search of adventure as a Texas cowboy. Like Robin Hood and many another highwayman and freebooter, he was "kind-hearted," according to popular tradition. He took away from the rich and gave to the poor as Sam's personal inclinations dictated. Truly, at all times, Sam was the "master of his fate, the captain of his soul." His home was in the brush; society had no claim on him. He distributed just as his fancy directed the wealth that he collected at the point of his pistol. In the distribution of wealth, so that every man will be a king, there must be a he-king, a brain-truster or what not, whose word is final. For several years Sam reigned supreme in northern Texas as he threw, according to legend, twenty-dollar gold pieces about that were his share when he and Frank and Jesse James and the Younger boys staged the famous Union Pacific robbery.

What wonder that the common people loved him and covered his tracks as he rode for years over Texas, robbing banks and holding up trains as his needs required? In the eighties there were no telephone lines to help locate him. Young, handsome, free-hearted, a matchless rider, he and his band of wild, hot-blooded young adventurers, aided and protected by an admiring populace, rode and robbed almost at will in the most thickly settled sections of Texas.

But finally, in an attempted bank robbery at Round Rock, Texas, twenty miles north of Austin, the capital, through the treachery of one of his companions, on July 21, 1887, he "met his fate." In a fight with a company of Texas Rangers Sam was mortally wounded, and he died the next day, refusing to the last to give the names of his associates who fled. His purse contained the last twenty-dollar gold piece of his share of the Union Pacific Railway swag. His pistol and belt, now in the University of Texas Museum, still hold the thirteen unshot cartridges found there at the close of the Round Rock battle.

Sam met his fate at Round Rock, July the twenty-first,
They filled poor Sam with rifle balls and emptied out his purse.
Some say he's got to Heaven, there's none of us can say;
But if I'm right in my surmise, he's gone the other way.

Sam Bass is buried in a lonely country graveyard near Round Rock. Some kindly person has carved on his headstone (the original tomb-stone has long ago been chipped to pieces and carried away by curio hunters), "Sam Bass, died July 21, 1887, on his birthday, aged 27." By his side a companion in the robbery who fell instantly in the fracas must forever carry the obloquy of being "killed," as his headstone relates. Sam "died" the day after the robbery. A well beaten path leads to his grave, seemingly the only grave frequently visited in the cemetery. A "Sam Bass Café" in the town wins a large patronage, and Round Rock, Texas, a prosperous village, is famous chiefly because Sam Bass, cowboy, horse-racer, free spender, robber, lost his life in an attempt to rob its only bank.

As for the song, it sprang from the people. No one has ever claimed to be its author. Its sources are as mysterious and unknown as the

Texas grasses that grow above his grave, rustling and whispering in the Texas northers that sweep through them on long wintry nights.

During cattle-trail days, in Texas, 1868–1892, every singing cowboy carried Sam Bass in his repertoire. The tune is typically of the western ballad breed, drawling, whiney, creepy, saturated with gloom. Negroes classed it among their lonesome tunes. My manuscript collection contains nearly forty versions of the words; all the tunes were much alike. Once, while lecturing at Coe College in Iowa, I referred to the Sam Bass story. At the conclusion of the talk a freshman came up and said proudly: "I thought you might be interested to know that my mother was a sister of Sam Bass!"

"Sam used to coin the money," he said, "and spend it just as free."

Like Robin Hood, Sam robbed the rich to give to the poor. One story goes that he rode up to a lonely ranch-house one day and asked its mistress for something to eat. She caught, killed, and fried him a chicken. On leaving, Sam handed her a twenty-dollar gold piece and told her to keep the change.

At another time Sam, when hard pressed by the officers, and when his own horse could go no farther, proposed to a ranchman to buy a horse running loose in the lot.

"He's not for sale," said the man.

"If he was for sale," inquired Sam, "what would he be worth?"

"A hundred dollars," was the reply.

"Here's two hundred," said Sam, counting out the money from a handful of gold, as he at the same time loosed his pistol from its holster. "Saddle him up quick, I've got to be on my way. And I'll give you my horse to boot."

Still another good story is told of how Sam and his men were given lodging one night at a farmhouse where the owner and his family were to be put out the next day by a money-lender who held a mortgage on the place. Sam paid off the mortgage when the man came for his money, and gave the happy couple a clear deed for their house, and then at the first turn of the road robbed the money-lender of the money he had just paid him.

For several years he robbed in Texas, always going on horseback, and never being arrested until "they pierced poor Sam with rifle balls" at Round Rock. The song is sung widely throughout the West and has also found its way back into the Ozark Mountains of Arkansas, as well as the mountain ranges of Tennessee and Kentucky.

During one of my early folksong hunting trips to San Antonio, I looked up the proprietor of the locally famous Buckhorn Saloon. He was a German with a penchant for collecting the horns of wild animals. The horns, literally thousands in number, festooned the walls of his place of business, even to the gambling quarters in behind the front room where drinks were shoved across an elaborately carved bar.

As I sipped a glass of beer, I noticed a stack of printed eight-inch slips, titled "Hell in Texas." I read one through and was reminded that a Texas newspaper once claimed that General William Tecumseh Sherman was reputed to have written the song as a faithful picture of what he had suffered when, as a young officer, he was stationed on the Texas frontier. On leaving Texas, General Sherman, again according to legend, had said that if he owned both Texas and Hell he would rent out Texas and live in Hell. Whereupon a Texan retorted: "Well, damn a man who won't stand up for his own country!"

In the song Texas is described as a special creation of the Devil:

He scattered tarantulas along all the roads,
Put thorns on the cactus and horns on the toads;
He lengthened the horns of a Texas steer,
And added some inches to the rabbit's ear.
The rattlesnake bites you, the scorpion stings,
The mosquito delights you with buzzing wings,
The sand is sprinkled with millions of ants,
And those who sit down need half-soles on their pants.

He quickened the buck of the bronco steed,
And poisoned the feet of the centipede;
The wild boar roams through the black chaparral,
It's a hell of a place that he has for Hell.
He planted red pepper beside all the brooks,

The Mexicans use it in all that they cook;
Just dine with a Greaser and then you will shout,
"I've Hell on the inside as well as the out!"

My pleasure in this modern broadside won the attention of the German saloonkeeper. "I've already given away 100,000 copies of the Hell in Texas song," he told me. Then he directed me to another drink dispenser, a Negro, who ran a place down near the Southern Pacific depot, out in a scrubby mesquite grove.

"He was a trail cook for years," declared my friend, "and he knows a world of cowboy songs."

That afternoon I found my man back behind his saloon shack with his hat drawn down over his eyes, his head tilted back against a mesquite tree. When I shook him awake and told him what I wanted, he muttered, "I'se drunk, I'se drunk. Come back tomorrow and I'll sing for you." I spent all the next day under the mesquites in back of the saloon with this Negro. Among the songs he sang was "Home on the Range." From the record I made that day in 1908, down in the Negro red-light district (they used stolen red switch lanterns to advertise their trade), Henry Leberman, a blind teacher of music in the Austin State School for the Blind, a few weeks afterward, set down the music which, touched up here and there, has since won a high place as a typical Western folk tune. The original cylindrical record of the song has crumbled into dust, but the music that Henry Leberman set down from the record still survives. First printed in *Cowboy Songs and Frontier Ballads* in 1910, the basic melody which the Negro saloonkeeper gave me runs through the many sheet-music versions of the song that have since been published. In 1925 Carl Fischer published for Oscar J. Fox, a composer of San Antonio, Texas, the first sheet-music version. Lawrence Tibbett and John Charles Thomas soon thereafter included it in their concert programs. For a time it became the number one tune on the radio.

The story goes that on the night that Franklin D. Roosevelt was first elected to the Presidency, New York reporters gathered on his doorstep and sang "Home on the Range." At a White House press conference, the President afterward called it his favorite song and at Warm Springs, Georgia, the custom grew of using the song to welcome his visits.

Admiral Richard E. Byrd told a group of San Francisco reporters a story of his six-month vigil alone near the South Pole:

"For entertainment I took along an Edison phonograph and a few records."

"What was your favorite song?" asked the reporters.

"'Home on the Range.' During the first months of my stay I gave myself daily concerts, always playing the song that tells about the land of sunshine where 'The sky is not cloudy all day.' Later, when the cold grew more intense, my phonograph froze up and wouldn't go. Then I found myself spelling my loneliness by singing 'Home on the Range' against the cold, black darkness of the South Pole."

I like to think that my San Antonio Negro saloonkeeper friend helped to make life more tolerable for the brave explorer amid the icy solitudes of the Antarctic. The words of the song which I pieced together make the precise framework and order universally employed today. Moreover, the tune sung by the San Antonio Negro and printed, along with the words, remains substantially the same in all current renditions. I have preserved the original sheet on which I jotted down the words taken from several sources. Yes, I know I did wrong, but I rephrased some unmetrical lines.

Even before I found and recorded the tune in San Antonio in 1908, scraps had come to me by mail from several states. In my file I preserve references to the song and quotations varying from a single line to several stanzas. The longest version of the song, sent to the *Journal of American Folklore* (printed volume 22, page 257) by G. F. Will of North Dakota, contains seven stanzas and the chorus—the same number used by me. The sharp variations in different versions, some stanzas entirely meaningless, show clearly that the song was passed around by "word of mouth."

In 1934, a suit for a cool half-million dollars for alleged infringement of copyright, brought by a couple of Arizona claimants, put "Home on the Range" in the headlines. A resourceful New York lawyer found that, in 1873, two lonely Kansas claim-owners got together and composed the song. From one dugout came the words; from another dugout the music. Fortunately it was printed that same year in the *Smith County Pioneer*. Faced with these facts, the pseudo authors withdrew their suit. The National Broadcasting Company and others breathed easily again. A contributor who helped trace the origin of the song was W. W. McGilvrey of Thief River Falls, Minnesota. In the song, "the buffalo roam," "the deer and the antelope play," "the wild curlews scream" and

> "The graceful white swan goes gliding along
> Like a maid in a heavenly dream."

Replying to a request for information about the song, the Thief River Falls man addressed a letter to "Fiddlin' Joe and all the rest of the Wild West Family" in which he furnished helpful facts. Then he added: "P.S. I might add that at that time there was antelope (in Kansas) in plentiful numbers, also the curlew was there, but *not nary a dang swan!* Buffalo had been gone about three years."

Writing to the San Francisco *Chronicle* from Redwood City, California, February 21, 1938, Mrs. S. Dimick says: "I read an obituary of Reverend Crandell, a Methodist Minister in Oregon, which said that he was the author of both the words and the music of 'Home on the Range.' Anyone familiar with the old church song, 'Home of the Soul' will recognize quite a similarity to that tune." Mrs. Sidney Cowell and others have recently written me that Vance Randolph told them that swans were common in Kansas in early days.

Meanwhile, in the Dallas (Texas) *Morning News* for May 24, 1940, William L. White of the Emporia, Kansas, *Gazette* wrote from Bucharest of a trip through the Balkans: ". . . the little bars are particularly nice because of their music. And they all know American songs. . . . And the nicest thing of all is that every one of them knows 'Home on the Range' and for the equivalent of one United States quarter in the local money, you can get them to play it over and over during the evening while you sprawl back in the soft leather cushions and drink beer and think about Kansas, or your lost youth, or some of the girls you used to know. . . .'"

I wonder if Mr. White knew that "Home on the Range" got its start in Kansas?

Late at night, hungry and tired, I leaned out of the car window as the train came into Deming, New Mexico, over the dusty route of the Southern Pacific railroad from El Paso, Texas. My friend, Roy Bedichek, met me at the train steps with his friendly Airedale dog, Hobo.

"Come over to the back room of the X–10–U–8 saloon," said Bedi. "They serve good steaks there and you may hear some singing."

As we ate, an impromptu quartette, made up of the bartender, a hobo graduate of Oxford University, a freight-brakeman just off his run from Lordsburg, and a cowboy from the Diamond A (Hearst) Ranch, sang "Casey Jones" with so many sad quavers that the dog Hobo howled mournfully as the song ended. Too perfect for a real ballad, I thought, though I have since found out that a Negro round-house worker at Canton, Mississippi, started the song on its way, when he found blood on the engine that killed Casey Jones.

Through the Diamond A cowboy I got an invitation to visit the Hearst Ranch about halfway between Deming and Silver City, where Billy the Kid reputedly added several notches to the handle of his Colt revolver. It is said that Billy killed twenty-one men, not counting Mexicans, before Sheriff Pat Garett got him. The next morning I rode northward out of Deming on a hired livery-stable horse. On the pommel of my saddle I balanced the fifty-pound recording machine, while tied up in a slicker behind the cantle of the saddle was the recording horn. No stranger-looking outfit, perhaps, had ever gone over that trail.

The Diamond A Ranch, at that time still a part of the estate of Senator George Hearst, father of the newspaper publisher, covered a large section of that part of New Mexico. The Southern Pacific Railway split it in halves. My business took me to the North Section. Darkness fell before my plodding steed stood at the front gate from which a long path led to a low, rambling dwelling house. I shouted, "Hello!" A man came to the door and answered, "Light, stranger, and look at your saddle." Then I felt at home, even at the Hearst headquarters in New Mexico.

After supper, my host drove me in a buggy behind two big, long-legged fast-moving horses several miles away to where a bunch of cowboys, camped in the open, had their campfire in a gully. The roaring wind sent streams of sparks across the open plains as the men sat about the fire in cowboy fashion with their backs to the blast. Here again I met my cowboy of the night before, Garland Hodges, a genial, friendly chap. Several men sang for me that night.

After a time the foreman said to the cowboy, "Jim, you old horn-swoggling cadaver of a pinto, say your piece for us, and put on all the tremolos. I'm pining for home and mother." And big Jim Swanson, still wearing his spurs, and marking the rhythm of the verses by waving his quirt, executed a bow to his eager audience and recited "The Cowboy's Ruminations":

Didn't have no dandy riders with their fancy-bosom shirts,
Didn't have no love-knot ribbon tied by gals upon our quirts.
Didn't pack no looking glasses in our saddle bags, to see
If the wind an' our complexion seemed inclined fur to agree.
Didn't wear no chaparejos trimmed with fringes an' with beads
An' to keep our tailor breeches from the bushes an' the weeds,
An' you bet you never saw us, it's as true as preachin', boss,
With a hundred dollar saddle on a twenty dollar hoss.

Warn't no shindigs at the ranches, as they have them nowadays,
With a lot of purty cowgals fur to jine in the hoorays,
Whar the music of the fiddle started every heart to prance,
An' the gods of fun and frolic ruled the sperrit of the dance.
Then we lived in tents an' dugouts, jest some blankets fur our beds
Used our saddles then fur pillows onto which to lay our heads,
An' our rifles an' our pistols right beside us we would lay,
So's to git 'em muy pronto if the Injuns made a play.

Finally Garland said, "Here is a short piece which I learned from a cowboy one night in Silver City":

Oh, the cow-puncher loves the whistle of his rope,
As he races over the plains;
And the stage-driver loves the poppin' of his whip
And the rattle of his Concord chains;
And we'll all pray the Lord that we will be saved,
And we'll keep the Golden Rule;
But I'd ruther be at home with the girl I love
Than to monkey with this goddamned mule.

Years afterward as a train took me into Concord, New Hampshire, where I was to lecture to the boys of St. Paul's School, I saw from the window a big sign over a large manufacturing plant. I read, "Concord Ironworks." On inquiry I found that this company had built the stage coaches (and the chains to pull them) that were famous in early western life. Thus I found out about the puzzling words "Concord chains" Garland Hodges sang that night in New Mexico.

On that same night one of the cowboys, speaking across the fire-light, vouchsafed, "Them 'Concord chains' reminds me of a song I knew about a fightin' son of a gun of a stage-driver." Then he sang *Bill Peters, the Stage Driver*, nine stanzas long:

Bill driv four pair of horses, same as you'd drive a team,
And you'd think you was a-travelin' on a railroad driv by steam;
And he'd get there on time, you bet, or Bill 'd bust a seam.

And Bill didn't low no foolin', when Injuns hove in sight
And bullets rattled at the stage, and driv with all his might.
He'd holler, "Fellers, give 'em Hell—I ain't got time to fight."

But he chanced one day to run agin a bullet made of lead
Which was harder than he bargained for, and now poor Bill is
　　dead;
And when they brung his body home, a barrel of tears was shed.

To protect me from the wind, Hodges had curled his body in half circle, I on the inside, while I scribbled as the songs went on. The flames of the fire, blown almost parallel to the ground, gave but feeble light, though I managed to get down all the words. He sang me the first tune I had ever heard to Larry Chittenden's *Cowboys' Christmas Ball*.

After arranging to go on a cow hunt with the boys next day, my host took me back to the Hearst headquarters ranch house. As he showed me to my room he said: "We used to keep this reserved for young William Randolph Hearst when he visited the ranch. But we don't see so much of him, now that he's running so many big newspapers."

The four huge, tall bedposts supported a mattress high up from the floor. I first stepped on a chair to get into the bed. Since that night one of my claims to fame has been that I once slept in the bed of William Randolph Hearst.

In the summer of 1910 Theodore Roosevelt attended the Frontier Celebration in Cheyenne, Wyoming. The year before he and Elihu Root, influenced by Professor Barrett Wendell, had asked a grant for me (which was denied) from the Carnegie Institution, in Washington. For me the Cheyenne visit afforded a happy chance to meet him. A letter I wrote home, just after the interview, tells the story:

"In the forenoon I sent a note asking for a moment's interview. Directly he came to where I was waiting in the hotel lobby and said: 'I should have answered the letter you wrote me [about two weeks before] if a moment's time had been left me. Now I must go to church. Can you meet me in my room at two o'clock this afternoon with a sheet of unruled paper (for a statement to be copied in the book)?' I said I could, and went my way.

"He was ready at the hour, and began by asking me just what I wished him to say. Thereupon I told him of the general attitude of unappreciativeness on the part of the West toward my work, and suggested that there was little recognition of the fact that the ballads throw light on western conditions and traditions. Whereupon

he interjected, 'Not only that, but they illustrate the curious reproduction of mediaeval conditions in the West.' I ventured to hint that
such a happy phrasing of the truth might go in outright; and he said,
'I am going to put it in.'

"Then he wrote, and chatted to me between sentences. Frank
James had been an ardent supporter of his in Missouri, and that suggested a line from Jesse James' ballad, which runs, according to his
version: 'The G—— D—— coward who shot Mr. Howard.'

"As he wrote on painstakingly, he remarked: 'Well, it is a tribute to the policies I stand for if the American people can read my
handwriting and still think there is any man behind it.' Meanwhile
someone knocked and he shouted 'Come in!' twice without turning
his head. When he had done, he introduced me to his visitor, a son of
Lyman Abbott, told him of my work, and then asked me to read what
he had written."

Mr. Roosevelt said:

You have done a work emphatically worth doing and one which
should appeal to the people of all our country, but particularly to
the people of the West and Southwest. Your subject is not only
exceedingly interesting to the student of literature, but also to
the student of the general history of the West. There is something very curious in the reproduction here on this continent
of essentially the conditions of ballad growth which obtained
in mediaeval England, including, by the way, sympathy for
the outlaw, Jesse James taking the place of Robin Hood. Under
modern conditions, however, the native ballad is speedily killed
by competition with the music hall songs; the cowboys becoming ashamed to sing the crude homespun ballads in view of what
Owen Wister calls the 'ill smelling saloon cleverness' of the
far less interesting compositions of the music hall singers. It is
therefore a work of real importance to preserve permanently this
unwritten ballad literature of the back country and the frontier.

The day before Boothe Merrill, a college friend, had given me the dance song, *Goodbye Old Paint.* Unexpectedly and joyously, one night we faced each other at the entrance of a noisy Cheyenne saloon. Boothe was coming out one swinging door as I was going in through the other. We grasped hands and chanted together the last verse of our college song, afterward sung by the Texans at Corregidor, "The Eyes of Texas."

Boothe was astounded to see me going into a saloon, and I was amazed to see him coming out. Then both doors swung inward and we found a quiet room at the back end of the place. I was running down cowboy songs and recording them; Boothe was on a vacation from his duties as prosecuting attorney for a county in western Oklahoma.

"Out in my country," said Boothe, "we do not dance *Home Sweet Home* for the last waltz at a cowboy breakdown; instead we stop the music and all sing and dance, to slow waltz time, *Goodbye Old Paint.*" He wouldn't let me "can" his voice, but he did sing the tune over and over again until I was able to carry it in my head back to Texas. Afterward I heard the same song at a rollicking play-party near Orville Bullington's ranch in Wheeler County, Texas.

Years later Oscar Fox, of San Antonio, Texas, set down the tune from my singing and from the melody used by Jess Morris of Dalhart, Texas; wrote the harmony and published it in sheet music. The song became popular throughout the country, especially over the radio, and won a place in *American Ballads and Folk Songs.* Since then I have often heard the song among West Texans where "play-parties" yet flourish instead of dances, fiddle music being thought sinful while the same tunes with dance music and precisely the same dance movements are not frowned upon by the churches.

To the stanzas sung to me by Boothe Merrill in Wyoming have been added other stanzas, all in loving tribute to a cow pony called Old Paint. A paint horse is a spotted horse, the favorite colors being a mixture of white and black, or white and bay. Such a horse in the "string" of a cowboy was usually reserved for his Sunday riding mount. Sometimes he was called a calico horse, "for to go to see my calico gal with a calico dress on," as one cowboy remarked.

The fact that a paint horse was a bit tougher, perhaps more given to pitching when first saddled, only increased his attractiveness to the fortunate youth who claimed him. Happy the lover if Old Paint pitched a "fence-row" from his sweetheart's door while she waved a happy farewell from her front porch. For her lover could ride, and tomorrow night were they not to dance together while they sang with the other dancers?

Old Paint's a good pony, he paces when he can,
Goodbye, Old Paint, I'm leavin' Cheyenne.
Goodbye, Old Paint, I'm leavin' Cheyenne.

His name was Texas Jack, ex-cowboy, stocky, massive in build, quick as a panther. For two days I had watched him bulldogging wild steers at the great Frontier Days celebration. Here in these days before immense crowds you could see the life of the West, especially the work of the ranch, unrolled before you in the contests between wild cattle, wild horses and wilder men.

For two afternoons I had looked on at Texas Jack, riding full tilt into the arena, just as a wild steer was turned into the arena in front of him. When Jack rushed by the center of the grandstand, he would suddenly dash up close to the fleeing steer, lean over, catch a horn with his right hand, leap forward from his horse, sending himself clear off the ground in front of the steer, with his own body, faced backward, lying high up between the steer's horns, his breast braced against the flat skull. At the same instant, with his free hand now clinging to the other horn, he would suddenly twist the animal's head and throw him in a heap to the ground. The two running animals, the wild leap of the cowboy, the steer lying helpless on the ground, the horse with reins dangling standing quietly by, it all happened too quickly to seem real. Texas Jack, the king of bulldoggers, as he told me, was to get $100 if he thus threw a steer on three successive days.

On the third day, after the last show, Texas Jack and I were to have dinner together and he was to sing cowboy songs for my recording machine. As I helped him dress for his last day's bulldogging, things looked bad. His right wrist was swollen to twice its size from a strain in a struggle of the day before with a steer of enormous size. He could barely bend his fingers. His face was twisted with pain. Before mounting his horse Jack handed me a hypodermic needle and gritted his teeth as I pumped morphine into three places in his swollen wrist. Then he rode into the arena. The steer was big and vicious, but Jack threw him just in front of the judges' stand in which sat Teddy Roosevelt. Jack galloped his horse to the door of the tent where I stood waiting for him, and, as he walked toward his bed, he fell flat on the ground, fainting with pain from his tortured wrist. Yet that night we had dinner together and afterward Jack sang for me many songs. Among them *Silver Jack*, a he-man of the West and of the cowboys and the hero of a ballad sent to me by Stewart Edward White.

Early in my folksong hunting days had come a letter and some songs from Mr. White, the first distinguished writer to pay any attention to my folksong project. He sent me a song about fighting Michigan lumberjacks with a rattling refrain: "Bung your eye! Bung your eye!" The last stanza ends a story about the heroine whose "front name stood for Kitty":

> I took her to a dance one night,
> A mossback gave the bidding,
> Silver Jack bossed the shebang
> And Big Dan played the fiddle;
> We danced and drank the livelong night
> With fights between the dancing,
> Till Silver Jack cleaned out the ranch
> And sent the mossbacks prancing.

I was soon to hear more about Silver Jack. From Bay City, Texas, Mrs. Hally Bryan Perry sent me a song, August 10, 1910, describing another fight of the trouble-shooting Silver Jack, which should put him high among frontier immortals. She wrote: "Colonel Abner Taylor, who built the $3,000,000 Texas granite Capitol at Austin, repeated it to us often, but under the cloak of confidence, as all of the parties concerned were at that time living, and at least one of them was in Washington, where we first heard it. He attributed the authorship, as I remember, to the late (then ex-) Senator Stewart of Nevada; and the redoubtable Bob you will probably recognize as ex-Governor 'Bloody-bridle Robert Waite'* of Colorado. The author declared the episode to have been history. Jackson was the state prison of Michigan, as you will know or infer."

Before I could decide just how to classify the stirring story of Silver Jack, Professor Edwin F. Gay, the first Dean of the Harvard Graduate School of Business Administration (he was on the committee that awarded me the first Sheldon Travelling Fellowship), wrote me from Cambridge:

"I sent the lumberman's ballads with which you favored me to another of my uncles in Michigan. One, you remember, had already written that it would be impossible to find any of the men who knew the ballads. He encloses a little poem, 'Silver Jack,' which was reported to him a number of years ago but which he does not think was an original lumberman's ballad, although Silver Jack was a real person who lived near Saginaw and was well known among the camp and river men as a hard case. His real name was Jack Driscoll."

Professor Gay's version of the song, almost identical with the Texas copy, is printed rather than Mrs. Perry's which contains many curiously variant lines, because I think the Michigan version is probably closer to the real source of the song than Texas or Washington, D. C. To me it remains a puzzle how a future Governor of Colorado could ever have had a fist-and-skull, drag-out fight with the deep-drinking, hell-roaring, "hard case" Michigander lumberjack, Silver Jack:

SILVER JACK

I was on the Drive in eighty,
Working under Silver Jack,
Which the same was now in Jackson
And ain't soon expected back;

---

*No record of this man is found. Davis H. Waite was
Governor of Colorado, 1893–1895.

And there was a fellow 'mongst us
By the name of Robert Waite,
Kind of cute and smart and tonguey—
Guess he was a graduate.

He could talk on any subject
From the Bible down to Hoyle,
And his words flowed out so easy,
Just as smooth and slick as oil.
He was what they call a skeptic,
And he loved to sit and weave
Hifalutin' words together
Telling what he didn't believe.

One day we all were settin' round
Waiting for a flood, smoking Nigger-head tobacco,
And hearing Bob expound.
Hell, he said, was all a humbug,
And he made it plain as day that the Bible was a fable;
And we 'lowed it looked that way.
Miracles and such like were too rank for him to stand.
And as for him they call the Saviour,
He was just a common man.

"You're a liar," someone shouted,
"And you've got to take it back."
Then every body started, 'twas the words of Silver Jack.
And he cracked his fists together
And he stacked his duds and cried,
"'Twas in that thar religion
That my Mother lived and died;
And though I haven't always used the Lord exactly right,
Yet when I hears a chump abuse him
He must eat his words or fight."

Now this Bob he weren't no coward,
And he answered bold and free,
"Stack your duds and cut your capers,
For there ain't no flies on me!"
And they fit for forty minutes,
And the crowd would whoop and cheer
When Jack spit up a tooth or two
Or when Bobby lost an ear.

But at last Jack got him under,
And he slugged him oncet or twicet
And straightway Bob admitted the divinity of Christ.
But Jack kept reason with him
Till the poor cuss gave a yell,
And 'lowed he'd been mistaken
In his views concerning Hell.

Then the fierce discussion ended,
And they riz up from the ground,
And someone fetched a bottle out
And kindly passed it round.
And we drank to Jack's religion
In a solemn sort of way,
But the spread of infidelity
Was checked in camp that day!

4

TWENTY YEARS INTERIM

Sturgis & Walton, first publishers of *Cowboy Songs*, asked to see the manuscript after the book had been turned down by Appleton & Company and by Doubleday, Page. The firm consisted of a couple of New Yorkers who possessed more nerve than capital. Macmillan later bought them out. I don't think *Cowboy Songs* brought about the Sturgis & Walton financial downfall since my first royalty check was half my annual salary.

The book had one distinction which no one recognized at the time: It was the first collection of native American folk songs ever printed along with the music of the songs. This music had been taken down in field recordings, and such music as there existed on the cylinders then transcribed through the use of earphones. Without the earphones, the squeaky, mouselike sounds bore little resemblance to music.

Sturgis & Walton would print the music of only eighteen of the cowboy song tunes from the hundred or more I had recorded. The tragedy of the situation came when, despite the best care, through the years many cylinders crumbled into dust. Some of the best tunes I found have been irretrievably lost. Folksong archaeologists of the future—if there be such—will find, however, copies of the genuine tunes of a few western songs, sung by genuine range riders, embedded in the dingy pages of the 1910 edition of *Cowboy Songs*. These records were not made in soundproof studios, but in dugouts, cow-camps and saloons where the cowboys felt at home.

Cowboy and other western songs first printed with music in *Cowboy Songs* have been well known and popular with radio singers: "The Dying Cowboy," "The Days of Forty-Nine," "Jesse James," "Git Along Little Dogies," "The Old Chisholm Trail," "The Texas Cowboy," "Sam Bass," "The Buffalo Skinners," "A Prisoner for Life," "Little Joe the Wrangler," "The Dreary Black Hills," "Jack o'Diamonds," "Home on the Range." *Cowboy Songs* also furnished the texts of many songs now occupying honored places in the American folksong field: "California Joe," "The Cowboy's Dream," "The Crooked Trail to Holbrook," "Hell in Texas," "Jerry, Go Ile That Car," "Joe Bowers," "The Trail to Mexico," "Sweet Betsy from Pike," "When the Work's All Done This Fall," "Night-Herding Song," "Zebra Dun," and many others.

So far as I can discover the word "dogie" was first printed in *Cowboy Songs*. George W. Saunders, the founder of the Trail Drivers Association, and at that time head of the San Antonio Stockyards, told me this story of the origin of the word: "When a young calf loses its mammy and is forced to eat grass before he can digest it properly, the calf's belly swells, his hair grows long, his legs wobbly. The calf gets puny and drifts behind the herd, where he gives the cowboys trouble in making him keep up. 'They ain't nothin' in your guts but dough' (because of the swelled-up belly), the cowboys first began to holler at the sorry-looking calves. Then they called them 'doughguts,' and 'doughguts' just naturally grew into 'doughies.' The spelling has become shortened to 'dogies,' the pronunciation being self-evident. You can spell it how you please."

While I was visiting Bryn Mawr College in 1933, Owen Wister wrote out for me a version of "Whoopie-ti-yi-yo" in which he spelled out the word "doughies, just as a cowboy thirty-nine years ago spelled it to me," said Mr. Wister, "while we sat under a mesquite tree near Brady, Texas." This version is printed, along with Mr. Wister's recollection of the music, in *American Ballads and Folk Songs*.

Many radio singers have pronounced the word "doggies." Even Will Rogers once made that blunder over the radio. Mr. Saunders' version of its origin is confirmed by Jack Thorpe of New Mexico, an authority on range manners and customs, and author of *Pardner of the Wind*, The Caxton Printers, Ltd., Caldwell, Idaho, 1945. In confirmation, Mr. Thorpe points out: "Stand a naked Mexican boy of four or five 'en profile' and you will see his little tummie sticking out—too many beans and not enough milk. Another who has nursed a goat will have quite a different figure."

But this is not all that can be said about this illusive and beautiful word. In New Mexico they tell it this way:

"Assuming that a ranchman is milking two cows, the calves are left in the milk pen and the cows turned out to graze. In the evening the milk cows enter the big corral and one of the calves is turned in with her to nurse. The milker puts a rope around the calf's neck and holds it back, letting it nurse but one teat. If grass is good, the calves are turned out at night and their mothers left in the corral. This custom, the Mexicans call *dogal*—a rope tied around the neck. Americans probably have corrupted it to 'dogy,' as most of the lingo we use about horses, saddles, cattle, etc., is derived from the Spanish, this is probably the explanation." There are other definitions, including the humorous one which I first read in *Time* magazine: "A dogie is a little calf who has lost his mammy and his daddy's run away with another cow."

When I put together the copy for *Cowboy Songs*, I planned to use as a tailpiece a fugitive stanza, recited to me one day in New Mexico, by a rider on the Diamond A Ranch. But, at that time, I was a member of the faculty of the University of Texas—and the bit of cowboy lore contained a naughty word. I took my problem to the President of the University, Sidney E. Mezes. After reading the lines he chuckled and said, "I'll stand back of you, Lomax. You'll spoil the book if you leave out that stanza."*

Early reviews of *Cowboy Songs* were none too flattering or numerous. I got my worst hiding from the book reviewer of the *Boston Transcript*, who called the book vulgar and cheap trash. In contrast, the St. Louis *Post-Dispatch* devoted an entire page in a Sunday issue to extravagant praise, reprinting many of the songs: "Frederick Remington had put the cowboy into art as Professor Lomax now puts him

---

*This was the stanza beginning "Oh, the cowpuncher
loves the whistle of his rope," p. 67.

into literature. One painted pictures of the cowboy in action while the Texan has gone about lassoing the songs." Sure enough, a drawing showed me careering along astride of a dangerous-looking mustang opposite a drawing of the famous artist.

A professor of English, Dr. A. H. Tolman of the University of Chicago, wrote in *The Dial* a warm and lengthy commendation of my effort to make known the brave, rough songs out in the cattle country. For years, however, the book received only scanty notice. (I do not now find any text of American literature that fails to give mention of *Cowboy Songs* as one of the "types," sometimes with liberal quotation of the verses.) Later, in 1914, the *Christian Science Monitor* of January 27 said editorially:

> For some time past Professor Lomax of the University of Texas, aided by professional and amateur students of literature, has been busy collecting the ballads and folk songs of the white people of the United States. . . . The days of pioneering from the Atlantic to the Pacific were rich in adventure and romance and naturally found expression in songs that are only now being recorded for the benefit of scholars. Among folk who live in the remote regions of the South and West today there is much of sentimental interest between the old and the young, between lover and loved one, and between the hero and his admiring fellows, that gets itself uttered in songs quaint in their phraseology and odd in their tunes. The white mountaineer of the Appalachians, the cowboy of the southwestern ranch, the worker in the western mine and the farmhand of the southern plantation, still rely on these aboriginal forms of self-expression.
>
> Realizing the value of such material to many groups of scholars, the Federal Bureau of Education is leading in an effort to make as inclusive as possible a study of the American variants of the old English and Scotch ballads.

Material was to be sent to Professor Alphonso Smith of the University of Virginia. Every public school in the United States was asked to send in the words of surviving English and Scotch ballads. The Folklore Society of Virginia thus became, at government expense, the depository of a large amount of material. But the more conservative scholars, at least until recently, have fought shy of showing any concern for folksong material indigenous to this country. What a grab bag of treasure would have been accumulated had the Bureau of Education asked also for songs of American origin. The "scholars" seemed interested only in the old stuff imported from across the seas.

Professor Smith's associate, Professor Arthur Kyle Davis, has since edited a handsome and scholarly collection of ballads that have a known English origin: *Traditional Ballads in Virginia*. Even now many American teachers of English show little interest in our nation's own folk songs. Witness Bryn Mawr College, where for many years no American Literature was taught—on the theory that there is no American literature!

When my income was no longer increased by the annual Sheldon Fellowship grant from Harvard University, the demands of a growing family forced me to give up active folksong collecting. Salary increases were small and came slowly to a frontier university striving to win public favor in the wide empire of Texas. My work as Registrar and Secretary of the University of Texas kept me busy the year 'round except for a month each winter when President Mezes allowed me to attend the Modern Language Association meetings and to lecture on Cowboy Songs at colleges and continue to collect folksong material.

On a bleak wintry afternoon in late December, 1911, a timid and uncertain young man stood on the platform in a circular auditorium in Cornell University to read a paper on "The Songs of the Cowboys." My book with the same title had just been published to a frozen-faced academic audience in Texas. I had traveled 1,000 miles to attend the annual meeting of the Modern Language Association of America. Professor Kittredge had wangled me a place on the program.

No one had greeted me. I had never before seen any member of my small group of hearers (when my paper on the program was announced, most of the audience had retreated to the corridors to smoke and gossip). I must have looked forlorn and lonely. My paper treated the rough songs of the southwestern frontier as a revealing expression of the life and experiences of cowboys at work on the open range and in trail-driving. As illustrations, I quoted liberally from the verses and, finally, I sang one or two songs. I didn't quite dare to ask the listeners to join in on the choruses.

Probably this group of professors had never before listened to a thesis so remotely foreign to their experience or so different from what they were accustomed to hear. When I finally ended my paper by putting the dogies to sleep with the line "Lay still, little dogies, lay still," and had given the long, eerie, lonesome night-herding yodel, I was greeted with a startled clapping of hands. I shall always hold in gratitude Professor F. N. Scott of the University of Michigan, who said that the songs I quoted were like a fresh breeze out of the west. "Good for our rusty mustiness," he added.

I drifted out into the cold darkness, glad that the ordeal was over and wondering whether I had failed completely. That night, following a dinner, came a smoker in the biggest hotel dining room in Ithaca. Louis Fuertes, the famous bird artist, made the Smoke Talk from the top of a long table, telling the story of an African adventure, the climax coming in a fight with a gorilla where as a culmination Mr. Fuertes fell flat on the table.

I sat alone, still abashed from my possible failure, a stranger among a jovial crowd. A friendly Yale man came over, called me "Texas," and invited me to join his crowd who were drinking beer and singing college songs. When Mr. Fuertes had plopped down on the long table, my crowd began to shout for me to sing cowboy songs. They carried me—resisting—to the long table and hoisted me on it. I sang all the cowboy songs I knew, including "Home on the Range," the crowd joining with special enthusiasm in "The Old Chisholm Trail." They shouted and laughed and begged for more. Then, I recited "Lasca." I had brought them something new, and they seemed to like it. Among those present I recall Raymond Weeks of Columbia, William Strunk of Cornell; E. W. Olmsted, Cornell; John Manly, University of Chicago; E. E. Hale, Jr., Union College; W. M. Chamberlain, Denison University.

From this incident came immediately two invitations to speak at Cornell. One brought me to the final and annual function of the Junior Class. The ballad talk I made for these boys a year later is now filed away somewhere in the "archives of gravity" in Cornell. When I came back to Texas, many letters followed asking me to come to colleges throughout the north and east. During the following ten or fifteen years I spoke to more than two hundred institutions of learning, in every state except three, for a total of more than five hundred engagements. Professor William Lyon Phelps used to have me visit Yale for every student generation, and always introduced me. Equally generous was Professor Kittredge, who once presented me to the Harvard Club in Boston. Also he turned over to me for an hour his class in ballad study. But far happier was I when Dean Briggs put me in charge of English 5. Many folk songs and tunes fell into my hopper as a result of these engagements.

More important was the realization that our native folk songs awakened interest among intelligent people. My newfound friends cheered me on and bade me keep on collecting. I needed this encouragement. After Cornell in 1911 I never lacked for friends among the Modern Language Association group. I read papers at their annual meetings in Cambridge, Cleveland, Philadelphia (twice), Madison, Baltimore and St. Louis. If my efforts contributed nothing to scholarship, I did perhaps add hilarity to the Smoke Talk period, at which I was frequently asked to speak and to sing cowboy songs.

In 1917, just as the United States entered the World War, a local political explosion on the University of Texas campus catapulted me from the state. James E. Ferguson, the picturesque and dynamic Governor, didn't like me. I landed in Chicago with my family and household goods, an exile from all that I held dear—the hills and prairies I loved, my half-paid-for home in Austin, Texas, the University of Texas that I had served since the day after I graduated in 1897.

I had come to Chicago to work for the investment banking house of Lee Higginson and Company, many of whose employees had recently joined the United States Army or Navy. Barrett Wendell, Jr., of that firm, whose father had taught me in Harvard, had offered me a salary almost twice as large as I had earned at the University of

Texas. "As much as the Governor of Texas gets," chortled my children, Shirley and John and Alan. I knew nothing of high finance; I know even less today. At that time I don't think I could have defined accurately the difference between a stock and a bond. My ignorance made me terribly self-conscious and unhappy. I didn't want money that I had not earned, and I soon discovered that as a bond salesman I possessed no immediate earning capacity. Christmas Eve, after I had begun work on September 1, 1917, I found on my desk one morning an envelope containing four one hundred dollar bills, crisp and brand new, together with a letter from the partners thanking me for my services, saying the money was my part of the year's bonus to employees. Up to that time I had probably not earned for the firm a total of half that amount. Such generosity humiliated and shamed me. I laid the money on the desk of Charley Schweppe, one of the partners, and told him I couldn't accept a bonus. He listened patiently to my halting, embarrassed explanation and then said:

"John Lomax, Lee, Higginson and Company think they know how to run their own business. You take that money and go back to work." A few days afterward he brought his wife from their Gold Coast home in Lake Forest to visit us in our rented cottage in Highland Park.

But I found little happiness in the money-grubbing toil of State Street. The excited barkings of brokers in the stock and grain exchanges, where I sometimes loitered, sounded like the yapping of coyotes. I had little sympathy for this sort of warfare. My life seemed drab and desolate as I walked from one building to another hunting for customers; the streets were cold, inhospitable. On the corners, the policeman's whistle in the murky, wintry darkness sounded like the cry of screech owls, dismal and forbidding. At times even now I seem to hear those shrill whistles, and my heart turns cold again.

For me Chicago held one bright spot—the home of Tom Peete Cross, one time fellow student at Harvard, a Virginian with a lovely wife and two daughters almost as lovely. As a student of Irish literature he knew ballads and folk songs scientifically. He cheered me on in my work as a collector. Almost every year we had met at the annual sessions of the Modern Language Association, where a group of like minds would meet and sing together some of my latest finds. Through Tom Peete Cross I met Lloyd Lewis, Alfred MacArthur and Carl Sandburg. These four men changed the color of my existence. Their friendship and sympathetic attitude kept alive my interest in folk stuff even amidst the deadening influence of the stock ticker. We met informally now and then, and swapped songs.

Carl Sandburg came out to see me on a holiday, taking away with him the *Letters of Harry Peyton Steger*. Steger, the literary executor of O. Henry, at one time high in the councils of Doubleday, Page & Company, was my friend and classmate of university days. Sandburg possesses a rare, unerring, instinctive feeling for the genuine ballad. When we remember that he has spent years of his life pounding pavements looking for news items, it is remarkable that the first large collection of folk songs, his *The American Songbag*, contains so few cheap tin-pan-alley maunderings. He loves simple folk, and his instinct for their real product is uncanny.

I leave it to Lloyd Lewis, who was then a star reporter on Chicago's best newspapers and is now managing editor of the Chicago *Daily News*, to interpret this quartet's reaction to me. Lloyd Lewis became nationally known through his "Life of General W. T. Sherman" and *Myths after Lincoln*. He will do other historical masterpieces, granted only that he has time from earning a living. Lloyd has written, without any thought of publication, a flattering summary of what I did as an avocation during the two years I was submerged in the financial vortex of Chicago, thus keeping alive my interest in folk stuff. Too personal, yes; but at least a fine tribute to the validity and appeal of cowboy music, is Lloyd's story:

"It was a Sunday afternoon, the year I suppose about 1920 (it was soon after you came to Chicago to work for Lee, Higginson and Company) that Tom Peete Cross brought over to our apartment at 5220 Dorchester Avenue the Texas folk-lorer he had so often talked about. I was curious, for you had but lately gained fame in academic circles at least, by defying Pa Ferguson on the matter of academic freedom, and were said to have been recommended to Lee, Higginson by Teddy Roosevelt. Then, too, I was curious about your songs, for Tom Cross and I, in our elaborately untrained voices, amused ourselves with folk songs. He knew more than I, being a Southerner, but in Indiana on the farm where I grew up, we had had North Carolina uplanders as farm hands and they had sung many ballads, most of them westerns, 'Jesse James,' 'Poor Dying Cowboy,' etc., etc. And I had been in northwest Colorado a summer or two at the time and learned a lot of cowboy songs from the sheep-herders and wild-horse wranglers.

"Anyway, Tom and I got you to singing right off, almost as soon as you got inside the door, and my mother, who was a Quakeress, and my sister, all sat listening. You were pretty timid about it, but evidently you saw we meant it when we said we wanted more, and that we weren't being polite.

"I fairly rushed to Carl Sandburg, who was a fellow newspaperman in town, and told him you were living on the North Shore, and he must hear you. He sang a lot, collected songs, and would go with Alfred MacArthur, Otto McFeely and myself to the sand dunes and sing hobo songs, all kinds of folk songs, over week-ends, fooling around, taking it easy.

"I don't know whether Carl had heard of your songs at that time. It seems to me that he had, but I am not sure. Anyway we had you and Tom over again, and Carl out—one evening, I think—and you and Carl cut loose. I remember that you sang 'The Buffalo Skinners,' and Carl rocked his granite head to and fro and shut his eyes and raised his eyebrows and made whistling little 'ohs' as he listened, and when you were done, he said, 'That's a novel—a whole novel—a big novel—it's more than a song.'

"I remember how Alfred MacArthur kindled when he came out not long after and heard you sing that same song. He had knocked around a lot, was a successful businessman and publisher, a hard-fisted Scot, and like Tom Peete Cross the scholar, and Carl and me, the newspapermen, couldn't sing a note in the conventional way, didn't know anything about music—none of us did, or give a damn for it, as such. But what we used to talk about was that you had what we took to be pitch, you could hit the sharp, often piercingly right note that gave the song character, made it descriptive, made it a picture of somebody, or some mood. We could see the characters who were singing—the buffalo-skinners killing old Crego, the Negro woman when her apron got too high, and then the role that I always thought you did best, the Westerner who when riding one morning for pleasure met a cowboy who was singing about the little doughies who wouldn't lie down.

"I remember it was this time when Tom and I had Carl with us that you cut loose with that yodel at the end—the yodel just after the cowboy had assured the little doughies that Wyoming will be their new home. It was one of the damnedest pieces of transporting of the imagination I ever experienced, and I had before that and since seen a lot of actors and heard a lot of singers. It was the same sort of thing that Bert Williams and Mary Garden did—the song without singing—the role established without great technical display—the singing voice made a medium and not a goal—the singing voice which isn't mechanically remarkable (perhaps not even good), but capable of making the listener get up and go where the singer wants him to go, and feel what the singer feels.

"Never has any singer of cowboy songs since then made me feel the dust, the great grass ocean, the harried, bellowing steers as you did in that yodel. It was strange, eerie and western. Your voice would break and hitch sometimes but would get right back on the pitch and go on, and that made it all the more real—and all the more imaginative.

"We kept you singing a long time that night. Tom would do 'Dese Bones Gwine Rise Again,' and Carl 'Hallelujah, I'm a Bum,' and 'Humble Yourself' in between times, then we'd get you on the plains again. There were two nights I can't separate in my mind—Tom was there both times and Mac-Arthur once. MacArthur and I had been making beginnings at the time of collections of cowboy ballads on the phonograph, and you set us off hunting more. There weren't many then, though in succeeding years more came on the market. The Tin Pan Alley boys took it up.

"I remember Carl, a day or two after hearing you sing the first time, saying, 'That Lomax, ain't he something when he drives the doughies?' We none of us knew what doughies were before you sang about them; had to ask you. I remember MacArthur and I showing his little boys soon after how you skinned the buffalo, and how their eyes shone even at the second-hand and highly unmusical imitation.

"Tom Peete Cross was, and still is, the most interesting talker about folklore I ever knew; has more information about legends, myths and folk sayings. MacArthur was, and is, as you know, one of the best of all tellers of stories that have a native tang. I was busy collecting legends and myths about Lincoln, after his death; and Carl was collecting songs from all the sources that the cultivated musicians scorned; so you met a set of men who were ready to recognize the authentic collector, the artistic characterizer when he came along.

"The time was ripe, too. Here were we in a modern metropolis, all farm boys or small-town boys, and all getting a little sick of the efficiency, the mechanism, the culture of the big industrial cities of the 1920s. A lot of people were turning to folk songs, too, at that time. A few years later, and the radio and phonograph began the rage for cowboy songs, rural songs, mountain music, hill-billy ballads, all representing an escape from the complexities of a civilization which was over-scientific, over-capitalized, over-mechanized. As theater goers or newspapermen, Carl, MacArthur and I had had our fill of sophisticated programs and artists. We were ready for realism, for the genuine folk music, and it seemed important, seemed nostalgic and natural when you sang it. I remember we told everybody we knew to meet you and get you to sing, but we couldn't get you to shoot to larger groups. It had to be casual and informal . . ." It was through the influence of those four men, I feel sure, that I put together in 1918 and sent to the publishers an overflow book from *Cowboy Songs*; another smaller volume, it was *Songs of the Cattle Trail and Cow Camp*.

As for my Chicago venture into the world of business, I guess I was a misfit from the beginning as a very small unit in an important group that, as events proved, was only one more important factor in that era of "Frenzied Finance." Of one thing I am certain: the firm was kind and indulgent to me—even to allowing me, now and then, to accept invitations from colleges to talk to the students about folk songs.

I found many folk songs during my lectures to college students; but I had other experiences too. One winter night I lectured before the students of Denison University in Ohio. The following morning, at eleven o'clock, I had engaged to speak at chapel services at the University of Indiana at Bloomington. Since I had no agent to look after my routine, before signing lecture agreements I would apply a ruler to the railroad map and decide whether I could make the distance required to meet the next audience. A railroad timetable always confused me. I could never figure one out. But sometimes my ruler got me into trouble, for the length of the line I measured did not always fit the timetable. This was one of the times.

My route led from Denison University, about fifty miles east of Columbus, Ohio, via the Pennsylvania Railroad to Indianapolis, Indiana, where I was to change cars and take a way train to Bloomington. Before reaching Columbus, however, the conductor told me that the train was due to leave Indianapolis for Bloomington ten minutes *before* my train would reach Indianapolis.

I couldn't make it. That meant the loss of a lecture fee, as well as disappointment to friends who were bringing me to Indiana University for the third time. On account of snow, an automobile was out of the question. I even considered hiring a special train. In desperation I told my troubles to a new conductor who had taken charge of the train at Columbus. He most kindly agreed to wire the train dispatcher in Chicago and ask that the train to Bloomington be held. "But who are you, and what is your business?" he inquired.

I told him that two thousand Indiana University boys and girls would be packed in the chapel the next morning to hear a Texan sing cowboy songs. I must not disappoint them. I did not mention my fee of $75. My earnestness moved him to such a degree that he promised: "If you will stay awake and remind me, I'll wire the Chicago dispatcher at every stop we make throughout the night. Maybe I'll impress him with your importance."

It was then past midnight. I was tired and needed rest; but there was no sleep for me. As the conductor swung off at every stop, I was at his elbow to remind him of his promise. Two or three hours passed, and he came to me, smiling. "I've found another passenger who also wishes to go to Bloomington, so my wire now mentions the two of you. Don't worry; your chances look better," he said.

I hunted up the drummer, hurrying home to Bloomington to spend Thanksgiving with his family. We talked the night through, as we wondered about our train. Dawn was just breaking as we rolled into the big Indianapolis station. Our friend the conductor directed that we stand on the train's steps, bags in hand, to be ready to jump off and make a run for it. Amidst the clanging of bells and the cheerful early morning roar of the station I heard, coming from a group of men, swinging lanterns, a cheerful and happy call: "This way! Hurry up, you Bloomington passengers. The train can't wait any longer!"

I ran and ran with two heavy suitcases, up one flight of stairs, down another, through two or three long corridors, up a steep incline—ran until I reached the blessed refuge of a day coach headed south, and, breathless, fell exhausted into a seat! The telegrams had done their work. I had made the Bloomington train. And so had my friend, the drummer!

I curled up on a seat and was immediately asleep. Soon a sound of violent altercation awakened me. Through the bleary haze of semi-consciousness I saw my erstwhile fellow traveler, whose destination luckily had helped me, being escorted, loudly protesting, from the train. The conductor and a brakeman were dragging along the angry man to unload him, ten miles outside Indianapolis, on a bleak and barren landscape. In response to my puzzled inquiry the conductor growled:

"Had a ticket for Bloomington, Illinois, and not for Bloomington, Indiana—the darned fool!"

Growing out of similar haphazard routings, I later faced another mixup in California, after a series of three talks at the University of California at Berkeley. The evening following the final date, I was to speak to the students at Stanford University. No troubles there. The fly in the ointment turned out to be an eleven o'clock morning engagement, the day following the Stanford lecture, at the University of California in Los Angeles. The four hundred miles distance had looked so short on the map.

"The Southern Pacific runs a lot of fast through trains, I can make it all right," I had comforted myself, as I signed the impossible-of-fulfillment contract; for, as it turned out later when I pestered various overworked and harried railroad agents, the only possible train that could land me for my lecture in Los Angeles (after the evening appearance at Stanford) was a non-stop train. It ran straight from San Francisco to Los Angeles without one pause to take on passengers at any station. "It shoots through Palo Alto at a mile a minute," one agent told me. When I listened to this ominous announcement, my serene confidence in the good fortune that had rescued me from other overhanging disasters was in no whit disturbed. "I'll just run down to Stanford and ask the President to stop that train. He'll know how; a railroad man founded Stanford University."

But President Wilbur could do nothing. "That through train won't stop for anyone. In the past I have tried repeatedly for many prominent people." He looked me over casually. "My trustees are supposed to exercise power and influence in California. Palo Alto and Stanford should be important to the life of the Southern Pacific Railway, but all of us together, trustees, faculty and students, can't stop that train. It *can't* be done; you'll have to break one of your engagements!" His big fist thumped, for emphasis, the desk in front of him.

I assured him that I would stand by dear old Stanford, and vanished into the gathering darkness, my vaunted confidence in my good fortune not shattered—but slightly slipping. On the train back to San Francisco I took serious thought with myself. Again a fat fee, though dangling four hundred miles away, was in dire jeopardy. I abhorred the telegraphic device: "Imperative business calls me back to Texas. Leaving immediately for San Antonio. Regretting, etc."

"No," I thought, "there must be some way."

Earlier that same year, at home in Austin, Texas, I had been busy preparing an ex-student catalogue of the University of Texas, sixty thousand names. I dug my knuckles into my eyes to assist concentration and attempted to resurrect the names of those "Texas-Exes" who had drifted to San Francisco—one of these might help. Suddenly, like a ray of sunlight through a rift in a cloud, flashed one name. Cy McLaughlin! I hadn't seen Cy for twenty-five years or more; as I was getting into the University of Texas, he was getting out—off on a fellowship to Columbia University to study geology. Men with money long since had come to believe that Cy's knowledge of what was under the earth had a cash value. Cy was now president of a big California oil company. To Cy I went with my tale of woe. I'll never forget the kindly crinkle about his keen black eyes as he heard my story.

"I think I can fix it up," said Cy, as he reached for a telephone. "Give me the General Manager of the Southern Pacific Freight Division. I want you to stop No. —— at Palo Alto next Friday night," I heard him speak into the phone. "Friend and college mate from Texas. Speaking to Stanford students, etc." A slight pause. "Thank you," said Cy, as he hung up. "Everything's all right, Lomax," he announced, as I stammered wondering gratitude. I had at last reached the place where sat the man who could punch a button and make the wheels go round—and stop.

I said my little piece in Stanford and, in due time, was standing on the platform watching the approaching head-light of the Los Angeles train that, in all the tides of time, had stopped for no man. As the train rushed by it seemed endless—a solid quarter of a mile of sleeping cars headed south. My heart was in my mouth, for I couldn't yet believe that all this terrific power, these tons of wood and iron and steel, would pause for me. Suddenly came the shriek of tightened brakes, the long train ground to a stop. I hurried for the first opening. From it swung two men in uniform.

"Shine his eyes with your lantern," said the deep-voiced conductor. "I want to see the color of the hair and the cut of the jib of the son-of-a-gun who had influence enough to stop a train that *can't* be stopped." Then, as he caught sight of my timid, inoffensive exterior, he gave me a half-friendly push: "Hurry up, son: get aboard. I thought you'd look like a combined Jesse James and Sam Bass, rolled into one. You don't even resemble a millionaire!"

Once while speaking before the students of Oberlin College on Negro humor, even in spirituals, I quoted some stanzas I had heard sung in a small wayside church among the big cotton plantations of the Brazos bottoms in Texas:

I am Baptist bred and Baptist born,
Jine de Heaven wid de angels,
And when I die dey's a Baptist gone,
Jine de Heaven wid de angels.

Methodist preacher, you are dead,
You poured water on the baby's head;
Baptist preacher, you are right,
'Case you take them candidates out o' sight!

I went to the river to be baptized,
I stepped on a root and I got capsized;
The water was deep and the preacher was weak,
So the nigger went to Heaven from the bottom of the creek!

Until I made this quotation the audience had followed sympathetically the illustrations I had given of the picturesque imagery and poetic phrasing found among the humblest Negro congregation of the backwoods. Now this vigorous defense of the Baptist doctrine of immersion and the story of an accident in a creek water-hole sent the crowd into gales of laughter. The last resistance between speaker and audience broke down, leaving me happy. Joining uproariously in the laughter was a portly young instructor of modern languages seated near the front. As I attempted to go on, suddenly he again exploded, taking the audience with him. He threw up his arms, tilted back his head and shouted guffaws. Again before I had spoken half a sentence his merriment erupted, this time louder than ever; and once more the audience followed him. Repeatedly the same thing happened until the play was out of my hands. Thereafter, it must have been a full five minutes that the audience, forgetting what first set them off, laughed at the antics of the hysterical young man. When he stuffed a hand-kerchief into his mouth, a blast from within blew it out as he and the sympathetic audience howled in unison. They had forgotten the lecturer entirely.

Meanwhile I found a convenient chair and sat down and waited. The audience was watching the helpless, fat instructor, not me. He did not disappoint them. Following explosions from him perhaps a dozen times they all shouted and laughed together. Finally, I hesitat-ingly began to talk, but once more, as if necessary to restore complete composure, the audience cheered me heartily, and again laughed with the hilarious young instructor.

This lecture, which, thanks to the laughing professor, should have been long remembered at Oberlin College, had grown out of a more serious paper that I had read some years before at Cleveland, Ohio, for the annual meeting of the Modern Language Association of America, in which I attempted mainly to show that the phraseology of Negro spirituals often contains poetic expressions of pungent wit, simple beauty, startling imagery, extraordinary vividness and power. All my life I have laughed with my Negro friends—never at them. In particular do I resent "takeoffs" of Negro religious ceremonies and spiritual singing such as I have often heard in northern cities.

Early in 1919 my career as a bond salesman ended unexpectedly and suddenly. Two of my college friends, Will C. Hogg and Dexter Hamilton, asked me to come back to Texas, at an increased salary, as Secretary of the University of Texas Ex-Students Association. Only a month after I first reached Chicago, swashbuckling Governor Fer-guson, my enemy, having been impeached and forever prohibited from holding any state office of public honor or trust, the Regents of the University of Texas re-elected me to my former position. At that time I could not desert my newly found friends, Lee Higginson and Company. Now, however, after a lapse of nearly three years I felt greater freedom. I had developed into a fair salesman, and for a year or so I had several times earned my salary. Moreover, I was devoted to the University of Texas; I loved my State and Texas people, and a chance to go home brought supreme happiness to me and my family. So again we packed all our goods and chattels and trekked back to our beloved Texas, all singing as we rolled across Red River, the state's northern boundary, John Lang Sinclair's famous song:

> The Eyes of Texas are upon you
> Till Gabriel blows his horn!

Will Hogg had led the fight against Governor Ferguson, who declared that Texas was "going hog-wild on higher education." He had told the Governor to his face that he had "rather go to hell in a hand basket" than be dictated to by him or any other man. Mr. Hogg got more than five hundred friends to join him in financing the Ex-Students organization in a minimum annual amount of twenty-five thousand dollars.

The offices of the association were established off the campus from where "we can freely fight any politician who dares to put the putrid paw of politics on the University of Texas," said Mr. Hogg. When he succeeded Dexter Hamilton as President of the Ex-Students Association, I well remember the first instruction he gave me. He told me to advertise in every newspaper in Texas that any returning service man of World War I could get money to attend the University of Texas.

When nearly two hundred applications came in I telegraphed to him in alarm and asked where the money was to come from. He boomed over the telephone: "That's my problem. You keep on doing what I tell you. You get the soldier students; I'll get the money." And he did—a lot of it coming from his own pocket. When a lad of great promise preferred a college outside of Texas, he financed his entire college course. His only stipulation was that I should never disclose the source of this money as long as he lived. He once wrote to me: "I find nothing else gives me half the satisfaction that I derive from the knowledge that I have gambled on the brains and ambition of young men and women. If I knew when I was going to die, beyond my funeral expenses I wouldn't reserve enough to buy a bowl of chili." Oil wells poured wealth into his lap faster than he could give it away in hundreds of beneficent enterprises. At his death he left the remainder, in excess of three million dollars, for educational purposes, including a loan fund for each of the twelve Texas state colleges.

My association with this man—a most difficult, lovable, explosive friend with a heart of gold—brightened ten years of my life, from 1915 to 1926. He was a worthy son of a great father—Governor James S. Hogg, a man-mountain in size and intellect. Alan Lomax and I dedicated our second book of American Ballads, *Our Singing Country: To Will C. Hogg, Classmate and Friend, Whose Life Was a Ballad.*

While Mr. Hogg was busy giving away his millions, building an Art Museum and a Young Women's Christian Association Building in Houston, buying parks and spending $30,000 a year for crape myrtle plants to beautify his home city, another Texas millionaire, Lutcher Stark, came along and attempted to use the University of Texas as a plaything. As President of the Board of Regents he called before that body Dr. H. Y. Benedict, Dean of the University. "Dr. Benedict," queried the President of the Board of Regents, "do you believe that God is good?"

Answered honest Harry Yandell Benedict, "Lutcher Stark, I hope so!"

At this point the investigation on faculty religious beliefs broke down.

Himself a recent graduate of the University, Regent Stark summoned the distinguished faculty and lectured them for two hours, on their duties and responsibilities. Repeatedly failing to have me discharged, he proposed to finance a rival Ex-Students Association. He made himself popular with the students of the University by cultivating the athletic department, buying blankets and gold footballs for the football team, bringing wandering football prodigies in to strengthen the football squad—students who promptly resigned when the football season ended. He sat on the players' bench at football games and was known to tell the coach what plays to call, and what substitutes to send in. The *Texan*, the student daily paper, partly financed by the University Athletic Department, continuously sang the praises of Regent Lutcher Stark. So one morning when a banner headline reaching across the front page featured a petition signed by sixty senior campus leaders, demanding my resignation, I knew that the end of my usefulness in the University of Texas had come. No longer could I get recruits from the graduating classes. Without these members the Ex-Students Association would shrivel and die. It made no difference whatever that the Executive Council could find no supporting evidence for the long array of charges of malfeasance set out against me. My local influence was gone. I was on a greased toboggan, no brakes working. In an American college no combination of men can break the clackers and the football gang on a rampage. Back of the students was an athletic department outraged because I had printed in *The Alcalde*, the Ex-Student Magazine, letters from alumni criticizing football management; and back of the football crowd was a millionaire Chairman of the Board of Regents distributing gifts and largess where they would do the most good. In his eyes a university was great in proportion to the number of touchdowns its football team chalked up. I couldn't buck the combination. This time I found it easy to fold my wings and again leave the University when I was offered a position in a young and vigorous bank in Dallas with a salary much larger than any I had ever earned. So to Dallas I and my much troubled flock moved in 1925. There we built The House in the Woods, a lovely refuge amid towering trees. For me it is the end of the trail, an anchorage for my four children for the past twenty years.

Leslie Waggener, Jr. was the Republic Bank executive who engineered the final Lomax move. I had known him only slightly during our student days. Now, perhaps partly through my favorable appraisal of his father as a teacher, I was to get a second chance in the world of finance. I went to work for the bank April 1, 1925.

First, I was sent on a month's trip to visit the outstanding banks of the nation, including, finally, J. P. Morgan and Company, with whom profitable arrangements were established. Even at that time the Republic Bank, now among the twenty largest banks of the country, was recognized as a conservative, soundly managed financial institution. Not long before, I had spent an entire week in New York City lecturing on folk songs in the public schools at ten dollars per lecture. My sleeping quarters had to be a hole in the wall. Now as the representative of the Republic Bank of Dallas my daily expense account amounted to more than ten dollars. "It's true but it's not so," I kept thinking. I was the same boy who paid his first year's expenses in Granbury College by selling flour made from wheat grown on eleven acres of land and salvaged from a field that had been ten feet under overflow water.

The Republic Bank officials seemed pleased on hearing my report when I came back to Dallas after a month's travel. As an understudy and close associate Mr. Waggener placed at a desk next to me his son, Leslie Waggener II, a Dartmouth graduate with one year of training in the Harvard Business School. As I look back now, this charming boy seemed to have caught up into his life and personality all of the worthwhile graces of the old South. His father was a power of the Republic Bank organization. In any controversy with his young son, I would be at a complete disadvantage. Never, however, was there any conflict, for the reason that young Waggener and I threshed out between ourselves any possible differences of judgment in policy or practice. I spent a happy year with Leslie II. He belonged to the debutante group, and often came to work when he had slept not a wink the previous night. "It's silly but necessary," he would grin. "I slip off and take naps between dances. I hide so my partner can't find me." Meanwhile he worked faithfully, asking no special favor. Along with other new employees he was on trial.

He and I worked shoulder to shoulder day after day. A few times we made business trips through Texas, riding in his car. He was a delightful companion. Neither of my two sons had ever talked so intimately with me. He didn't stop to ask me not to tell, but talked on and on straight into my heart.

At two o'clock one morning my telephone jangled. Leslie Waggener II had been accidentally killed! My son, John Jr., drove me through the darkness to the Waggener home. My friend, the son of the man who at college had given me many words of encouragement, said to me quietly, "Lomax, you have lost your best friend."

The Republic Bank had grown almost overnight into a hundred-million-dollar organization with two hundred employees housed in an eighteen-story building with a cupola just topping its chief rival. I came late into the group of employees where cross-currents of clashing ambitions and jealousies thrived.

The bond department of the bank prospered throughout the wild speculation days leading to the final crash in 1931. John Lomax, Jr., after graduating from the University of Texas and spending a year in the Harvard Business School, joined my force. When the cataclysm struck the country, I had made my share of mistakes, but the involvements of the Republic Bank went far beyond the contracts of its bond department. It weathered the storm. Day after day bond buyers came to my desk: "You recommended this security. I bought it from you. Now its market price is less than fifty per cent of what I paid for it." Then they would pause and look at me: "You recommended it." I couldn't take my troubles to other departments of the bank. They had troubles of their own. I was forced to sit and take it. The market in New York had gone mad. What could I say? Nothing. And I said nothing.

Then the president of the bank came to my desk and said: "Sell everything, all the bonds we own, for what you can get on the New York market." I called New York and found that for some of the bank's securities there was no market at all. No buyers, only sellers. And now the Bond Department had nothing left to offer our customers, many of whom hovered around and looked at me with sad, sometimes indignant, eyes. Down in the bank lobby were many white faces—faces of those who had speculated and lost. The bank was calling for more security for their loans, security that they couldn't put up.

One morning I staggered to my desk, whence I was led to a doctor. Fever 104. To bed. After two months I went to the bank and resigned. Back to bed for six months. Then Bess Brown Lomax, the sweet mother of my children, died.

It is impossible to overestimate what her intelligent and enthusiastic aid had meant to me. Without it I should probably have made little headway in sustained folksong collecting. When I first began seriously in 1907 to bring together a collection of cowboy songs she found time to keep up with the heavy correspondence involved despite the care of two very young children and the duties of a house-keeper when our total income was thirteen hundred dollars a year. She it was also who deciphered and typed the often dim and penciled manuscripts sent in by contributors, as well as my own hurried and almost illegible field notes. Moreover, she was orderly and system-atic, so that when I sat down to put together my first book, all of the material was ready at hand. Certainly to her belongs full credit for the folk songs uncovered during the first twenty years of my work. Whenever I faltered, her unflagging interest and energy kept the project going.

In 1910, just after *Cowboy Songs* was published, I was sched-uled to deliver a paper on "The Songs of the Cowboy" at the first meeting in Dallas of the Texas Folk Lore Society when I received a telegram from Professor Kittredge. He had secured an invitation for me to read a paper on the same subject before the annual meeting of the Modern Language Association at Cornell University. I was very anxious to accept, but the date on which I was invited to speak at Ithaca was identical with that of the meeting in Dallas. My wife, as always, rose to the occasion. I traveled to Ithaca and read my paper, as I have already recounted, while she mounted the platform in Dal-las and read the same paper on my behalf.

Her interest in folk songs was, I feel sure, increased by the fact that her people for generations had been born and bred in the moun-tains of North Carolina and Virginia. They were folksong singers; perhaps also they helped to make folk songs. The reader will find a dozen of her family's favorite ballads printed in *American Ballads and Folk Songs*, the music and words having been written down as sung by our daughters, Shirley Lomax Mansell and Bess Brown Lomax Hawes, who had learned them at their mother's knee.

5

AMERICAN BALLADS AND FOLK SONGS

During the late spring of 1932, at the nadir of the general financial collapse, my fortunes had reached their lowest ebb since the day I left college. At those two periods of my life I was in each case worth less than nothing; I was heavily in debt, I had no job. When I was graduated from college I did possess youth and health; while in 1932 I was barely recovering from an exhausting illness, with a home broken by the death of my wife, my four children scattered, and two of them, Bess Brown and Alan, nine and sixteen years old, respectively, still financially dependent on me.

I had reached New York on a long lecture and folksong collecting trip undertaken partly to restore my health. John, Junior, drove my Ford car. By night we had camped by the roadside and we had done our own cooking. Lecture fees were scarce and small. Cowboy songs had gone almost into a total eclipse.

One morning I drifted into the offices of The Macmillan Company at 60 Fifth Avenue. Mr. H. S. Latham, a big, healthy, wholesome man, whom I knew slightly, received me with gracious courtesy. I told him that for years past I had hoped to edit a volume of American folk songs but that until that time I had never had the leisure to round out a collection that had been growing steadily for more than thirty years. Mr. Latham had spoken more than once of his fondness for my two books of Cowboy Songs published by Macmillan. Both these books had had a steady if slow sale for several years. I watched Mr. Latham's face as I unfolded my story. I was desperate and I think he realized it.

"I like your plans," Mr. Latham said, "but we cannot tell in advance how we will regard the book you will submit. Have you any sample songs?" I was ready for just that question. "I can't sing them," I said eagerly, "but let me read you three."

I tried him first on the tragedy of "Big Jim," which had come to me from Vicksburg, Mississippi. It begins:

Cold and chill is de winter wind,
Big Jim's dead and gone—
Big Jim was my lovin' man.
Long, long, long are de years—

and ends:

Big Jim's dead and gone now,
Listen to my song;
Soon I'll be going too—
And I hope it won't be long.
Long, long, long are de years.

Next I read the long ballad of Adam and Eve in the garden stealing apples, pinning leaves; read it all, and read it in the elocutionary style that Mrs. Carrie Cox Langston had taught me in Texas when I was a boy in Granbury College. (Tom Peete Cross of the University of Chicago gave me that ballad. At the Modern Language Association meeting he used to recite it to uproarious applause with the fourth drink coming up.) In the concluding stanzas the Lord takes the situation energetically in hand, and shouts when he discovers an apple missing:

"Adam, Adam, where art thou?"
Dese bones gwine to rise again—
"Here, my Lord, I'se a-comin' now—"

Dese bones gwine to rise again.
"Stole my apple, I believe?"
Dese bones gwine to rise again.
"No, my Lord, but I 'spec it was Eve"—
Dese bones gwine to rise again.
Of dis tale dere aint no mo'.
Dese bones gwine to rise again.
Eve et de apple, gave Adam de co'.
Dese bones gwine to rise again.

Then I fired my third and last shot—a ballad I had found on the Texas Gulf Coast in the district between the Colorado and Brazos Rivers where the river bottoms spread out and overlap, where Negroes are thicker than mustang grapes. The story of "Ida Red" is personal and direct. It hits like a rifle bullet. When it is ended, you don't know whether to laugh or to cry. This time again I read more stanzas than I am printing.

I went down town one day in a lope,
Fooled around till I stole a coat,
Then I came back and did my best,
Fooled around till I got the vest—
Oh, weep, oh, my Ida,
For over that road I'se bound to go.

They had me tied with a ball and chain,
Waitin' all ready for de east-bound train,
And every station we passed by,
Seemed like I hear little Ida cry,
Oh, weep, oh, my Ida,
For over that road I'se bound to go.

If I'd a-listened to what Ida said,
I'd a-been sleepin' in Ida's bed,
But I paid no mind to my Ida Red,

And now I'se sleepin' in a convict's bed.
Oh, weep, oh, my Ida,
For over that road I'se bound to go.

I wash my face an' I comb my head,
I'm a'mighty fool about Ida Red;
When I git out-a this old shack
Tell little Ida I'se a-comin' back.
Oh, weep, oh, my Ida,
For over that road I'se bound to go.

As Mr. Latham laughed he was also mopping the lower part of his
brow. But he said no word. I was almost praying by this time. At last
he spoke.

"When do you think you could have the copy ready?"

"In one year."

"I am very much interested," he said. "The matter must go before
our Editorial Council. Where are you stopping? I'll let you hear
tomorrow."

I cannot recall how I got from Macmillan's to the home of Dan and
Jean Williams up near Columbia University. Consciousness came
back to me fully only when the mail was delivered two days later. My
letter was in a long important-looking Macmillan envelope containing
a contract for the book. Also it held a check to bind the contract. And
that's the how of *American Ballads and Folk Songs*, and the moment at
which I turned the corner to where a little light was shining.

For a long time I had planned to bring out a general collection of
folk songs. Now Macmillan had contracted for the book. I was ready
to fill in the gaps of my store of material. First I visited the Harvard
Library and the Library of Congress to read the books that had been
published in the folksong field during recent years. At Harvard I also
examined private collections, not yet catalogued, that had come to
the Library through the work of Professor George Lyman Kittredge.
Also I turned through the recently acquired popular ballad collection of Brown University and the large collection of Civil War songs,

nearly all anti-slavery, in the University of Wisconsin. Meanwhile I traveled to the University of California and was again disappointed with their barren folksong shelves. It required six months to make the survey necessary to avoid duplications.

During my stay in Washington, Librarian Herbert Putnam and the Music Division Chief, Carl Engel, interested themselves in the project and, finally, through the promise of funds from the Council of Learned Societies, agreed to secure for my use an electrically driven recording machine. Mr. Engel sent me to New York to examine the models (all new and untried). I fell among thieves and recommended an outfit, later bought for me, which was never satisfactory. Delays from breakdowns came with such frequency that I finally took the machine to Professor Paul Boner of the University of Texas who, after various tests, declared it to be a mass of junk, a low order of junk at that.

He threw the entire machine into the scrap heap and designed a brand new one, which was soon built under his direction. Thus I was saved much time, many long drives looking for a competent radio mechanic, outlays of money that I could ill afford. By agreement, all the completed records were to be deposited in the Library of Congress, in return for which the Library furnished the blank records and the recording machine.

While waiting for our first machine from New York, Alan and I made our first venture with a large Edison Dictaphone. We drove out of Dallas early one June morning in 1933 from the country home of Mr. and Mrs. Walter P. Sharp with our Ford car packed to the guards. I was at the wheel. At my side sat Alan, a seventeen-year-old college Junior, a tired, sleepy traveling companion after the festivities of commencement week. Soon, in the blessed refuge of youth, he slumped and slept.

Stored in the rear of the car were two army cots and bedding, a cooking outfit, provisions, a change of clothing, an infinite number of "etceteras" which will manage to encumber any traveler. Later, as a crown to our discomfort, we also carried a 350-pound recording machine—a cumbersome pile of wire and iron and steel—built into the rear of the Ford, two batteries weighing seventy-five pounds each, a microphone, a complicated machine of delicate adjustments, coils of wire, numerous gadgets, besides scores of blank aluminum and celluloid disks, and, finally, a multitude of extra parts, of the purpose and place for which neither Alan nor I had the faintest glimmer of an idea.

For four months this overburdened Ford bore us through Texas, Louisiana, Mississippi, Tennessee and Kentucky. Later in the same brave little car we also visited Alabama, Georgia, Florida, North and South Carolina and Virginia. Sometimes we camped by the roadside and slept under the stars. In Louisiana, bitten by malaria mosquitoes, I suddenly collapsed from violent attacks of chills and fever, the "shaking ague."

While I was yet in the hospital, Alan fell ill from the same malady, and, while he was recuperating, we treated ourselves to a leisurely stay in a comfortable tourist camp on the outskirts of Jackson, Mississippi.

We both worked hard, made long night drives over strange rough roads, camped only when we were too tired to go farther, ate rough and too-quickly-cooked food. Sometimes we dined alongside of convicts, more often with the trusties or guards. We worked late every night and often throughout Sundays. Meanwhile, except from Negro convicts, we found little interest or sympathy manifest for our project. Crisscross over the South our journey carried us. Often we doubled back to visit a community we had missed. Before the end of this particular trail had been reached and Alan and I were again back in Austin, Texas, we had traveled a distance of 16,000 miles.

The main object of this journey was to record on aluminum and celluloid disks, for deposit in the Library of Congress, the folk songs of the Negro—songs that, in musical phrasing and in poetic content, are most unlike those of the white race, the least contaminated by white influence or by modern Negro jazz. Folk singers render their music more naturally in the easy sociability of their homes and churches and schools, in their fields and wood yards, just as birds sing more effectively in their native trees and country. To find such songs, we visited groups of Negroes living in remote communities, where the population was entirely black; also plantations where in number the Negroes greatly exceeded the whites, as in the Mississippi Delta (one town there of 2,000 inhabitants, Monte Bayou, has not one white resident). Another source for material was the lumber camp that employed only Negro foremen and Negro laborers.

However, our best field was the southern penitentiaries. We went to all eleven of them and presented our plan to possibly 25,000 Negro convicts. Most of these men and women saw in us hope that once more they might get out into the "free world." At every opportunity they told Alan and me their pitiful stories. Alan seemed to want to set them all free. Perhaps they sang for us in the hope that we could help them. They did sing in every instance that we asked them.

In some states the convicts work on large cotton, corn and cane plantations, where they are segregated into companies of three or four hundred men, living in groups of houses, situated in different parts of the plantations. The Negro convicts do not eat or sleep in the same building with white prisoners. They are kept in entirely separate units; they even work separately in the fields. Thus a long-time Negro convict, guarded by Negro trusties, may spend many years with practically no chance of hearing a white man speak or sing. Such men slough off the white idiom they may have once employed in their speech and revert more and more to the idiom of the Negro common people.

As he made his work songs, the Negro cleared the land of the South, worked its plantations, built its railroads, loaded its steamboats, raised its levees, and cut its roads. When he worked with a group of his fellows in a situation where a regular work rhythm was possible, he sang simple, highly rhythmic songs; and every axe, pick or hoe in the group fell on the same beat. When he picked cotton or did some other form of work in which it was not possible to adhere to a regular rhythm, his songs rose and fell with the free and easy movement of his breathing. These songs were not designed for the ear of the Lord, nor for the ear of the white boss. In them the Negro workman is likely to speak his free mind. If he touches on religion at all, his mood is apt to be, at one extreme, submissive devoutness, and at the other, a horse-laugh.

Booker T. Washington, wise, tolerant, a gifted orator, a great leader of his people, urged Negroes to preserve their glorious spirituals as well as their rhythmic songs of labor. Often in his addresses he cast aside the white man's hymnal and led the audience in singing the songs of the Negro race. "Develop yourselves as Negroes, don't merely imitate the whites," he urged. One has to go to the back country, to the Negro in confinement or to communities where the churches are not large enough to attract the educated or the semi-educated minister, to hear these songs sung with the emotional fervor and vigor that gives them their chief charm. "We have grown beyond such crude songs," said an educated Alabama Negro to me when I asked for help in collecting Negro folk songs. What I have said does not apply to such great Negro artists as Dorothy Maynor, Marian Anderson, Roland Hayes and Paul Robeson, or to many other intelligent Negroes who are beginning to appreciate the richness of their own racial heritages.

At Terrell, Texas, thirty miles from Dallas, Alan and I made our first recording. A Negro washerwoman, as she rested from her work, sang a baptizing song:

Wade in de water, wade in de water,
Wade in de water, chilluns;
Gawd goin' to trouble de water.

Though her voice was high-pitched, it had a liquid softness that made the effect beautiful and moving. Alan blinked his eyes as he bent over the machine. Long afterward he told me that from that moment he felt no further doubts about enjoying ballad-collecting. He suspended his college career and worked with me steadily for the next two years. Alan also became my equal partner in three books of folk songs.

After one other stop in a Negro community, we reached Huntsville, the main unit of the Texas penitentiary system, where I hoped to test my theory that Negro convicts could sing the fast-disappearing gang songs of labor. My friend, Superintendent Lee Simmons, being away, I called on the Warden, long an official of the prison. He looked at me with surly contempt as he listened to my request for a chance to talk to the Negroes after working hours, and made no attempt to soften his emphatic "No" as he turned away to other work. So the sad little Ford trekked away to Austin to get help from Governor "Ma" Ferguson.

Often, we were afterward "slapped in the face" along our way but at no time with such brutal directness as by our fellow Texan. A year later we came back to Huntsville more than once, always backed by authority to which the unfriendly Warden was forced to yield. We endured his cold disdain, for we did find many interesting singers in the Texas penitentiary.

From this point of our journey I made frequent reports by letter to my folks back home. I include excerpts from them here since they give a first hand account of a trip which was more or less typical of many others I was to make in the next decade with Alan, with others, or alone. I shall have more to say later of some of the characters whom we met on this trip, but I introduce them here since this was my first encounter with them:

Prairie View, Texas, June 28, 1933.—Presently we are to meet a group in the "Music Hall" of Prairie View State Normal College, a Texas tax-supported college for Negroes, to get the songs for which we are looking. About seven hundred teachers, chiefly from the rural districts, are here. They seem suspicious of us and somewhat ashamed of the creations of their people—the uneducated group known as the "folk." Because some of these songs sound tawdry and cheap, these critics of their own people are apt to be blind to the beauty of the music, and the grace and sometimes lyric quality of the words of their songs.

The prospects seem to justify our staying over, and we are occupying comfortable quarters in the "Committee Rooms" provided for white visitors. We have been very courteously received by the Principal and find comfortable beds and a private bath to compensate for the loss of cots under the starry skies. *Later:* We are back from a gathering of interested people summoned by the Professor of Music. The going was hard, though we did find one distinctive tune which may go sounding down the ages.

Sunnyside, Somewhere in the Brazos Bottom, twenty miles from Hempstead, Texas, July 1, 1933—Time: sunrise.—Alan still sleeps with face covered from the sun. I sit in the shade of an abandoned garage facing a dingy house where lives a Negro family of fourteen, including the parents, a very abundant, motherly black woman and a mouse-colored man (also mouselike in spirit and demeanor). Yesterday, under the guidance of Professor Mills, we came down to this remote Negro settlement in search of survivals of real Brazos Bottom singing.

At the first place we stopped, the Professor, in explaining his sudden decision to come with us, told our host that he had come "sposmadically." The word struck Alan so forcefully in the midriff that he hastily refastened an already securely tied shoestring as a cover-up for his face, purple from suppressed giggles. Then presently a handsome mulatto woman sang with emotion, more effective because you felt the repression, the beautiful song:

I want to meet Death smilin';
I want to cross over in a ca'm time.
Deep River, Deep River, Deep River, Lord,
I want to cross over in a ca'm time.

To me and to Alan, there were depth, grace and beauty in this spiritual; quiet power and dignity; and a note of weird, almost uncanny suggestion of turgid, slow-moving rivers in African jungles.

We later found an excellent guitar-player seated under the shade of a large mulberry tree. Alan wrote down the words of picturesque songs until his hand became cramped with weariness. Meanwhile a group in the house sang "saints' songs" to me:

Three stars in the East, three stars in the West,
Show the gates of our home.

We took down the music of the best of these songs, working till the sun went down; and then we were summoned to a supper of fried chicken, fresh roasting ears, sweet milk and "ground peach" preserves—served in advance of the spread necessary for this huge family of children, ranging from two-and-a-half to twenty-eight years. We slept for the night on our cots under the mulberry tree in the front yard.

Last night we drove our musical, guitar-picking friend to a birthday party, where he thrummed away until midnight for a crowd of dancers, packed into a small room. As I sat in the car and listened to the steady, monotonous beat of the guitars, accented by handclaps and the shuffle of feet—the excitement growing as time went on, the rhythm deeper and clearer—again I felt carried across to Africa, and I felt as if I were listening to the tom-toms of savage blacks. When I peered through the doors and the windows the whole house seemed to throb with the movement of the dancers. I saw the grotesque postures and heard the jumbled and indistinguishable cries of jubilant pleasure, and I realized that Alan and I were now enjoying a unique experience amid a people we really knew very little about. We drove back after midnight through dark forests with a "yellow half-moon, large and low," peeping at us through the towering trees. The exhausted musicians slept on the back seat.

From my letters home describing our experiences I quote:

Galveston, Sunday Afternoon, July 2, 1933.—Here I am facing the Gulf with a strong inland breeze—a late afternoon breeze—sweeping in to make us forget the heat of a quiet, restful Sunday. Alan, who has worked steadily, needed some diversion and my suggestion brought us here where we hope to find some material tomorrow from the Negro longshoremen. We slept last night with our bed spread on the warm, springy beach sands near a tongue of deep water from the bay, which gave us a swimming place last night and again this morning before breakfast. We slept within sound of the breakers, and this morning the complaints of water birds waked us. Alan turned and begged for more sleep. I let him lie quiet in our remote camping spot until nearly nine o'clock. Today we made our salaam to civilization by dressing up and treating ourselves to a good meal at a beach hotel.

Darrington Convict Farm, thirty miles from Houston, July 7, 1933.— Alan and I drove direct through Houston to the Duncan Farm at Egypt in Wharton County. We enjoyed a chance again to sleep on a springy bed. We were busy through July 4 visiting the Negroes on the plantation, winding up the day by hearing a rousing Negro sermon, followed by some fine singing of Negro spirituals. The next morning we visited our first large prison farm—the Imperial—where we had many unforgettable experiences, tragic, comic, and of the deepest human interest. We added a number of good songs to our stock, both words and music. Alan and I worked with those men until we both were exhausted from long nervous tension. Last night we slept again under the stars down near the Gulf.

Wiergate, Texas, July 11, 1933.—Yesterday I heard for the first time the wail of the Negro woodsman as a fine tree that he is cutting sways and then falls to the earth with a shuddering crash. Shrill, swift, wavering, the shout swings to a sudden and dramatic conclusion, just as does the tree when the cry ends as the tree surrenders and lies prone on the earth that has fed it. It is a dirge of the dying pine and at the same time a warning signal to other woodsmen.

There is music in that cry, and mystery, and wistful sadness. After we had listened for a while, a group of glistening ebony figures, their torsos naked, came and sang the requiem of the falling pine into our recording machine.

Today I am staying over so that Alan may follow the different groups of woodsmen far out into the hills, some felling trees, others skidding the logs to the railroad, others laying new steel. The words of the work songs seem to fascinate Alan. In the new songs we are finding, I believe some of the unquenchable spirit of men at work in the open has been imprisoned.

After another night here we shall drive direct to Baton Rouge, whence, when our new machine has been tested, we shall travel, probably by short stages between big plantations, on to New Orleans. I am hoping Alan will not be disappointed about the boat trip up the Mississippi. As yet I do not know certainly that the boats will carry our car, or even that large freight boats yet ply the river. One of the charms of this trip is that we never can tell what the turn of the road will uncover, nor have we tried to find out things that we might possibly have known ahead of time.

"The little green leaves would not let me alone in my sleep" last night. I rested fitfully, now and anon looking into the forest nearby, with its towering, brooding trees. I dreamed of "Iron Head," "Clear Rock," "Mexico" and "Lightnin'," all noteworthy characters we have met on this trip.

Baton Rouge, Louisiana, July 13, 1933.—The night before we left Wiergate Alan and I spent at the cabin of Henry Truvillion, one of our star finds. We had a difficult task, for his wife objected to his singing other than "sancrified" tunes. We worked inside with the aid of a kerosene lamp, for Henry said that his members would expel him from the church if they heard him singing the blues. The night was sultry and I sat outside for a while on the porch and watched the moon shining through the tops of some of the lovely pines that crowned the hills to the south.

New Orleans, Louisiana, July 21, 1933.—Last Sunday afternoon Alan and I visited the Negro women prisoners on the Angola (Louisiana) State Farm, in number nearly a hundred. All were neatly dressed, many in white in tastefully chosen, ready-made costumes.

I stopped at the gate to chat with the "Captain" in charge while Alan went on into the dormitory. Later I found him seated in the dining room, a bunch of comely colored girls grouped around, singing beautifully the story of the Crucifixion—how Christ took his persecution, the crown of thorns, the cruel nails through his feet and hands, with no word of complaint. After reciting each trial, these clear and musical voices chanted: "An' he never said a mumblin' word!"

The girls swayed as they sang, their young and supple bodies moving in perfect unison to the rhythm of the song. At each end of the long table at which Alan sat, two other groups of Negro women played cards, now and then joining in on some moving line of the music. To me it was a strange, strange picture, for the manager had told me that nearly all these girls were from New Orleans or Shreveport, life-termers for murder. One young amazon, shiny black, handsome, eighteen, vibrant with vitality, was doing her best to attract Alan's attention. They crowded around us both until the time came for us to go, like eager children starved for the outside world.

We worked four hard days on this Louisiana farm of 18,000 acres, planted in corn and cane. On this farm Negro prisoners are not allowed to sing as they work, so we found the fountains drier than they are in Texas. One man—Lead Belly—alone, however, almost made up for the deficiency. He knew so many songs which he sang with restraint and sympathy that, accepting his story in full, I quite resolved to get him out of prison and take him along as a third member of our party. The prison records at Baton Rouge proved unfavorable, showing, in fact, that he had also served part of a thirty-year term in the Texas penitentiary for murder.

New Orleans, Louisiana, July 23, 1933.—Yesterday my fever continued, the rain poured, our project languished. But I did find Bertrand Cohn, a University classmate, who gave us cards to the New Orleans Athletic Club, a pleasant loafing place where Alan can swim in salt water as he wills. Moreover, Cohn had assigned to us a plainclothes man who will go with us tomorrow night into the jungles of Negroland where we hope to find some ballads and ballad music devoted to the seamy side of Negro life in the city.

This job has engrossed Alan entirely. You see, every turn projects us into the unknown and unexplored. The people we meet never fail to do or say the unexpected.

I keep thinking of hard-faced Iron Head as he leaned against the doorjamb (at a Texas prison farm) and cried in heart-breaking sobs. As Alan told him good-bye, Iron Head playfully dropped the red inside rim of each eye entirely over the eyeball. The shocking horror of the sight terrified Alan. "Dat's de way I looks when I'se a bad nigger," chuckled Iron Head.

This little interlude probably was to please Alan or to cover up his own emotion in saying goodbye. He had the dignity of a Roman Senator. While other Negroes swarmed around us begging for money, even for a penny apiece, he did not ask for a tip. When we paid him something for his time, he thanked us with grave courtesy, saying that he had little use for money except for one purpose. And the garrulous, conceited, sycophantic, able and utterly unreliable Clear Rock stalked around as a beautiful foil and contrast.

New Orleans, Louisiana, July 28, 1933.—(Alan's version [I'm in the hospital] of the New Orleans experience.) "New Orleans must, as the fellow says, have a black-cat bone. It has rained every day for a week. Father has been afflicted with a series of aches and pains and fevers. Neuritis, indigestion, sciatica, have been climaxed by a bad attack of grippe, which has sent him to the hospital. He is better now, but for a while I was mightily worried. And then, too, I haven't heard a Negro sing all week.

"I've ransacked the town, scoured the barrel houses, the redlight district, the French Quarter, the steamboat docks, the Creole section, and always there's a singer and always he's just around the corner, just stepped across the street, or, if I find him, just too busy. I even broke into a nunnery one night to the great surprise of all the sisters, and, I say this without conceit but on the basis of careful observations and correlations, to the great delight of the young girls who boarded there. But that is a story all by itself, and my purpose in writing this letter was to let you know that father is ill and due to stay in bed for another week, anyway. You see his fever was at one time as high as 104½. Use your nimble pen to persuade him that he ought to stay in bed. His years have made him think that he knows how to live his own life. Strange?"

Jackson, Mississippi, August 5, 1933.—As we rolled out of New Orleans, I felt like saying, in a different mood though with the same finality in which the words were first used:

Ave in perpetuum, frater,
Ave atque vale!

The experience was miserable in every respect. We both suffered from high fever (malaria) and now Alan's sickness is aggravated by a severe and persistent cough. I brought him this far to get him away from the miasma and mosquitoes of the lower country; also to run away from Tulane doctors who dose one with the same medicines used forty years ago.

If Alan has no fever tomorrow we will go Monday to Vicksburg and then to Parchman. . . . I am much pleased at one angle of my illness. When I learned that Alan was lying in our room with fever at

104 degrees, I jumped out of bed (I wasn't due to leave the hospital until the next day) and went at once to nurse him. Although I had had fever up to 104 for seven successive days, I showed no physical sign except a drawn and somewhat pale face. I was alert and strong as before the sickness. And I still am.

Jackson, Mississippi, August 7, 1933.—Alan still sleeps, free of fever but wan and thin. Yesterday, in fact, we spent the entire day working in a Negro prison camp twenty-five miles away. Alan made some fine records and we found several melodies hitherto unrecorded.

The day being Sunday, we naturally were more successful in finding spirituals. Some of the singing we heard was overpoweringly moving. I saw Alan blinking back the tears while his body swayed with the Negroes to the rhythm of the songs.

Nearly a hundred were in the dining room, nearly all shiny black. These faces, some cruel, some crafty, some of the older ones grim-looking and solemn, many boys with round jolly countenances, all, without exception, had rapt expressions of intense devotion. Wave after wave of melody flowed from the group, with never a false note, the voices blending exquisitely, even despite some high tenor, or deep, deep bass, breaking through the massed volume with an individual excellence.

Our machine won't take this mass singing. It overflows the microphone and drowns the harmony. However, we picked out a group of eight or ten of the best singers to have them sing for recording. Were it possible for the world to listen to such a group singing, with no vestige of self-consciousness or artificiality, the songs that seem to have sprung full-panoplied with beauty and power from the emotional experiences of a people—I say that the world would stop and listen.

Yesterday I jotted down a few nicknames I heard among our group of singers; for example, Highway (a marvelous voice and strong face), Tight Eye, Rat, Breadline, Log Wagon, Iron Jaw, Black Rider, Buckeye, Goat Face, Spark Plug, etc. The Sergeant told me that, within twenty-four hours after his arrival, each convict earned a new name that stuck. I'm getting 5,000 nicknames for Professor Kittredge.

This morning we go on to Parchman, where thousands are locked in. After Memphis we will call on the Governor at Nashville. We will spend one night at Harlan, Kentucky, and a day or so at the University of North Carolina.

Parchman Convict Farm, Mississippi, August 10, 1933.—"Lifetime" looked at me with his one good eye—a sinister, immobile face rendered more unattractive by a white film-covered orb. He was singing in a deep and tremulous voice an epic about *The Midnight Special* (train), which suggested to him freedom with all its opportunities. Over and over again came the throbbing refrain:

Let de Midnight Speshul
Shine hits ever-lovin' light on me.

And then the terrible story of the fear of the Negro as he sees the "Cap'in" riding up with the bull-whip in his hand. Here the chorus consists of the line

Great Gawdamighty!

uttered in a voice that mingled terror with entreaty and the horrible shrinking from physical pain.

The simple directness and power of this primitive music, coupled with its descriptions of life where force and other elemental influences are dominating, impress me more deeply every time I hear it. A play built around the imprisoned black and the songs he has made about his life and work would probably have more appeal than did "Green Pastures."

Over in the corner, meanwhile, Alan is trying out a heavy-jawed Negro, appropriately named Bull Dog. (We test out voices before recording songs.) The interested and curious men in stripes crowd around, while the guards look on condescendingly, sometimes with amused tolerance. To very few of the guards do the Negro songs make any appeal.

Yesterday morning we recorded in a sewing-room where women convicts sat at their machines and sang pathetically many "spirituals," among them a beautiful one, "If I could hear my mother pray again." Nearly all of them were young women. The Captain told me that most of them were there for murder growing out of troubles about their "man."

The male convicts work from 4 A.M. until dark. Thus our chance at them comes only during the noon hour and at night before the men are sent to their bunks for sleep, at nine o'clock. These periods are strenuous for us, for each group is timid, suspicious, sometimes stubborn. By tomorrow night we shall both doubtless be tired enough to move on. It would require many months to secure all the song material available among these two thousand black men.

Richmond, Virginia, August 22, 1933.—At last over in Kentucky we found him—the blind bard, with a good voice, for whom we had been looking since we left Texas. For, as you know, blindness brings a retentive memory. Near Harlan, Kentucky, where feuds are still active, he lived in a rocky gorge in a typical mountain home, and there he sang for us until all our records were filled. Alan put the microphone and the singer out under a shade tree in the yard where he sat leaning forward in a rocking chair, playing softly on his fiddle as he sang ballads—blood-stirring ballads of love and life in the mountains.

His name was James Howard. He was kindly, keenly intelligent, without formal education. His handsome face would light with pleasure as Alan played back for him the recorded songs, executed almost as perfectly as if sung in a soundproof room under ideal acoustic conditions. Lying around in the grass, as attentive and shy and observant as little animals, were a lot of mountain children, while the smiling wife peered from the doorway. The experience was unforgettable.

The day before as we recorded in precisely the same way before another cabin, Alan whispered to me, "Look at that beauty in the door." There she was—starry blue eyes, very fair, with wavy hair, neatly dressed, seventeen, a mountain rose just emerging from the bud. It was all over for Alan! That afternoon he disappeared and again that night. Now he is busy with plans to help her with her education, for she turns out to be artistic. She draws excellently, and her singing voice is as lovely as she is herself.

Leaving Harlan we drove on to Chapel Hill and Duke University, where at both places I saw friends who might help with our project. One night in our drive of two hundred miles through wonderful mountains we spent in a beautifully furnished log cabin built on the edge of a stream that made music to sleep by forever. Tall pines shut us out from the world as they bent and sighed in the stiff wind which blew the night through.

Tomorrow morning we go on into Washington, where we will set to work to put our book into final shape. The summer's adventure is ended.

When Alan and I delivered to Macmillan's the copy for *American Ballads and Folk Songs* (the manuscript filled an old laundry box), the officials of the company made us happy by unlooked-for attentions. As my mother used to say, they "made a to-do over us." We had put together in the Library of Congress from September 1 to October 15 the entire copy for *American Ballads and Folk Songs*—a remarkable task for six weeks' work.

At the same time Dr. and Mrs. Charles A. Beard had brought in an important manuscript. We met both these distinguished writers and shared with them the honors of a Macmillan cocktail party. Following this gathering we were overnight guests, through the courtesy of Macmillan's, at the National Arts Club. A dinner was served to a small group including the Beards, after which about two hundred people came in to see and hear the exhibit of the authors. Alan Lomax, who had not then learned to thrum a guitar, sang with abandon "Po' Laz'rus," "The Gray Goose," "Black Betty," "Shorty George," and "Yaller Gal." In reporting the occasion for the *New York Herald Tribune*, Jack Beall, a Texas newspaperman, filled out his story with lines from these songs.

Another evening Mr. and Mrs. James Putnam invited Alan and me to their home, where a group of their friends listened to some of our records. Alan also sang several of the songs that we had recorded on cylinders before our electric recorder was ready. Worn out from day and night work, Alan and I relaxed under this kind recognition.

During this same visit Mr. George P. Brett, Jr., President of the Macmillan Company, suggested that the Carnegie Corporation might be willing to help finance further recordings of folk songs. Until then I had borne all the expenses of our work. Armed with a letter to Mr. Keppel, Alan and I called at the Carnegie Corporation offices on Fifth Avenue. There we met and talked with Mr. Robert M. Lester, who told us that Alabama was his native State.

When he mentioned Alabama, I recalled with dismay that I had found little interest among Southerners in Negro work songs. Afterward I told Alan that we had little chance of a favorable report from this gentleman. Yet, as he dismissed us, he asked us to submit our request in written form. We recklessly requested $2,400 to cover our joint expenses for a year of travel in our automobile, including the purchase of records, repairs to our machine, tips to singers and all other necessary outlay for a year on the road. Our letter read in part:

"The Negro in the South is the target for such complex influences that it is hard to find genuine folk singing. His educational leaders, broadening his concepts and thus making him ashamed or self-conscious of his own art; his religious leaders, turning away from revival songs, spirituals, and informal church services to hymns and formal church modes, ranting against any song that has to do with secular subjects; prosperous members of the community, bolstered by the church and the schools, sneering at the naïveté of the folk songs and unconsciously throwing the weight of their influence in the balance against anything not patterned after white bourgeois culture; the radio with its flood of jazz, created in tearooms for the benefit of city-dwelling whites—all these things are killing the best and most genuine Negro folk songs.

"We propose to go where these influences are not yet dominant; where Negroes are almost entirely isolated from the whites, dependent upon the resources of their own group for amusement; where they are not only preserving a great body of traditional songs but are also creating new songs in the same idiom. These songs are, more often than not, epic summaries of the attitudes, *mores*, institutions, and situations of the great proletarian population who have helped to make the South culturally and economically. We propose to give our time. We are asking you for an appropriation of two hundred dollars a month to defray our traveling expenses."

Later, Alan and I met Mr. Waldo G. Leland of the American Council of Learned Societies, in the office of Oliver Strunk, Chief of the Music Division of the Library of Congress. Before the interview was over we both had concluded that Mr. Leland's inquiries showed that he knew of our petition for funds addressed to the Carnegie Corporation. Since then we have discovered that he passed finally on all requests for aid in similar American projects.

Mr. Leland was kind and sympathetic, yet, when the conference was over, neither Alan nor I felt sure of the impression that our project had made on him. All doubts were resolved when some months later, while we were visiting on the Callaway Ranch in Comanche County, Texas, came a letter from the Carnegie Corporation announcing that we had been granted for a year's expenses the sum of three thousand dollars.

Eight years afterward Mr. Leland, whom I have not seen since the day of our conference, wrote:

"You and your son have gone far beyond our expectations in the work that you have undertaken for the nation through the Library of Congress. . . . You ask as to why we decided to endorse your undertaking and to try to secure support for it. . . .

"In the first place, we had reached the conclusion that folk art and especially folk music should receive far more attention from American scholarship than it had previously received. We believed that the scholarly study of all kinds of folk expression is essential to any real understanding of America—and of course of any other people. Perhaps it is peculiarly true of America because of the very diverse character of our population. Of course folk music is the most universal expression, and the most revealing.

"But the study of folk music requires that it be collected, and at the time of our talks there were few collections; especially there were few collections that had been made under such circumstances as to make the materials useful for scholarly study. The Library of Congress had endeavored to start an archive of folk music, but it seemed to be making no progress. So a second decision growing out of our first was that collecting on a large scale should be undertaken, and that the Library of Congress was the logical national institution to sponsor such work.

"Third, and of prime importance, was our belief in you and your work. We were convinced that you had not only the intuition and the flair that distinguishes the born collector, but that you possessed also the ideals of scholarship, so that whatever you might do would contribute to the scholarly study of the subject. This belief was, I suppose, the determining factor in our decision.

"At that time we knew little about your son Alan, but we were glad to understand that he would be able to assist you. It is a matter of the greatest satisfaction to us now to realize that he, too, is in the great tradition and that his scholarly qualities, intuition and inspiration are worthy of your own, and that your work is assured of continuity as you yourself would wish."

Alan drove me and the Ford back to Texas in early December, 1933. We had many relatives and friends, but no home. Whatever the outcome of our application for financial aid from the Carnegie Corporation, I was determined to continue the work of collecting folk songs to add to the meager store which then made up the Folk Song Archive of the Library of Congress.

From Lubbock, Texas, we traveled at Christmas time to attend the annual meeting of the Modern Language Association in St. Louis. I had been invited to speak before the Popular Literature Section, while Alan was scheduled, in cooperation with the maker of our recording machine, to play some of our records. Much to his embarrassment, because of a breakdown in the electric connections, this program proved a failure, though my story of our adventures and Alan's singing of some of our songs drew applause. As one result we were invited to deliver one of the Moody lectures at the University of Chicago.

An hour or so after our appearance before the Popular Literature Section, a gentleman interrupted me while I was writing letters in the hotel where all the meetings were held.

"When you have a moment of leisure," he said, "I'd like to talk with you. My name is Stevens and I am associated with the Rockefeller Foundation." My letter-writing could wait; I could talk now.

"I heard your talk a few minutes ago. I heard your son, Alan, sing some of the songs you have found. You are working right down my alley. I wonder if you would like to have the Rockefeller Foundation finance your project for five years?"

When Professor Barrett Wendell, one of my teachers at Harvard, first told me that cowboy songs were worth preserving; when I tore the covering from a five hundred dollar check from Harvard University making me a "Sheldon Fellow for the Investigation of American Ballads"; when long before at Cornell University the Modern Language Association members had shouted their approval of my rendition of "Whoopee-ti-yi-yo, Git Along Little Dogies"—I had felt somewhat as I did then when Mr. Stevens expressed his interest in our undertaking. I was, for a moment, paralyzed with combined amazement and gratitude.

At last I told Mr. Stevens of my previous request for help from the Carnegie Corporation. Maybe I only imagine that he looked disappointed. I do know that here again was another occasion when it was hard for me to tell the whole truth. What progress I could make in five years backed by the Rockefeller Foundation!

Mr. Stevens' disappointment took a practical turn: "While you are waiting to hear from the Carnegie crowd, isn't there something we could do to help your project along?" I told him that the recording machine we were using was so heavy that, in order to save undue strain on our Ford car, we should tear out the back upholstery and build a framework for the machine; also that we needed a "converter" for use when we were far out in a section where no electric connections were available.

"How much cash do you require?" asked Mr. Stevens.

"About a hundred and fifty dollars," I hazarded.

Not more than a week afterward, while I was staying with my friends, the Oscar Callaways, at their ranch in Comanche County, Texas, there came a check from the Rockefeller Foundation for the amount of money I had suggested.

The work of a ballad collector in the field does not divide itself neatly into a chronological sequence. In looking back on the years I have spent collecting folk songs and ballads, and particularly those years in the 1930s and early 1940s when I was most actively engaged in the field, I find that certain incidents and individuals stand out in my memory as typical of the work which I was doing and of the people with whom I came in contact. Sometimes it was merely a single encounter, which brought a rich reward in new songs or introduced me to someone, old or young, whom I cannot forget. Other encounters led to friendships which lasted over a period of many years and which I still cherish. In the following chapters I shall try to share some of these incidents and friendships with my readers.

6

PENITENTIARY NEGROES

When Alan and I called to deliver to the Governor of Mississippi at Jackson our letter of introduction from the Governor of Texas, we discovered that the Mississippi Executive was not in the city. After waiting a day, we appealed to the Governor's secretary. That gentleman kindly forged his Chief's signature and sent us happily away to the big farm penitentiary at Parchman, bearing a request that the superintendent allow us to hear the Negro convicts sing, and also asking for our entertainment. Our letters swung open the big farm gates and brought us comfortable quarters in Superintendent Timm's home.

Parchman is located in the central north section of the rich Delta lands of the Mississippi River, land as level as the Texas Panhandle, as fertile as the Nile. Night fell before our journey ended. We had come to where in the darkness ahead we could see huge bright spots of light breaking through the blackness. Afterward we found that each patch of light marked the home of two or three hundred convicts. A ring of white arc lights surrounds each group of buildings. The lights burn the night through. Over across the Mississippi and further down in Louisiana, the convicts have a song beginning: "Angola, Angola, where the lights burn all night long."

"The brighter the lights, the fewer guards are necessary," said our genial host. Lead Belly went to bed at night with a bright light shining in his face.

The first night we set up our machine on the gallery of the big dormitory of Camp No. 1, just across the railroad from the Superintendent's home. A lot of curious guards and trusties crowded around, for our recording machine was the first to visit Parchman. The singers on the ground in front, with hoes and axes and a log pile, staged work-gang songs. That night Alan and I heard for the first time "Big Leg Rosie," "Stewball," "Po' Lazus," the "Bad Man Ballad," "Diamond Joe," and many another. Our machine was not handling the aluminum disks without considerable scratching and sputtering, but we captured the tunes accurately enough to be transcribed, and we both knew that we were again finding vital material. Not since we had left Lightning and his gang at the Darrington Farm in Texas had we heard such dynamic singing of work songs.

Excited Alan was exhausted by the eleven o'clock zero hour and went quickly off to bed. Superintendent Timm and I sat out in the moonlight on his front lawn and talked for an hour or so. I asked him about two broad, four-foot leather straps I had seen hanging in the hall of the dormitory (in Texas convicts call these straps Red Heifer or Black Betty).

"Do you really whip convicts or do you use those straps only as threats?" I asked.

"We whip them," he replied.

"Both the whites and the Negroes?"

"Yes, the whites oftener than the Negroes, because the whites are harder to control."

It was difficult for me to believe that this soft-voiced, quiet-spoken, kind-faced man could use a lash on a human being. He had told me how four men would hold the offender face downward flat on the ground, one man to each hand or foot, while a man applied a strap to the bare back and buttocks.

"The broad strap burns but does not cut the flesh," he explained. "We don't hurt the man so that he cannot at once go back to work. We need all our field hands."

"But, Mr. Timm," I protested, "how can you justify such acts of barbarism in controlling criminals?"

The moonlight poured down through the branches of the over-hanging elm trees. Through the peace and quiet of the night it seemed that I could hear the screams of a tortured man. Mr. Timm smoked on and, after a moment, answered quietly:

"Most white prisoners come here from good families. Their ages usually run from eighteen to twenty-five years. They have grown up petted, indulged and spoiled. To them discipline is unknown; many have never done an honest day's work in their lives. They first flouted order and law in their homes, and then got caught breaking the laws of the State. Then they are sent to me. I try first to handle all these cases myself. When I tell one of these young convicts to take a hoe and join the field squad, I am often met with a haughty refusal: 'I've never worked and I never will—certainly not for you.'

"When I insist I am met with insults, curses and abuse. We have tried the dark cell, a bread-and-water diet, standing them on a barrel. Such methods don't work. I've tried 'em all. It's a waste of effort and time. When persuasion fails, I order the rebel stripped and whipped. Then I give him a day to think it over. The second morning, on another refusal, he is whipped again. Perhaps the third day the same program must be followed, but not often does the man hold out longer than that. Then when he yields and does his job faithfully for a time, I begin to give him responsibility. Only today I sent a convict with a wagon and team, unguarded, on a fifty-mile trip across the country; yet six months ago when he first came here he endured the lash for six successive days before he would agree to work.

"The practice may seem cruel, but it cures these white boys. I don't know of anything else that will. A Negro sometimes gets punished for repeatedly breaking prison rules, but the bad boys of the black race present no such problem as the whites. One white convict gives more trouble than three Negroes.—Time to go to bed if we expect to work tomorrow."

The week following I wrote from Parchman: "To hear in one day—Easter Sunday—more than two thousand voices of black men singing in reverential tones the spiritual songs of a race is possibly a unique experience. In the company of a white Chaplain and a Negro Assistant

Chaplain, on one 16,000-acre penitentiary farm in the Delta Country, in one day between sun and sun, I saw and heard what few persons have witnessed. For when I close my eyes, I yet see crowds of black men in stripes and hear waves of melody and deep voices chanting:

I'm troubled, Lord, I'm troubled,
Troubled about my soul,

Whatever the convicts sang, their chief troubles lay in their loss of freedom. They were using the phrasing of their hymns to voice these troubles. The Mississippi Delta Negro is a wonderful singer of spirituals.

The two Chaplains held Easter services that Sunday at nine different camp headquarters for the Negro convicts at Parchman, the largest unit of the Mississippi Penitentiary system. As a compliment to me the Easter exercises were changed to song services, and the men were asked to name their favorite spirituals, usually led by an individual or by a quartet. Throughout the day, every convict sang. I saw no mute lips. When the Negro Chaplain led in the Lord's Prayer, the responses were hearty and unanimous, and the final "Amen" almost lifted the roof. Probably no other audiences in the world were in more perfect emotional accord than the men who made up those seas of black faces.

Our first visit was to the women's camp, eighty Negroes, five whites, the latter all convicted murderers, as were indeed the majority of the Negroes. A big mulatto woman, weighing 250 pounds or more, "histed" the tunes. The peculiar long-meter rhythm, which they give to the old standard hymns, is most beautiful. Slow-moving waves of sound rise and fall, sometimes almost fading out and then speeding suddenly to life in cascades of melody; low moaning voices hold long notes to breathless length when, as the tone seems almost about to fade entirely away, a sharp falsetto voice breaks in, grabs the melody and carries it to new life.

If evil had left its mark on these bright young faces, no trace appeared as they sang about a "Motherless Child," or found comfort in the hope of "Hearing My Mother Pray Again." "So Soon, so

Soon, I'll be at Home" was the theme of another song—no Heavenly home, but some cabin on the Mississippi shore with a dirt floor, with no windows, perhaps, but the home they left behind when hard luck came knocking at the door. Another song with a lovely, lilting tune called on Gabriel to hand down a silver trumpet, its office probably to blow in a new order, to bring confusion to the guards, again with getting back home in view. "If you can't hand it down, Gabriel, throw it down, any way, so you get it down," the singers earnestly pleaded. They needed that silver trumpet.

At each camp I heard spirituals hitherto unknown to me. The convicts came from every part of Mississippi, and the best songs of many communities survived among these singing, black men. Again I found the practice of the Negro composer who takes a few highly colored words, usually an apt phrase from the Bible, fits them to tune, and a new song is made by grouping these words around "father," "mother," "sister," "brother," "cousin," "auntie," "uncle," "elder," "deacon," etc.

"Way beyond the moon" lies Heaven; and all the family dwellers in Heaven "outshine de sun"—fathers, mothers, brothers and sisters, on and on. Thus in a few expressions you have the flesh and bones of many of their songs. One vivid stanza of a song definitely locates Heaven as the place of eternal rest, where Negroes may "set down at de welcome table":

Oh, when I get to heaven gwine to set right down,
Ask my Lord for a starry crown—
Settin' down 'side of de Holy Lamb.

Some songs give lists of possible sins: "You'd better stop dat way of drinking 'shine," the word "'shine" fixing the prohibition times as the date of the song. Other ways of sinning are shooting dice, singing songs (all songs not religious are "sinful"), gossiping, backbiting, stealing, failing to support the pastor.

The breaks in "dis old buildin'" (the body) must be stopped soon by good deeds. "You must work on de buildin' soon," shouted Dobie Red of Camp No. 1, at Parchman. Although it is a grievous sin to drink moonshine liquor, one of the new songs I heard that day declared in a rousing refrain that Heaven is a place where one will sit and drink wine for a long, long time: "I'm goin' to be there ten thousand years, drinkin' of the wine." The Negro gets up to Heaven by riding "on de mornin' train." It has only one track, which runs "straight up to Heaven an' right straight back."

"Jesus is a dyin'-bed-maker," and, hence, makes dying easier. And "Jesus don't hate nobody." Even in the penitentiary, "All in my room I heard de angels singin'."

Other songs are addressed to the unbeliever. "What you goin' to do when death comes creepin' in your room?" "When de world's on fire, don't you want God's bosom to be your pillow?" "Jes' look down dat lonesome road; you spy trouble on de way." "Walk away, mourner; you stay at de mourners' bench one day too long!"

Graphic sentences formed themes for other songs sung that day: "There is strange things happ'ning in dis world"; "Long as I am in de world, I am de light of de world"; "Oh, you see dat golden circle around de sun"; "They have taken my Lord away and won't tell me where to find Him"; "King Jesus wuz dat stone dat heaved outa de mountain"; "Where th' flowers are bloomin' forever, de sun will never go down"; "King Jesus was de stone dat come rollin' through Babylon"; "Some come crippled an' some come lame, An' some come limpin' in my Jesus' name"; "Dis is de way I pray when trouble is in my home"; "If I never see you more, I'm goin' up de shiny way"; "In dat great gittin'-up mornin', gamblers goin' to be gone."

These songs and others I heard that day I shall carry in my heart forever. And those earnest black-faced boys, dressed in grisly gray stripes, who sang them, I shall never forget. The reaction from a high pitch of emotional excitement gave me a sleepless night.

Later I came back and made records of the tunes. A chance encounter with a Negro horseman in the Delta country suggested the possible origin of spirituals. He had stopped when I was resting by the roadside. Yes, he knew plenty of spirituals, but he had ruined his voice preaching loud. He was sitting on the ground; he leaned his elbows back and, punctuating his remarks with jabs of a straw between his teeth, he gave an interesting and perhaps authentic version of the rise of Negro spirituals:

"Way back in slavery times when us nigger folks couldn't read, the white folks tried to teach the slaves about the Bible by songs. They could remember it better if they sung it. So they taught them Bible stories that way—about Noah an' Jonah an' Samson an' all them. And the niggers, of course, they didn't know no better; they'd make up verses that didn't have nothin' to do with the Bible, like about animals, an' sometimes funny things that happened aroun' the quarters." He illustrated his points with snatches of spirituals and variants.

At one camp I asked the names of a quartet so I could call for them on a second visit. The first man gave me his name, so did the second; and then the third startled me by saying: "My name's John Lomax."

"That's my name, too. Why are you bringing our name to such a place?" I demanded.

"Jes' got inter a little trouble." He looked embarrassed. "The jedge jes' give me two years."

"Where did you come from?"

"Holmes County, Mississippi, near Durant."

Holmes County was also my birthplace. That boy's mother may once have rocked me to sleep.

Across the flat fields I noticed a line of small cottages facing the farm, just outside the high fence. Some of the houses were set back in the trees, though none was nearer than a mile from the camp headquarters. I asked my host, the Captain, who lived in this remote community beyond the farm limits.

"The wives and families of the Negro convicts of the prison camp," he answered.

"But who supports them? Where do they get clothing and food? I see a lot of children."

"So far as I can tell," he smiled, shaking his head, "they draw their rations from the men of this prison camp. You see, all our guards are Negro trusties who guard the regular line men day and night. Try as we may, my white assistants and I cannot stop the flow of food from our commissary to the Negro families living out there in the woods.

"One afternoon some weeks ago," he went on, "we had driven a young steer into our stock pens near the prison barn, planning to slaughter it the next day. Our field hands needed fresh beef. The following morning the pens were empty. The animal had vanished, leaving no trace behind. I summoned all the trusties who had been on duty the night before. No one could tell me anything. In advance, I knew they couldn't or wouldn't talk. I have never broken through their secretiveness—though I keep on trying.

"I got on my horse and rode over to that Negro settlement. Packed away in the kitchens I found our lost beef steer, neatly butchered and cut into equitable portions. How that thousand-pound animal could have been slaughtered in the night and the entire carcass carried across that open field through a line of guards armed with rifles is quite beyond me. And nobody saw or heard anything. What did I do about it? Nothing. There was nothing I could do. Magic, says I. Their skins are black all right, but don't fool yourself. Negroes are smart."

Later I discovered that once a month on Sundays Negro women are allowed to visit their convict husbands and boy friends. On these days the convicts are turned loose inside the high stockades provided at each camp, where they receive their visitors. Numerous one-room shacks stand around inside the prison fences, where privacy may be had by any couple. The men work more contentedly and cheerfully and are more easily controlled, I was told, when they can be with their women once a month. Texas and Louisiana have similar rules. I found no instance of such liberty being allowed to white convicts.

While at Parchman, Harris Dickson, outstanding among Mississippi writers who portray Negro life, told me that he once sat on a special commission, headed by the Governor, to consider pardons for State convicts. Only those men who had been in the penitentiary for ten years or longer without receiving a letter were asked to appear. The commissioners were looking for the friendless, the forgotten men. For three days they heard story after story. Subsequently the Governor issued a large number of pardons to the unfortunates. During the hearing, the Executive asked one black boy:

"Mose, why are you in here?"

"They accuses me, Guv'nor, uv killin' er man."

"Did you kill him?"

"Yes-suh, Guv'nor."

"Why did you kill him?"

"We wuz shootin' craps, Guv'nor. I made my p'int an' he wouldn't reckernize it!"

Just as the sun went down, I drove across the fields, tired and worn from a long, exhausting day. I passed a small and very old Negro convict driving a herd of milch cows down the road, and stopped to chat with him.

"My trigger got loose, Boss," he answered, when I asked him why he wore stripes. "I shot dat man nearly half in two, but I didn't go ter do it. De gun jes' went off. My trigger got loose." His lips trembled and his eyes begged me earnestly to believe him.

When I had asked for the best song leader at Parchman, the vote of the men was unanimously for Dobie Red, dark brown in color, with a thick bristle of straight red hair. His voice carried the shock of a bugle call. "I sings both kinds, the spirituals and the sinful," said Dobie Red. He was a natural leader, considerate, forceful, cordial in manner and speech. The men he chose to sing with him followed his lead with vigor and enthusiasm. Some of the best tunes in the Folk Song Archive carry the imprint of Dobie Red. That Sunday morning Warden Thames sat by in the big dormitory dining room and listened. Perhaps he was watching too. A year or two later I came back to Parchman to re-record some of the songs. I then missed the leader.

"Where is Dobie Red?" I asked Jim Henry, who had sung with us on the former visit.

"Well, suh, you know when you wuz here befo', the Warden noticed how us boys followed Dobie Red. So the Warden makes Dobie a trusty an' lets him be a guard. One night when Dobie wuz on guard they couldn't fin' him the next mornin'. He jes' sashayed away and nobody has ever seen him since. I heard he went to Detroit."

As for me, while I love the spirituals, I can feel the power of the sinful songs since I have listened to Dobie Red and his eight "podners" sing about Big Leg Rosy:

I see Big Leg Rosy in my midnight dreams,
Oh, Rosy, Oh, law, gal!
Wuzn't for de powder an' de sto'-bought hair,
Mississippi girls wouldn't go nowhere,
Oh, Rosy, Oh, law, gal!
Oh, Rosy, Oh, law, gal!

Well, this keepin' Rosy sho' is hard,
Dress she wo' it cost a dollar a yard.

Well, I come in here wid a hundred years,
Tree fall on me, I don' a bit more keer,
Oh, Rosy, O-ho!
Oh, Rosy, Oh, law, gal!

Along with the singing you hear the beat of their hoes on the hard ground, the shouted explanations at intervals in the song. "Talk it to time, now!" "Explain it to 'em!" "Dat's all right, now!" Over all throbs the strange, wild harmony; as you see in the background the somber iron bars, groups of men in striped clothes, black guards idling, listening, watching, guns on knee.

The Warden of the Arkansas Penitentiary was young, opinionated, able. He had won his appointment as a reward for an act of supreme courage, when, as sheriff, he killed in fair fight three bank robbers armed with rifles. He shot quicker and straighter. But I thought the Warden was just a bit short on Southern hospitality even when he read the letter which I presented to him from the Governor of Arkansas. I could sense him thinking, "What is the human race coming to when a full-grown white man spends his time making records of 'Nigger' singing?"

"It's up to you, my Texas friend," the Warden said briskly, putting the letter into his pocket. "I've no time to spend with you nor any place to sleep you. You can eat with the guards, and trust to luck to spend the nights at the home of one of the six Farm Captains. I am giving you a pass that will permit you to visit the six camps where the convicts are housed at night. If you can't lodge at a camp, there's a hotel in Pine Bluff, thirty miles away. Good luck and goodbye." He waved his hand as he dashed away on his big bay horse, leaving behind a not very happy visitor; though several years later, when I again visited this penitentiary, the Warden then entertained me in his own home.

Late that afternoon I finally found a Captain, an ex-Texan, who invited me to stay all night at his home. Among his group of convicts he had a singing cotton-picking bunch. After supper I set up the recording machine in the entry of the big dormitory where the men slept. Before the first song was completed, some electric doodad, thrown out of gear by bumpy roads, refused to function. The convict who looked after the electric power of the camp couldn't help.

The following day I hauled the lame machine into Pine Bluff to a radio repair shop. After a wait of six hours, back I went again to Camp Number 5 just at sunset. Although the machine seemed to work satisfactorily before I left Pine Bluff, once more, when I set it up in the entry of the prison dormitory, it broke down completely and refused to budge before the singing was well under way. A strange, uninvited guest, I felt sick at heart. The Captain, too, was plainly out of patience. I even overheard mutters of disgust from the convicts. The next day, after another weary trip to Pine Bluff over the worst roads in Arkansas, I returned to camp about the middle of the afternoon. I set up the machine out back of the barn on a grassy plot near a great pile of pine logs, where the men could use their axes while singing their chopping songs. The Captain first sang into the microphone. The recording, to my relief, was excellent.

"Bring the men in from the cotton patch," the Captain ordered. A guard went galloping off on his horse, leaving me waiting in the dust.

Presently I heard excited whoops. Down the road and around the bend ran at top speed a group of laughing, shouting convicts with the guard loping behind, a shotgun braced against his saddle and pointing straight up. At last these exulting boys were to "git on dat machine." They came up panting from their wild race. Soon a picked group gathered about the microphone and sang a wonderful cotton-picking song, a song about a Southwestern railroad, the rhythm of which fits into the movements of swift hands grabbing the white locks from the bolls of cotton and stuffing handfuls into their dragging sacks.

Eight to sing, and one to whistle like a locomotive. They picked that cotton so fast they seemed to feel as if they were on an express train tearing through the cotton patch on the famous Rock Island Line:

> Oh, the Rock Island Line is a mighty good road,
> Oh, the Rock Island Line is the road to ride;
> Oh, the Rock Island Line is a mighty good road,
> If you want to ride,
> You've got to ride it like you're flyin'—
> You'd better buy your ticket on the Rock Island Line.

The music is spirited. A hearer feels the train dashing through Arkansas pine forests, around wide, sweeping turns—

> The train left Memphis at half past nine,
> It made it back to Little Rock at eight forty-nine—

and then the long, lonesome whistle. It took one convict to run the whistle.

Axes were lying around. "Kelly Pace," I said to the leader, "can you sing axe-cutting songs like the ones I heard in Mississippi? *Stewball, Rosie* and songs like that?" "Them's old common songs," Kelly said. "We'll give you some old Arkansas, jumped-up songs. Get your diamond blades, boys, we'll set him afire." As the men sang and swung their axes, the diamond blades, they shouted to each other in sheer ecstasy, the blood running warm in their veins.

Partners—four men and four axes—faced each other across the big pine logs. A double-time axe rhythm, each partner on the opposite beat. The axes glittered in the sunlight, shining arcs of steel. "I got a rainbow round my shoulder," called Kelly, meaning an ax blade red-hot from being swung so hard and so fast. The boys meant business. Real chips, big chips were flying all around us. I trembled for the fate of my mike. "Drive it on, boys, drive it on," at regular intervals the chorus rang out, and the song ended with the log cut through. At this point I made the singers happy by playing their records back to them. They whooped and hollered and slammed their hats on the ground; slapped each other on the back and said: "Ol' Kelly Pace put it over that time, didn't he?" And the locomotive whistler said, "Yeah, but they gonna hear me whistlin' clear to Washin'ton."

And just at that time the head rider, a convict trusty ranking in authority next to the Captain (he had been quiet all this time), stepped up to me and said somewhat timidly, "I can sing you a steel-drivin' song, a song about John Henry. He's the man what win the race with the steamdrill and died wid the hammer in his han'." Then he began a stanza of this famous song that I'd never heard before:

> Every Monday mornin' when th' bluebirds begin to sing,
> You can hear them hammers a mile or mo',
> You can hear John Henry's hammer ring, O Lawdy,
> You can hear John Henry's hammer ring.

And the head rider ended with another new stanza:

> They took John Henry to Washin'ton
> An' they buried him in th' sand,
> An' th' people from the East and th' people from th' West
> Came to see such a steel-drivin' man.

> Some say he come from England,
> Some say he come from Spain,
> But I say he's nothin' but a Louisiana man
> At the head of a steel-drivin' gang.

The Rock Island song, found only in the Arkansas penitentiary, has been on the radio throughout the country, while this version of *John Henry* has a place of honor in Dr. B. A. Botkin's important book, *Treasury of Folk Lore.*

All that afternoon and until midnight I recorded the fine singing of Kelly Pace and his cotton-pickers. The wild harmonies I had heard, the ringing of the axes, kept me awake through the night. Six years later I drove into a cotton field to see Kelly Pace. He came up to my car on the turnrow and called my name: "I knew my boss-man wuz comin' when I saw your car a mile down the road." Kelly had served one sentence and now was again in trouble—sentence, forty years.

In Nashville, Tennessee, a kind and understanding Governor made easy our entrance through the grim gates of the penitentiary, a few miles away. There the Warden vacated his office for our recording machine. We worked two crowded days until midnight.

The second afternoon the Warden came in and asked about our progress. Among the singing convicts we had met Black Samson, a giant of a man with an engaging smile, a singer of unusual quality, who refused amiably but firmly to sing any of the songs he had learned as a railroad and levee worker. "I'se got religion, boss, an' I'se quit all dat." When we told the Warden that Black Samson knew one song that we wanted especially, he sent a guard for him, and the frightened Negro shuffled up and took his place before the microphone. Alan started the machine, and said: "Shoot, Black Samson." But Black Samson didn't sing. He closed his eyes and prayed:

Oh Lord, I knows I'se doin' wrong. I cain't help myself. I'se down here in the worl', an' I'se gotter do what dis white man tells me. I hopes You unnerstan's the situation an' won't blame me for what I gotter do. Amen!

Then he sang his sinful work song:

Ham and eggs, pork and beans;
Would-a et mo', but the cook wuzn't clean.
I gotter roll, roll in a hurry,
Roll on de side uv de road.

The microphone captured both the prayer and the song. That aluminum record in the Folk Song Archive in the Library of Congress will tell for many years the story of Black Samson's implicit belief and also his cleverness in a difficult situation. Throughout the day he asked me many times, after he had heard his song played back to him: "Boss, does yo' like my song? Boss, does yo' think some of dose big Washin'ton men, when dey hears my song, won't do something to help dis po' nigger? Sorta have mercy on him?" As I shook hands with him late that night at the big gates of the penitentiary, where he had helped carry our heavy machine, he said earnestly: "Boss, cain't yo' help me git outa dis place? I jes' nacherly don't like it." Black Samson had just begun a twenty-year sentence.

We found another very lovely Negro singer among the convicts in the Nashville Penitentiary. He had a silver tenor voice, clear as a bugle note, and we made records of six or seven notable songs from him. A mild-mannered, gentle-faced man, his name was Allen Prothero. "Allen," I said to him as I told him goodbye, "you don't look to me like the kind of man who should be in this terrible place. What in the world did you do to get in here?"

"Boss," he replied, "I was raised a country nigger down near Chattanooga, Tennessee. When I growed up to be a man, I went to Chattanooga and got me a job driving a dray for the City. I saved my money, found me a sweetheart and married her, and bo't me a little home. I was gettin' along mighty fine until one of these uppity town niggers got to messin' up wid my homely affairs, an' I blowed him down."

"But boss," he added earnestly, "when de jedge stood me up for sentence, he said, 'Allen, I ain't sendin' you to de pen for ten years fer killin' dat nigger who ruint yo' happy home, but yo' had no right to kill dat other nigger, his fren', who had come down to talk to you, and who wuz stan'in' there with his han's in his pockets.'" When I looked shocked at his story, Allen again explained, "Boss, I jes' got to shootin' niggers an' I couldn't stop."

Unlike many convicts, Allen Prothero did not ask us to try to have him freed from prison. But I couldn't forget the look he gave us as we parted from him. Later when his records were played, I was again reminded. Three songs in *American Ballads and Folk Songs* are credited to him. A year later I revisited Chattanooga, after again seeing Prothero in the Nashville Penitentiary, and talked to Judge Miller, who had tried him. Colonel Richard H. Kimball and his wife, Mildred, became interested in the Negro, she requesting his parole in her name. On May 10, 1936, Colonel Kimball sent me Prothero's clean-conduct record, but a week afterward he wrote: "Enclosed is a letter from Governor Hill McAlister which brings the distressing news that your Prothero died in the tuberculosis hospital April 9." The prisoner had been unable to take advantage of the parole that was being prepared for him.

Of Allen Prothero's favorite song, "Pauline, Pauline, I don't love nobody but you," Alan Lomax has written:

> This song will stand as a monument to him. It shows its kinship with a whole school of work songs, but it has its own highly individualized arrangement and we think is one of the tenderest, most delicate love songs that ever came out of a human throat.

A volume could be written about the receptions given me by wardens of Southern penitentiaries. I once had an amazing experience at the State Penitentiary at Columbia, South Carolina. It all grew out of a letter. Surprisingly enough the courtly and diplomatic Herbert Putnam, Librarian of Congress, had a hand in the composition and circulation of this letter. In fact, it went out as a franked official document from the Library.

After completing my visits to nearly all the penal institutions of the southern states, the idea occurred to me that prisoners in Federal penitentiaries might also know folk songs. Thereupon I prepared a letter, addressed to the heads of all Federal prisons, and submitted it to Librarian Putnam. He polished my English a bit, kindly added his endorsement and authorized me to go ahead. Through error a copy of this letter was sent to the State Penitentiary at Columbia, South Carolina.

Our joint composition read as follows:

Library of Congress
Division of Music
Archive of American Folk Song
Dear Sir:
I am collecting for the Library of Congress the words and tunes of songs and ballads current and popular among prisoners, or "made up" by them and passed around by "word of mouth" rather than by the printed page. Many of these songs—though by no means all of them—relate to experiences in prison, to the life of criminals in jail or in the "free world." They grow in length or change verbally as they are passed around. I wish to secure copies of them all, *no matter how crude or vulgar they may be.* Where a visit seems justified I plan later to visit your institution to record the tunes of these songs on an electric recording machine. The material I wish to secure is especially plentiful among Negro prisoners. Will you, therefore, be good enough to make inquiry and let me know whether such songs are current among the persons under your charge? May I also ask you to forward to me at this time the words of those songs that are available, with such remarks and suggestions as may be helpful? Even short scraps will be welcome. This proposal is part of a plan of the Library of Congress to collect and make available to properly qualified students the words and music of American folk-songs.

I shall greatly appreciate a reply to this communication.
JOHN A. LOMAX
Honorary Curator and Consultant
in American Folk-Song.

Compliance with the above request will be a service to the
Library of Congress, and appreciated.
HERBERT PUTNAM
Librarian

From this letter there came in a batch of unique manuscripts, none
of which have seen the light, many of which are of the type librarians
keep locked away from young and innocent readers. But long before
any replies reached me, this letter on one occasion was flung back
into my face under circumstances that made the incident one of the
most embarrassing and unhappy moments of my life.

At Columbia, my friend, Professor Reed Smith of the University
of South Carolina, had introduced me to the Governor. That gentleman gave me a note to the Warden of the big, gloomy state prison,
which I had missed on other trips, located on the outskirts of the city.
At the prison gates the guards bluntly refused entrance to my companion and chauffeur, Lead Belly. I left him in the car gloomy and
uneasy because so many "Laws" were close by, angry probably at
another instance of "race discrimination," and still more miserable
from an aching tooth he had refused to have treated. I remember,
when I came back, the car was spattered with blood. Lead Belly had
been trying to pull his molar with the automobile pliers. "I couldn't
get a good holt," said Lead Belly; "the pliers kept slipping off."

From the reception office I sent the Governor's note in to the Warden. Almost instantly the messenger returned. He took me to a room
where five or six grim-faced men sat about a table. I sensed trouble
in their cold greeting. No one shook my hand. The Warden shoved
a copy of my circular letter at me and asked, "Are you the man that
wrote that letter?"

"Yes, sir"—very timidly.

"Then you are the very man we are looking for. These gentleman
and I are here discussing the best ways and means to handle an incip-
ient riot in this prison. We already have six of the leaders confined in
solitary cells for provoking trouble. That letter is the source of what
may become a serious prison outbreak. And here comes the man who

has brought it all about with a request from the Governor that I allow the prisoners to sing for him!" He flung the papers on the table and, in his nervousness and excitement, rose from his chair and paced the room. The other five inquisitors sat and smoked slowly, boring me with unfriendly looks from unfriendly eyes. Suddenly the Warden turned and added,

"Why, sir, if I should let the convicts know that the 'man from Washington' had come, and then permit you to walk across the prison yard, a riot would be on in five minutes. I couldn't be responsible for what would happen. You get away from this place at once, and don't tell anyone else who you are. And go quickly."

I didn't wait for a second invitation. As I was leaving, he fired a final blasting shot.

"I notice, too, that in your damned letter you asked us to send in to the Library of Congress all the 'vulgar' songs these men know. What in the hell do you want with dirty songs? And did you think we would violate postal laws to send indecent stuff through the mails?" I don't believe Professor Kittredge, who had advised me to save all types of folk stuff, could have appeased that angry and outraged warden. I didn't try. He was still pointing to the door. This time I left without more ado.

Later, I heard the details of the story. When my letter came, the Warden had referred it to an assistant, he to a junior and he to a trusty. Instead of posting the letter on a bulletin board, this trusty had read and interpreted it to the group of trusties. By the time the mass of convicts heard of the letter its import had been completely lost. A letter far different had taken its place. Like wildfire the news spread through the "grapevine" that a man from Washington was coming to investigate the prison system of South Carolina. Any prisoner who had a complaint against the food or the brutalities of guards, or thought he should be pardoned, would be given a hearing. The New Deal was going to be extended to the convicts. For days past the prisoners had talked of nothing but my coming. Violent altercations had occurred in the prison yard about who was to see me first, who was to be the official spokesman, what each should tell, etc. Desperate for freedom, hungry for a chance to talk with an officer of Uncle Sam, these men were ready to revolt against the authority of the State of South Carolina.

I have always wished I might have heard the story direct from the convicts also. That was impossible. Better for me and Lead Belly to head North. So on we went to the convict camp out of Canton, South Carolina. These men, fortunately, hadn't heard any news from Washington.

Joe Lee, growing old, a grim, silent man, with an inscrutable face, sang some beautiful Negro hymns for the record. His comrades reported with awe that Joe had buried a thousand dollars in gold. No one knew where it was.

"Have you no Negro friend you can trust?" I asked.

"Not one," answered Joe.

"And no white man?"

"I put a lot of my money in one of their banks, and they shut the doors in my face," Joe said bitterly.

Harold Spivacke, Chief of the Music Division of the Library of Congress, helped to record Joe's songs. When Joe heard his voice coming back from the loud-speaker, he was mightily moved. His body shook, he dashed about the room shouting over and over, "My soul is wrapped up in the care of the Lord and nothing in this world can harm me!"

I called to Spivacke to bring the microphone closer so that we could record what Joe was saying, but poor Spivacke, terribly frightened, thought Joe had gone crazy and held the precious microphone clasped close to his breast until the excitement was over. He has written of the incident:

I shall never forget that week-end trip to the Virginia State Farm with you. It was one of the most pleasant experiences in my life, and it is remarkable how many details I can remember as I think back on it. We drove to Richmond in your car and both on the trip down and on the return trip, you sang for me and taught me many folk songs. I had before this, of course, listened to many records and developed a great love for the field of folk music, but I never did get the "feel" of them until that trip with you. As you remember, the weather was fine and perhaps hearing them from you on the open road made them seem so much more "alive." At any rate, we arrived in Richmond, had lunch, and you then expressed a desire for some liquid refreshment. However, I still remember your tactful approach to the man in the service station, who seemed to know exactly where the dispensary was. Thus armed, we set out for the State Farm over some beautiful rolling country.

The Warden had expected us and prepared for us a reception in typical Hollywood fashion. He and his family were sitting on the veranda of his house, while on the lawn in front he had a Negro quartet which burst into song the minute we appeared. On the steps of the house was sitting a blind Negro strumming a battered banjo [Jimmie Strothers]. On hearing the quartet, you said something to me about "trouble ahead" which I did not understand but which became perfectly clear to me later. For the next two hours, you sat on the steps with the blind Negro, whom you soon recognized as a real talent for folk singing, and did nothing but get acquainted. Your reference to "trouble" was caused by the fact that the Warden's quartet was very poor; and I admired your tact in getting rid of them after half an hour or an hour and at the same time obtaining from the Warden permission to roam the yard at will. But it was when you sat for over two hours with the blind Negro, just getting acquainted, that I realized what a consummate artist you are. You encouraged him to tell you his life's history, you swapped songs with him, you did everything but make records. Being a novice at the game, I several times suggested to you by whispered hints that we might start making records because time was short, only to have you wave me away. In fact, I do not believe we made any records that Saturday afternoon before returning to Richmond for the night.

It all became clear to me the next day, however. We returned to State Farm early Sunday morning and set up our recording machine in the armory. (I have never been so close to shooting irons in such quantity before and all through the day I must confess I was a little uncomfortable as the guards came in and loaded up their cannon.) You then brought in Jimmie Strothers and told me to go ahead and make records. You left me to visit another camp in the neighborhood and to do some scouting in the yard. I thought this was a dirty trick at the time, and felt pretty much like the boy who was being taught to swim by being thrown in the water; but after a few minutes it became obvious to me what you had done on the previous day. It was a cinch. Jimmie Strothers had been so well prepared by you on Saturday afternoon that all I had to do was ask him to sing one song after another and turn over the records and set the needles, etc.

You returned before lunch and began surveying the yard at State Farm proper. By the time we had finished our lunch, you already had quite a few singers lined up; Joe Lee was one of them, and there were several quartets. Everything went along smoothly until you played back for Joe Lee his songs. I happened to be on the porch with a guard, setting up the microphone for a duet we were planning with Jimmie Strothers when I suddenly saw Joe Lee begin to throw himself around the room, beat his head against the wall, burst into tears, screech at the top of his voice, and do everything but foam at the mouth. What surprised me at first was the calm expression on your face and the laughter of the guards. I had never seen anything like it. I rather expected the guards to clamp handcuffs on the men and expected you to run for your life; but instead, you turned to me and said, "Get the microphone." I, being sure that you meant for me to protect the microphone from this raving maniac, picked it up and held on to it for dear life, prepared to run if necessary. Seeing this, you burst into laughter, whereupon I realized that I was doing something very wrong. At any rate, by the time you straightened me out, Joe Lee had calmed down considerably and you asked him to repeat into the microphone some of the hysterical statements made before, but of course the true scene was lost forever, as he merely recited them. As you well know, the expression "Get the microphone" has had a special significance between us two ever since.

At any rate, we got a lot of beautiful records which have given many people much pleasure ever since. As a matter of fact, considering that we were gone only two days and had spent one full day in recording, it was probably one of the most successful trips ever undertaken by the Archive. Furthermore, I as an administrator have always been grateful because it gave me an insight into the collector's problems.

"We call him Lightnin' because he can think faster than the Warden," said his companions.

Lightnin's eyes blazed as he sang. He was the leader of a quartet of black convicts brought from their cells into the vacant hospital room where Lightnin' stood leaning forward toward the recording horn, his three companions in a group just behind him. His color was deep black, "a blue-black, bad nigger," the stolid guard whispered to me. Lightnin' was still young—not yet thirty—serving his second term. His strong, graceful body swayed with the rhythm and the fervor of the singing.

Lightnin' was leading a song describing the days when convicts were leased by Texas to owners of large cotton and cane plantations, sometimes to be driven under the lash until they fell from exhaustion; many, according to rumor, dying from sunstroke amid the sunbaked rows of corn and cane, in "dem long, hot summer days, you could find a dead nigger on every turnrow." The song pictures what went on in the minds of a gang of field workers, one of whom they thought was about to be punished.

The Negroes see the "Cap'n" riding up on his horse with a "bull whip in one hand and a cowhide in the other." They work faster. "Better go to drivin'," says the song. After each excited ejaculation of Lightnin's, the chorus rings out, "Great Godamighty!"

Ridin' in a hurry.
Great Godamighty!
Ridin' like he's angry.
Great Godamighty!
Well, I wonder whut's de matter?

Great Godamighty!
Bull whip in one han', cowhide in de udder,
Great Godamighty!
Well, de Cap'n went to talkin',
Great Godamighty!
"Well, come on here an' hol' him!"
Great Godamighty!
"Cap'n let me off, suh!"
Great Godamighty!
"Woncha 'low me a chance, suh?"
Great Godamighty!
"Bully, low' down yo' britches!"
Great Godamighty!
De Bully went to pleadin',
Great Godamighty!
De Bully went to hollerin',
Great Godamighty!

The listeners in the room grew tense as the four strong voices blended in the terrible sweep of the song. Again the stolid guard whispered to me: "The goose pimples always come out along my spine when I hear niggers sing that song." Even outside in the adjacent iron-barred dormitory the chatter and clamor of two hundred black convicts became stilled into awed and reminiscent silence as the song swept on, growing in power to the end, while Lightnin', blue-black, vivid, poised as if for flight, leaned forward and sang with his three comrades,

"Great Godamighty!"

Every once in a while Father Finnegan walks down a corridor of the Huntsville, Texas, Penitentiary side by side with a man on his way to the execution room; on and on through the little green door to where stands the cruel chair, the "hot seat." "I have been taking that walk for years," he said; "sixty-eight times in all." But there have been more times since he talked with me. Recently Father Finnegan told a

Dallas *News* reporter that he had gone through the little green door 133 times.

The night before a convict must die he knows that within call close by waits Father Finnegan. Up to that time the condemned man may have refused to see or to talk to Father Finnegan. However hysterical or stricken dumb by fear or grief the man may be, he finally yields to the thought that a sympathetic friend is near to sit with him, and sends for Father Finnegan. And Father Finnegan always responds. If wanted, he goes into the cell and spends the night before the execution with the condemned man, sometimes baptizing him and taking him into the church. When the fatal moment comes shortly after midnight, without exception throughout the years of Father Finnegan's ministrations, each man has walked quietly alongside the good priest to his death. Not one man has struggled and fought. No more struggles, shrieks and curses. Father Finnegan promises to stand near and whisper consolation to the end. What else he has said to the convict, what the convict has said to him, no one knows or will know.

One day while we were recording Negro folk tunes in the Huntsville Penitentiary, Alan, my son and collaborator, and I met Father Finnegan. Later we had lunch with him. He is an impressive man of middle age, a native of Ireland. Manager Simmons had spoken of his voluntary and unique service, and we listened eagerly to his stories of life in the raw as he had found it.

He told us that his appeal to the men about to die was to meet the situation bravely. With every door of hope closed, with every effort rendered futile, with death inevitable, they could do nothing better than to meet the end calmly, without struggle or protest. Further resistance was useless. Some would tell him their stories, and some who wished the consolation of the Church would make full confessions and receive whatever comfort the Church had to give.

There was no Catholic church in Huntsville. One night just before the execution hour, a condemned man made his final confession and asked for absolution. The necessary articles could be had only in a neighboring church, miles away. Father Finnegan hurried off in his car through the rain and darkness. Far out of Huntsville on a lonely road through the woods his automobile broke down. Despite his efforts the car refused to budge. The moment when the man was to die was near at hand, one minute past midnight. "As best I could," Father Finnegan said, "I arranged some substitutes in my car." "I did the best I could," he repeated. No man can do more, I thought.

"Did you ever in all those confessions you have heard"—I hesitated, for I did not wish to go too far; I went on, "Did you ever take that terrible walk through the little green door with a man you believed to be innocent?" He held up his hand as if in gentle protest and did not reply directly. "Several times," he said, "after hearing a condemned man's confession, I have driven in the night to Austin, two hundred miles away, to see the Board of Pardons and the Governor. I may have done some good. Who knows?"

"But after you have gone through this ordeal," I went on; "after you have listened to the man's story, after you have worked to save him, after you have spent the last night with him and watched the scene in the death chamber, how can you rest or sleep?" "I am utterly worn out," replied Father Finnegan, "and I fall asleep like a little child. I have already done my best; there is no use to worry more."

"One night," he added, "I led to his death a Negro boy who had lived in the country. He was young and untutored and had had but little experience with the world and its ways. The thought of death was overpowering; his grief grew uncontrollable. He caught at some of the words that I used in my effort to steady and comfort him and clung to them pitifully, repeating over and over again, 'No more sorrow! No more pain! No more sorrow! No more pain!' When just at midnight the Warden came in for him and read the death warrant, he fell to the floor shrieking for mercy. I took his hand and began to repeat the phrase. And again he took it up. He spoke no more to me as we walked to the place of execution, but louder and louder his voice rang repeating these six words. It rose until the corridors rang. Then the death mask covered his face. Even at the last instant, as I leaned over to listen, just before the final shock came, I heard him faintly mumble: 'No more sorrow! No more pain!' Sometimes I think of that boy," said Father Finnegan.

James Avery Lomax and Susan Cooper Lomax, parents of John Avery Lomax. John Avery Lomax Family Papers, Dolph Briscoe Center for American History, The University of Texas at Austin (JAL/BC)

Six-year-old John Avery Lomax eyes the world. (JAL/BC)

The Lomax boys: John at age twelve, Jesse, Robert and George (clockwise from top left), ca. 1879. (JAL/BC)

John Lomax, ca. 1902.
(JAL/BC)

Bess Bauman Brown Lomax,
ca. 1906. (JAL/BC)

Family portrait: John and Bess Brown Lomax with their firstborn child, Shirley,
and the family menagerie in College Station, Texas, 1905. (JAL/BC)

John (front row right) and University of Texas Press Club colleagues, 1911.
(JAL/BC)

John with younger son Alan, ca. 1920. (JAL/BC)

Ruby Terrill ("Deanie" to her family) during her days as Dean of Women at the University of Texas, Austin, and before her 1934 marriage to John. Terrill was a founder of Delta Kappa Gamma, the honorary society dedicated to woman's education. (JAL/BC)

John and Ruby at their 1934 wedding in Commerce, Texas, the city where they first met thirteen years earlier. (JAL/BC)

John and twenty-five-year-old John Jr. in New York City, 1932.
Courtesy of John Lomax III

Lightnin' Washington and his singing group at Darrington Convict Farm, Texas, 1934. "Lightnin' was leading a song describing the days when convicts were leased by Texas to owners of large cotton and cane plantations, sometimes to be driven under the lash until they fell from exhaustion." (137) Photograph by Alan Lomax. Library of Congress, Prints & Photographs Division, Lomax Collection (LoC/LC)

John's best-known discovery, Huddie "Lead Belly" Ledbetter, and his wife, Martha Promise Ledbetter, Wilton, Connecticut, 1935. "He knew so many songs which he sang with restraint and sympathy." (104) Photographer unknown (LoC/LC)

The Bogtrotters, Galax, Virginia, 1937. "They play and sing three hundred pieces, a lot of them mountain ballads, using the violin, guitar and autoharp." (262) Photographer unknown (LoC/LC)

Richard Amerson, Doc Reed and John Lomax working in Livingston, Alabama, 1940. "Doc Reed . . . furnished me with some beautiful spirituals not found in any other community." (265) Photographed by Ruby Terrill Lomax (LoC/LC)

Harriett McClintock and John Lomax, with Ruby Pickens Tartt and McClintock's great-grand children in the background, near Sumpterville, Alabama, 1940. "Aunt Harriet McClintock, who, according to rumor, knew a cotton-picking song. . . . I sat on the ground beside her while the machine was running, holding the microphone ready to catch everything she said." (165) Photographed by Ruby Terrill Lomax (LoC/LC)

John, Alan and Ruby relaxing at home in Dallas in the 1940s. (JAL/BC)

Three generations of John Lomaxes: John III (John M.) eyes his grandfather's autobiography while father John A. Jr. looks on in this 1947 photo taken in Houston. (JAL/BC)

John and longtime friend J. Frank Dobie (r.) discuss J. Evetts Haley's biography of Texas rancher Charles Goodnight. (JAL/BC)

Painter J. Anthony Wills's portrait of John Lomax,
based on a photo taken around 1935. (JAL/BC)

Joseph Franklin Lomax, John Lomax III, Anna Lomax Wood and Susan Mansell with Shirley Lomax Mansell, John A. Lomax Jr. and Alan Lomax at the dedication of J. Anthony Wills's portrait, Austin, Texas, 1964. (JAL/BC)

STATE HISTORICAL SURVEY COMMITTEE

TEXAS

1/4 MILE WEST TO BOYHOOD HOME OF
JOHN A. LOMAX (1867–1948)
ONLY A LOG KITCHEN NOW MARKS
THE HOMESITE OF JOHN LOMAX, ONE
OF THE FOREMOST COLLECTORS OF
AMERICAN FOLKSONGS. HERE, ON PART
OF THE CHISHOLM TRAIL, YOUNG
LOMAX HEARD COWBOYS CROONING
AND YODELING TO RESTLESS HERDS;
NEGRO SERVANTS TAUGHT HIM JIG
TUNES, CHANTS, WORK SONGS, AND
CALLS; AND ON WINTER NIGHTS HIS
FAMILY SANG SONGS AND SWAPPED
STORIES AROUND A BLAZING FIRE.

LOMAX BEGAN TO WRITE DOWN
THIS MUSIC WHILE STILL A BOY;
AND WHEN HE LEFT BOSQUE COUNTY
AT AGE 20, HE CARRIED WITH HIM
A ROLL OF COWBOY BALLADS—THE
NUCLEUS OF HIS LIFELONG WORK.
(1970)

The official state marker close to the Lomax homestead outside
Meridian, Texas. (JAL/BC)

7

IRON HEAD AND CLEAR ROCK

I first saw Iron Head, aged 63, convict No. 3610, late one afternoon when I was recording Negro folk tunes in the hospital of the Central Farm of the Texas Penitentiary System near Sugarland, Texas. Captain Gotch had told me that Mexico, a Negro convict and steward of the hospital, was the best singer on the farm. Only two or three convalescents were in the hospital, so the recording machine could be set up in the quiet of their large bedroom. Among the curious faces pressed against the window bars while Mexico was singing, a low, solidly built Negro listened intently. This man beckoned to me.

"I'se Iron Head, I'se a trusty," he said. "I know lots of jumped-up, sinful songs—more than any of these niggers."

That night and throughout the long day following, Iron Head proved that he did know the work songs of the black men. He and his "pardner," Clear Rock, turn and turn about, sang rhythmic, surging songs of labor; cotton-picking songs; songs of the jailbird; songs of the "bloodhoun's" tracking the fleeing Negro through the river bottom; songs of angry "Cap'n"; songs of loneliness and the dismal monotony of life in the penitentiary; songs of pathetic longing for his "doney," his woman; songs of the bold black desperado with his trusty fo'ty-fo' in his hand, with his enemy lying dead in the smoke pouring from its barrel; songs of his woman, dressed in "green, lavender and red," who waited hopefully outside the prison walls for her man, and many another, including English ballads found in the great Child collection.

Few of these songs were gay in tone. Most of them were dominated by brooding sadness. Here was no studied art. The words, the music, the rhythm, were simple, the natural emotional outpouring of the black man in confinement. The listener found himself swept along with the primitive emotions aroused, and, despite himself, discovered his own body swaying in unison with the urge of Iron Head's melodies:

"De roughest nigger what ever walked de streets of Dallas. In de pen off an' on fo' thirty-fo' years." Six times convicted, a "habitual" as he called himself. "I'se a H. B. C.—habitual criminal, you know," he explained proudly. "Not even Ma Ferguson can pardon me." Iron Head failed to look the part. Only some deeply graven and grim lines about his mouth and eyes made you stop and wonder if any tenderness had ever touched his life. He had a quiet dignity and reserve. Amid the clamor of a room full of black convicts, hearing for the first time their voices coming from the recording machine, he preserved his composure.

"Sing *Shorty George*, Iron Head," begged his companions. *Shorty George* told about the short passenger train that ran from Houston to the farm once a month on a Sunday, bringing visiting wives and sweethearts. The men were sad when they saw the train depart:

> Shorty George, you ain't no fren' of mine,
> Take all de wimmens, leave de mens behin'.

The convicts insisted and urged him until Iron Head's quiet negative flamed into an outburst of anger: "You niggers know dat song always tears me to pieces. I won't sing it." And he walked away from the crowd to the iron-barred door, where he stood, leaning against the jamb, looking out into the soft Texas moonlight. Soon he motioned to me.

"I'll sing dat song low for you," he said, as if in apology for his outburst. "It makes me restless to see my woman. I'se a trusty an' I has a easy job. I could run down one o' dem corn rows an' git away, any day. But when de law caught me, dey would put me back in de line wid de fiel' han's. I'se too ol' for dat hard work."

Then he sang the story of the convict who gets a letter that he can't read for crying. It tells him that his "woman ain't dead but she's slowly dyin'." The convict breaks out of the penitentiary and goes home to his wife's funeral, as the song relates. When Iron Head reached the last couplet, his low-toned voice swept along with lyric power into the tragic finale:

When dey let my baby down in de groun'
I couldn't hear nuffin' but de coffin soun'.

Then Iron Head, a perpetual jailbird, a condemned prisoner for life, broke down and sobbed aloud.

I put my hand on his shoulder: "Some men lose their wives forever, Iron Head. They can never see them again. Your woman is alive." Iron Head looked out-of-doors over broad fields of tall corn shimmering and whispering in the moonlight. Bitterness came back to his voice: "She might as well be dead; I can't go to her an' she's scared to come to me."

Alan and I had been attracted to this man because he knew many folk songs which he sang well. We always stopped to see him when we passed by Central State Farm No. 1. He was unlike the ordinary Negro convict; he confessed that he was guilty of other crimes than those that had put him in prison. "Mos' of de times dey didn't catch me," he modestly admitted. He had no complaints against his Captain and the guards; he wanted to be free again, but he offered no extravagant promises of reform. "I'se foun' out dat I cain't beat de law," he said quietly, "an' I ain't gonna try no mo'." Meanwhile he had become a trusty. In a little house set aside for him he worked all day, weaving from corn shucks the collars worn by the mules on the farm, as well as cleverly contrived door mats, one of which he sent as a gift to Miss Terrill.

There were no serious charges of prison misconduct against him. He had served more than eight years of his last sentence, to which had been added a credit of six years for good conduct. Captain Flanagan had already spoken a good word for him to the Board of Pardons. When I went to them, asking that he be paroled to me, my request was granted.

"Good Gawd A'mighty, de Lawd will provide!" Iron Head exclaimed when Captain Gotch of the Central State Farm read to him a four-months parole which I had brought down from Governor Allred. Iron Head, the friendless life-termer, a daytime burglar in the homes of his own people, was to have his chance. Iron Head was not the forgotten man. No one had ever cared enough about him to know him and forget him. No one could forget him, for no one had ever given him a thought. Even the Houston judge who had tried him last and the attorney who had prosecuted him were unable to recall him. No letter had come to him in ten years.

He had pleaded guilty to all the charges that had sent him to the penitentiary six times. "I wuz stealin' all de time. No use tryin' to beg off." Yet, in less than an hour, he sat smiling in my car, speeding to my home in Austin, two hundred miles away. (Later I drove with him down Fifth Avenue, New York City, while he held on to me in terror.) Presently I saw his lips moving.

"What are you saying?"

"Prayin'," said Iron Head.

"Say it out loud," I said; so he began:

"I ask de good Lawd while me and Mistuh Lomax went 'round through diff'rent parts of de country that He may go with us an' throw 'roun' us de strong arm of His protection what keeps us from all harm, hurt or danger. Move all hind'rin' causes, all stumblin' blocks; make our hilly ways level an' our crooked paths straight. An' take care of his dear-loved companion an' also dear-loved daughter an' son an' de cook, an', O Lawd, I humbly 'seech Thee, deliver him back safe an' soun' in physical health. An' when time is ended an' we cain't go no mo', 'ceive an' save us somewhere in Heaven. My prayer, Christ our 'Deemer's sake, Amen an' thank Gawd."

"I always said my prayers in de penitentiary," said Iron Head, the expert crap-shooter, a cooncan player much feared.

The next day in Austin, Governor Allred asked him, "How did you get the name of Iron Head?"

"I wuz cuttin' wood on de Ramsey State Farm at Angleton at a place called de 'lifetime cut.' A live-oak tree fell down dat I wuzn't 'spectin'. Some limbs hit my head, an' it broke 'em off; didn't knock me down, an' it didn't stop me from working. De boys name me Iron Head."

Thus I picked this Negro singer of English ballads, of *Ol' Hannah, Little John Henry, The Gray Goose, Black Betty, Shorty George, Pick a Bale of Cotton, The Ol' Lady,* and other "sinful songs," to be my chauffeur and companion on a hunt for folk songs among the Southern penitentiaries and remote Negro communities. Iron Head's singing was to inspire other Negro songsters to strive to excel him. If he went straight, I would ask the Governor to extend his parole or to pardon him. Should he fall back into thievery, I was under contract to deliver him back to Sugarland and to Captain Gotch, who doubtless would again put him to work weaving mule collars.

A few days later Iron Head and I headed out of Dallas bound for the Mississippi Delta and Parchman, where is located the 16,000-acre convict farm with more than two thousand inmates. Throughout the first day and on past Marshall, Texas, where we spent the first night in a tourist camp, Iron Head talked and sang gay tunes:

Me an' my wife kin pick a bale of cotton,
Pick a bale, pick a bale, pick a bale a day.
Me an' my podner an' my podner's fren'
Kin pick mo' cotton than a gin kin gin.

Always he smiled. He wondered "what dem niggers down at Sugarlan' would think if they could see me ridin' in a spang-new Primer [Plymouth] car, settin' up 'side a big white man like I wuz somebody." We passed by farms that were "too po' to raise a fuss on." A speeding car that passed us was driven by a man whose "wife had run away an' he wuz tryin' to ketch her." Of a young Negro woman dressed in red, whom we met on the highway, he said, "She's got a figger that won't wait." Proud of his ability to read, he shouted out the words on billboards as we dashed past. "Ambassado' Hotel, Grill in Connection." The word "Ambassador" floored him. After I prompted, he repeated,

"Ambassador Hotel, Girls in Connection!" Then: "Dey furnishes girls in dat hotel. Is dat whar we's gwine to stop tonight, Boss?"

For two days we camped on the bluff overlooking the Mississippi River just south of Vicksburg. After supper Iron Head started on a "ramble," claiming he wanted to see the "big river" running far below. Soon he came back. "I couldn't see nothin' but dark," he said. "I always has to be keerful of de dark." During the day we watched thirty roustabouts unload from the *Tennessee Belle*, just up from New Orleans, a carload of miscellaneous freight. I had hoped to catch some of the river tunes that Mark Twain wrote about. But no sound came from them as they shuffled up and down the gangplank in a long, ever moving line. Not one river "holler" did I hear.

"They never sing any more," the Captain told me. "They don't have life enough."

The river songs indeed seemed gone, for I had already searched the New Orleans docks. Soon the gang songs of the black men would follow suit, as a part of the advance of the machine age. On the penitentiary farms, where Negro labor must be done in groups, the plantation "hollers" yet live. To Parchman, Mississippi, then, I must travel to find them.

First it was necessary to drive by Jackson, Mississippi, to carry the greetings of Governor Allred of Texas to Governor White, and to seek permission to visit again the convict farms. On the way out of Jackson two young roadside minstrels sang about a gold-digger's victim, with the refrain:

When I got money, it's "Hello, sugar pie!"
When I git broke, "Go way, country boy!"

Iron Head grinned in appreciation.

In Yazoo City, on the way from Jackson to Parchman, I stopped to talk to a group of Negroes loafing in town for the Saturday holiday. Their spokesman attracted me. "You must be an educated man," I suggested. "Yes, sir, boss, I ain't much edjucated but I got good learnin'."

"When do the guitar pickers come in?" I inquired. "Jes' about fust dark," he replied.

For more than a hundred miles the highway runs due north from Yazoo City to Parchman, through one of the world's largest and richest deltas. In much of this section the Negro population is from five to ten times greater than the white. Town follows town with laughing, gaudily dressed Negroes crowding the sidewalks and overflowing into the streets. At last our car stopped close to the grim red building of Camp No. 1 at Parchman, to which I came for my second visit.

The day's journey was done. We could see the men in stripes lounging about the buildings. "Feels sorta like home," reflected Iron Head.

I was shown to a comfortable room in Superintendent Timm's home. The Negro boy in stripes who carried my baggage said, after we had unpacked my valise and as he turned down the bedcovers, "I'll turn over the mattress in the mornin' an' make you another sweet bed."

Meanwhile Iron Head was lodged with the "head shooter," a tall black man, the chief trusty. In Mississippi only the trusties carry guns and guard their fellow convicts. Late that night through the open window, I heard a Negro trusty singing:

Yonder comes Rosy in her mornin' gown,
An' the trimmin' on her apron, how it do hang down.

The ex-bellhop who had shown me to my room the night before tapped at my door early and stuck his head into the room.

"Night's out!" he announced. Another day of adventure was on among Negroes whose field "hollers" and gang songs are unexcelled.

As we had ridden along en route to Parchman, Iron Head often sang. One day his song was an appeal to "Ol' Hannah" (the sun) to go down. As he explained, "About three o'clock on a long summer day, de sun forgits to move an' stops. Den de mens sings dis song":

Been a great long time since Hannah went down,
Oh, Hanna, go down;
Been a great long time since Hannah went down,
Oh, Hannah, go down!

She's gone behin' dem western hills, (etc.)

I wonder where is de Capt'in gone? (etc.)

He's gone to de house to ring de bell. (etc.)

Bullies, did you hear what de Capt'in said? (etc.)

Bullies, if you work, I'm goin' trust you well,
An' if you don't, I'm goin' give you hell. (etc.)

You orta come on dis river in Nineteen-fo',
You'd find a dead nigger on ev'ry turnrow. (etc.)

You orta come on dis river in Nineteen-ten,
Dey was workin' de wommens like dey was workin' de men. (etc.)

Go down, old Hannah, don't you rise no mo',
Oh, Hannah, go down;
If you rise any mo', bring Jedgement Day,
Oh, Hannah, go down!

It is a far cry from Iron Head in the penitentiary to the time of one of
the early English ballads he sang:

Once I knows an old' lady,
'Round Tennessee she dwell;
She had a lovin' husband
But she loved other young mens as well.

Love my darlin', oh!
I love my darlin', oh!

I'm goin' down by de doctor's shop,
Jes' as straight as I kin go,
See if I can't fin' some instrument 'round dat place
Dat'll run my husband blind.

She only foun' two marrow-bones,
She made him eat 'em all.
An' he says, "Now, my dear wife, I'm blind
An' jes' can't see at all."

Says, "I would go to de river an' drown myself,
Honey, if I only knew de way."
She says, "No, my dear, come an' go with me,
Mother 'fraid you'll run astray."

She got away down on the river side,
She wanted to see her ol' man drown.
He says, "My dear kind wife, I cannot drown
Unless you shoves me in."

She gits way back, taken a long, runnin' start,
She goin' shove her ol' man in,
Ol' man step jes' a little one side
An' headlong she jump in.

Ol' man bein' so kind-hearted,
Knowin', too, de sweet wife couldn't swim,
He reached right back an' he got a long pole
And he shove her further in.

Says, "Come all you young hasty women,
Take warnin' after me;

Don't never try to drown a po' ol' man
Says he's blind an' cannot see."

Love my darlin', oh!
I love my darlin', oh!

Less than a year after the Governor set him free, I found Iron Head
in the garden squad of the Ramsey State Convict Farm in Texas. He
peered past me through the iron bars of his cell. Once more he was a
convict longing for the "free world." I asked him what had happened.

"Well, I got hard up, an' I did a little mo' porch-climbin'." (The
swag amounted to more than a thousand dollars.)

He once had explained to me why he first became a thief: "Dem
Jew merchants on Deep Ellum in Dallas had so many goods dey piles
'em out on the sidewalks. I jes' took what I wanted. I never done no
work. My grandma raised me. Ev'ry day she giv' me my dinner in
a bucket an' sent me to school. I never got there. But mos'ly I stole
from niggers. De law don't pay no 'tention when niggers lose their
things. I'd watch a house till de womenfolks go away. Den I'd go in
an' take what I wanted."

During our trip, when Iron Head's singing brought him some
money, I suggested that he save it, go back to Dallas and restore the
value of the stolen goods. He rejected the idea: "Dey has money. Dey
never miss what I took." He often expressed a wish to hunt for some
stolen jewelry that he had buried in a Dallas back yard. "I dug up de
whole yard an' couldn't fin' de place no mo'."

Iron Head often paraded his virtues. We were leaving a tourist
camp in South Carolina, where he had made his pallet on the floor
by the side of my bed. On other occasions when such an arrangement
was impossible, he would sleep in the automobile and have me lock
him inside the car, as a terrible fear seemed to harass him when darkness fell. He could get out but an intruder could not get in.

As we drove away from the South Carolina camp that morning,
he said: "Boss, you don't think I notices, but I watches ev'ything. I
knows where you keep yo' money. You leaves it all in yo' pocket an'

hangs yo' clothes in de closet, an' you goes off to sleep while I stays awake. I could git up any night an' knock you in de haid an' take yo' money. You wouldn't know nothin' about it. Then I could take de car an' drive away. I ain't never killed you yet, now has I?"

Despite his threat to drive off in the car some night, I could never teach him to manage the automobile. After many trials I had him take the wheel one day in Florida, where the road ran straight for ten miles. There was no traffic. I let him drive until I happened to see his hands trembling as he grasped the wheel. When we swapped places, Iron Head staggered as he walked around the car. "My legs feel funny," he complained. Thereafter I became the permanent chauffeur.

After two months together as automobile-touring companions, I wrote of him: "Iron Head has assured me earnestly that the Good Lord must have him especially in mind, since He has thus far not permitted him to be killed, although shot at repeatedly and hit twice! 'He watches over me,' says Iron Head without a shadow of regret for his past, or sorrow for the cruel losses he has caused to poor washer-women away from their homes at work while he robbed them. 'I'd rather be a dog and bay at the moon' than to try to set him right on any of his philosophy. Just as was Lead Belly, he is entirely satisfied with himself and has no spark of gratitude in his make-up. We get along and I am not complaining, only I know now that you can't make a silk purse from a sow's ear."

When we finished our work among the Negroes where Iron Head's singing had been useful, I proposed to send him back to Austin where, according to promise, I was to set him up in the business of weaving rugs from corn shucks. He was bitterly resentful and hinted at reprisals on my family. Neither was he willing to find a job and work in Washington. So I bought a ticket, gave him money and sent him back to Texas.

He never reported at my home in Austin. Another friend found work for him in the country. But he couldn't stay away from Austin honkytonks and low company. Finally, I learned, he had deserted his job on the farm and become a street-corner bum. Then quickly followed the "pen" for the seventh time—and life.

When I last saw him it was a sad meeting and a sad separation. Ramsey Farm is the State's home for the long-termers and the incorrigibles. I should have left him at Sugarland to weave from corn shucks horse collars and rugs for Captain Gotch and Captain Flanagan.

"Gimme room, niggers, gimme room. Let me git at dat singin' machine. I'se de out-singin'est nigger on dis here plantation. I'se been in de pen forty-nine years off and on, an' I ought to know all de songs. Git out o' my way!"

I saved the microphone of the recording machine from being overturned by the big, eager, confident, self-important copper-colored man as he pushed through the throng of Negro convicts.

"Wait, Clear Rock," I said. "Later we will try you out."

"Ready right now," he insisted, and I hardly had time to start the machine before he plunged into a patting song, "Dat's All Right, Honey," where his big hands helped to carry the melody:

"'Way up yonder, darlin', 'bove the sun, sugar,
Girls all call me honey, sugar plum, sho' 'nuff!
Got a horse, sugar; buggy, too, baby;
Horse's black, darlin', buggy's blue, sho' nuff!
Dat's all right, honey, dat's all right, baby."

The crowd cheered, for the tune was catchy. Where he got the words and tune he did not know. I have not found the song elsewhere. Here was evidence that among Negro convicts Alan and I were to find an easy source for folk songs, for Clear Rock was among the first group of Negro convicts in our search.

Afterward when I talked alone with Clear Rock, I asked him what brought him to the penitentiary as a life-termer.

"I th'owed three niggers."

"I don't understand."

"Well, I got three of them. I got 'em with rocks. That's why they calls me Clear Rock."

"Do you mean to tell me that you killed three people with rocks?"

"No, boss, I th'owed three when a bunch come at me. [A convict doesn't like to say "kill."] I used to be a powerful rock th'ower. I th'owed three, an' the law sont me to the pen. Then the Governor pardoned me."

"And the second time?" I inquired.

"I was jes' misfortunate, boss, jes' misfortunate. It might 'a' happened to anybody."

A buxom yellow girl; some question of her age; an enemy or two; and here was Clear Rock, a seventy-one year old water boy, a satisfied prisoner for life. Unable to read or write, he afterward sang *"Bobby" Allen*, as he called the old English ballad, true to tune, but hopelessly mixed with a famous cowboy song entitled "The Streets of Laredo." His song buried "Miss Allen" in a desert of New Mexico with six pretty maidens all dressed in white for her pallbearers, though there seemed water a plenty for a rose and a briar to grow over her head till they met and "got twined in a knot and couldn't grow no higher." In another rendition he buried "Bobby" Allen out of Dallas with the mourners "hollerin' and a-squallin'."

Clear Rock seemed to have caught in his capacious memory the floating folk songs that had been current among the thousands of black convicts who had been his only companions for fifty years. He had a store equal in continuous length to the *Iliad*. He did not sing any song through. Always I had to stop him and ask for another tune. Nor did he hesitate for a word. If he ever forgot (I could not discover), his quick invention supplied a word or line without a moment's hesitation and in the spirit and rhythm of the song he was singing.

He sang a new version of *The Old Chisholm Trail*, an endless ballad describing the experiences of a band of cowboys driving a herd of Texas longhorn cattle from Texas to Montana. One of the cowboys in his song, riding an unruly horse, was thrown high and left hanging on a limb of a tree along the trail. Clear Rock sang four stanzas describing this incident and then ended his song.

"That's rather hard on that cowboy," I suggested, "to go on up the trail and leave him sprawling on a limb in what is doubtless an uncomfortable position."

"Lemme git him down, boss; I'll git him down!" And at once he sang in perfect tune:

Cowboy lyin' in a tree a-sprawlin',
Come-a-ti-yi-yippy, yippy yea, yippy yea,
Come a little wind an' down he come a-fallin',
Come-a-ti-yi yippy, yippy yea.

"Could you let me have a quarter, boss? I jes' lef' my crap game to help you out. I wants to fade one of dese biggety town niggers who thinks he knows how to roll de bones." And Clear Rock, whistling cheerily, started away, as I handed him half a dollar. He quickly readjusted himself. He hadn't expected more than a dime.

"Boss, can't you make it a dollar? I could 'a' made lots more money than that if I hadn't stopped shooting craps." Once, he told me, he had won the spending money of all the men in the camp, two hundred convicts. "Cleaned 'em spang out," boasted Clear Rock. The total amount was $27.85.

On our second visit to Clear Rock and his crew, late one wintry Saturday afternoon, Alan and I stopped at Sugarland, Texas, and took from the express office a new recording machine that had just come in from New York City. Then we drove on out to Central State Farm, Number 1, of the Texas Penitentiary system, where Captain Flanagan agreed to let us bunk that night in the dormitory with the prison guards. After supper about a dozen Negro trusties who were to sing for us helped unload and unbox our machine and carry it into the farm blacksmith shop, which stood some distance away from the main group of buildings. The men crowded around eager and curious as a bunch of children as they watched Alan test the connections, adjust the gadgets and doodads, and unwrap and set up the microphone.

"Now we are ready for a singer," Alan said as he turned on the electric current and set the turntable spinning. "Oh, I forgot—where is the cutting needle?" This minute steel plug, with a diamond set in the smaller end to cut the line of sound in the aluminum disk, could not be found. We turned over every scrap of wrapping paper, shook out the excelsior and looked carefully into the cracks and crannies of the boxes and machinery. No cutting needle. Without it no records could be made.

"The singing tonight is off, boys."

Our eager "songsters" showed their disappointment as Alan and I discussed telegrams to New York City and the chance of finding in Houston some substitute for the lost cutting needle. But tomorrow was Sunday, and no shops would be open either in Houston or in New York. We might be in for a long delay.

"Well, boys," I said, "the men who shipped this machine probably would not trust a diamond in an express package, but, instead, doubtless sent it by registered mail. We didn't ask at the post office. We'll get it in the morning and record songs all day Sunday. Let's tell stories. How many of you believe in ghosts? Have any of you ever seen a ghost?"

By that time a steady rain was pouring down on the sheet-iron roof above us. Outside black darkness; inside the white-clad Negroes sat around on empty nail kegs. The dirt-floored shop, with its anvil and old-fashioned bellows, piles of rusty iron in the corners, a blackened workman's bench, showed dim from a single dust-covered light globe. It was a gloomy place; a dark and dismal night. The sound of rain on the sheet-iron roof boomed as the torrents poured steadily down.

When I said "ghosts" the black men stopped their chatter.

They looked at each other and no one spoke. Iron Head got up and moved his seat to the other side of the room, away from the two big Edison batteries that now and then suddenly popped from escaping gas. He had not been able to locate the sound, and I saw him continue to peer at the dark corner where they stood. Finally, Burn Down, the big blacksmith, said, "Well, suh, I don't exactly believe in ghosts. I never seen one. But when I'se out in de fields by myself nights an' has to come by dat lonesome little graveyard where dem convict boys is buried what didn't have no friends to come and git 'em when they died, I jes don't come dat way. I takes a wide 'roundance. Dem white lumber tombstones seem like dey is runnin' along in de dark behin' me. Yassuh!"

Nobody laughed. But tongues were loosened, and for more than an hour Alan and I heard stories to rival those of Gulliver and Munchausen. Clear Rock from "Taylortown," Texas, seventy-one years old, "Been in de pen forty-nine years goin' on fifty," told three stories, "Each one," as Alan said, "better than the other."

"One time," Clear Rock said, "'fo' I got in de pen, I wuz livin' out in de country close to Bastrop, Texas. In dem days I wuz a sort-o' jack-leg Baptis' preacher. Well, over 'cross de road fum where I live there wuz a sick man come from Georgy. He wuz sick fur a long time. Dat day some wimmens fum de house come over an' say dat de sick man wuz dead. Dey ask me to he'p wid de settin' up wid de corpse, 'cause dey had to set up wid de corpse until de man's kinfolks could come fum Georgy to moan over him and see him buried. An', bein' as I was 'greeable, I went over to de house where de dead man wuz at.

"De wimmens an' de mens wuz all settin' scrooched up aroun' de fire, mighty sleepy. Dey wuz plum wo' out fum settin' up wid de sick man so long. Dat dere man wuz lyin' over in de corner on his coolin' board wid a white rag wropt aroun' his jaws. It was a mighty cold, lonesome night.

"'Clear Rock,' de wimmens says, 'we's all tired out an we's gonna lay down. Dere is about a waggin load o' yam pertaters in de corner by de chimbly. Ef you gits hongry, you might cook you some.'

"Den de wimmens huddle demselves togedder down in de middle ob de flo' and kivers up wid a ragged quilt. De mens was sittin' befo' de fireplace in deir cheers, leanin' back, noddin' an' bowin', dey was so sleepy.

"I picked me out three o' dem yam pertaters, about so long an' so wide [measuring with his big hands]—jes' good eatin'-size yams, an' I stuck 'em in de ashes an' kivers 'em up wid de emmels [embers]. Den I lean my head on de back o' my cheer an try to sleep. Well, I was sort-o' nappin' 'long, noddin' an' nappin', till lastly I did fall asleep. Long 'way in de night I wakes up an' looks 'round de room. All de mens was settin' in deir cheers sound asleep, wid deir haids th'owed back an' deir mouths open. De wimmens was huddled up on de flo', 'cause it was so cold. Dey was all scrooched up asleep, kivered up wid dat ragged quilt. Dat daid man, he was jes' layin' over in de corner on de coolin' board wid a white rag wropt 'round his jaws.

"'Clear Rock,' I says, "spec dem yams o' yo's is done.' So I retcht in de emmels an' took out one o' dem yams. You know, when you cook a young yam, de sap comes out all over it an' sticks to de ashes. So I takes my foot an' whacks de yam agin' it, 'Whock, whock, whock,' so de ashes would come off. Den de man dat was daid, layin' over in de corner on de coolin' board wid a white rag wropt 'round his jaws, he raise up an' he say: 'Is dey done?'

"I say, 'I don' know whedder dey is done or not, but I'se done wid dis place!' De do' was too fur away, so I went out th'oo de winduh. My feet was itchin' an' my body was honin' to move on. As I was a-purceedin' up de big road, I pass by one dem German school-houses where de mens was practicin' music. 'Bout de time I pass by deir house, one o' dem mens poked a big brass horn out de winduh on de side where I was at and blowed 'da-ti-da-da-ti-do!'[Clear Rock imitates taps.] I wasn't expectin' nothin' like dat an' I leaned over, and when I riz up I was in Ardmo', Oklahoma, fo' hundred miles away! My eyes was stickin' out an' shinin' like de spy glass on a loco-mobile. I was goin' so fas', splat-splattin' it down on de asphalt, dat when I crossed de T. P. tracks in Fort Worth my shirt-tail ketch afire an' make me run faster. Dat's what I calls runnin' yo'sef lost. Befo' I could perteck myself I had run outa Texas clean over into Oklahoma."

Before the men quit shouting Clear Rock was off on another story about his ability as a runner:

"Me an' a bunch o' boys one time went to pick cotton out from Taylor. So we walked and we walked till we got tired, an' we hunted for a place to lie down and sleep. So we was searchin' and lookin' for a lodgement place where we could lay down, an' we come to a' ol' vacant house away from the road an' we laid down on the floor on our cotton sacks. Well, being hungry, I was cookin' some eggs and meat in the fire-place when a black cat pop outen the chimney into the skil-let an' jump from there over in a corner of the room. His eyes was turnin' over just like some buggy wheels. Some boys went out the winduh an' some went out the door, an' all was hollerin'. I wound up in Floridy, an' my feets was so sore I had to lay down by a' ol' dotten log. An' that same ol' black cat ask me, 'Didn't we have a good race?' An' I say, 'Ain' nothin' to de race we gwine have!' (At this point, I, who had heard the story before in one of Clear Rock's innumerable improvisations, remarked that he hadn't told the story in the same way at all as he had the first time. I reminded the obsequious and delightful Negro that in his previous telling the cat had stood on a little built-in shelf in the corner, a shelf that is typical of the houses of poor country farmers, and that at last it had spat out the fire. Clear Rock with his never-ending desire to please and his inexhaustible energy, began again at the dramatic entrance of the black cat.)

"I was cookin' at the fireplace," he said, "an' I look over my shoulder an' see a li'l black kitten on a little shelf in de corner of the room, an' dat kitten was turnin' roun' an' roun'. Seem like de mo' I look the bigger he got, ontil it got de size of a yellin' [yearling]. An' he jump down off de shelf an' come over to de fire an' spit it out, 'whoosh!' Dat lef' it all dark in that place, an' one o' de boys, hearin' me stumblin' roun', say, 'How you comin' out?' And I say, 'Ain' comin' out, gwine out!' We was all scramblin' roun' in dat place trying to get away from that cat an' out de door. So boy holler out, 'Where's de door?' An' I say, 'I don' know, but jes' follow me and I'll find daylight somewhere.' Dis time I ran to Africy on my hoss and when he cross de Dead Sea, between here an' Africy, dat hoss wuz goin' so fas' he didn't sink down over his hocks!"

The wind dashed the rain against the thin walls of the blacksmith shop.

"Jes' one mo' little one," begged Clear Rock:

"One time I went to town huntin' a job, up in a little old town they call Rogers. And so I went to a lady's house there and asked her for some work. She says, 'Can you cut yards?' an' I says, 'Yes, ma'am.' She says, 'Go 'roun, go 'roun to de back and look under de house, you'll find a lawn-mower there, and then begin cuttin'.' I told her, 'Yes, ma'am,' and I went 'round and got de lawn-mower and started on de back cuttin' grass.

"And so—she had some geese out into a vacant park there, she had. And so—under a tree laid a goat. And this old geese in de heat of de day raised up and said, 'We's havin' a *hard* time!' Goat says, 'Ungh-Ungh.' So de geese kep' a-pickin', and they raised up agin and says, 'We's havin' a *ha-ard* time.' Goat say, 'Ungh-ungh!' And so de geese raised up agin and says, 'We're havin' a *ha-a-ard* time.' And de goat says, 'ba-a-d managin'!'"

Let your imagination picture Clear Rock as his fingers imitated the geese snipping grass, the flock protesting against the hard facts of life, the solemn, taciturn billy goat passing final judgment on the situation.

Some years afterward, resourceful Clear Rock caught the attention of Governor "Ma" Ferguson when she visited the convict camp. He sang about Long John, a runaway Negro, who wore a wonderful shoe: "Had a heel in front and a heel behind, so you never could tell where that nigger was a-gwine." According to Clear Rock, "One day some of my friends in Taylor heard that Miz Ferguson wuz goin' down to Central Farm a-visitin' an' they sont a car down there with a letter signed by 30,000 peoples; they wuz de names of all de prominent lawyers an' officers and all the other whichocrats around Taylor, an' Miz Ferguson sot me free." (The population of Taylor is less than 5,000.)

I hunted for Clear Rock for several hours in Taylor one night. The next morning I found him seated on the running board of my car in front of the hotel.

"How did you know my car?" I asked.

"Looked jes' like you," chuckled Winedot, alias Clear Rock. "Winedot's my new name," he added. I got no other explanation, even though I was driving the car for the first time.

Clear Rock, then on the WPA rolls, complained that the "release hardly don't give us nothin' to eat 'cept grapefruit." And his pastorate (he was shepherd to a flock of Baptists) did not pay much, though he had added four sisters to his board of deacons "to take keer of de money, 'cause de men mought take de collections an' lose 'em all shootin' craps." He was handy man around the Courthouse and the post office. Also he exhibited proudly a soiled perpetual petition for funds written out by a lawyer, dictated and circulated by Clear Rock:

Taylor, Texas, March 8, 1939.

We certifies that we knows Mose Platt, Clear Rock, and that he has been up to this time a good hardly working man. He is sick and his wife is sick, he is unemployed and aint go no job, and not able to demand no job whatever, and his doctor is Mr. Doaks and Doaks, and the judge of Williamson County, which he is worked for, is Mr. Judge Burnap, and his boss lawyer Mr. Lawhon, and also Captain boss Mr. Booth of the bank, also Mr. Richards and Judge Davis, also Mr. Challener, also Mr. Connolly, also Mr. Speegle, also Mr. M. B. Connolly, also Mr. Howard Bland, also Mr. Prewitts, in fact all Prewitts, also Mr. Lloyd Payne, also Mr. Hewitt, the drugstore man, also Mr. Brunner the postmaster, also Mr. lawyer Fox, also Mr. Wofford, the lawyer, also Mr. Judge Black and so he has been sociable with his fellowman, this Mose Platt, and also trustworthy. Also Mr. Judge Governor Allred, and also Governor Ferguson. We hereby wish you would contribute to him, and we thank you very much; also Mr. Judge Roach.

Although his petition indicated a low physical state, he assured me: "I ain't got no sickness nowhere. My whole body is as clean as de pa'm o' yo' hand." When he introduced me to his wife, "Miss Reverend Mose Platt," he whispered: "She weighs 250 pounds. She's my seventeen" (meaning the number of his marital ventures)—probably quite untrue but in keeping with this black Munchausen. It required a four-hour session to secure one nugget, a lapse into Clear Rock's renewal of theological reflections:

"De fus' man de Lawd made was bound to be a nigger. My ma, who come a slave f'om South Ca'lina, tole me dis, and she say her mammy tole her dat no white man could 'a' lived naked all by hisself wid nothin' but fruit to live on. Especially widout no nigger to wait on him. De white man is higher up den de black man, and de Lawd made de best last. He made all de creatures fust, den He made a black man. Den He made de white man. He made de nigger outer red dirt mixed wid dis black swampland dirt, and he stood him up and blew into him, and dat nigger begun to walk. (I 'spec he strut, being as he was de fus' man and named Adam.) But de nigger couldn't get 'long by hisself. He let de devil fool him. Now de white man would 'a' sho' fooled de devil. Dat's anudder p'int, and 'cause everything gets better and better, when de nigger dies, he is gwine be white like de white angels."

Clear Rock added: "I got a clock in my stomach an' a timepiece with ideas which will, tell me to de minute when eatin' time comes. I ain't got but two teeth, and dey don' fit. When I gits t' heaven my teeth are going to fit, and I's gwine have a bowl of good, greasy greens."

8

ALABAMA RED LAND

One day in 1936 while I was working in my cubbyhole in the Music Division of the Library of Congress, Dr. Luther Evans, who later succeeded Archibald MacLeish as Librarian, called on me in behalf of the Writers Project administered by Mr. Henry Alsburg. This project had collected a lot of folklore material from all over the country. Would I evaluate it and make suggestions for its enlargement? I undertook the assignment on condition that I be allowed time and opportunity in my journeyings to continue making records for the Archive of American Folk Song. Through this arrangement I came to meet Mrs. Ruby Pickens Tartt of Livingston, Alabama. Mrs. Tartt has since written the immortal Negro story about Uncle Josh and his "Pair of Blue Stockings," published among the *Best Short Stories of 1945* by Houghton Mifflin and Company. She sent the story first to me and I sold it to the *Southwestern Review*, Dallas, Texas, for fifty dollars.

With the help of Mrs. Tartt, during four visits, I made records of three hundred and five folk songs, all the songs coming from a district of worn-out farms covering not more than ten by twenty miles. Without her help I could have made but little headway. She knew her Negroes, and they loved and trusted her as they had her father before her. Everywhere they greeted her as "Miss Ruby," and she called them by their first names. She had helped bury their dead, had repaired their shambling church buildings, counseled them in their troubles, enjoyed their stories, loved their songs, greeted them with smiles, always leaving a shining token of her affection when they shook her hand.

Mrs. Tartt usually had a good story for us. Fond of her Negroes, she could laugh at them also. "How many children have you, Auntie?" Mrs. Tartt inquired of a colored farmer's wife.

"Le's see; nine, I believe. Yes, I got nine head o' chilluns."

"Isn't that pretty hard on you, to take care of nine children?"

"No'm, dey ain't much trouble. The only thing that bother me: it sho' do make me mad when a baby come in pea-pickin' time; sometimes I loses as much as fo' days!"

On another occasion Mrs. Tartt passed on a story told her by a railroad conductor:

The conductor came to an old Negro on his rounds. The Negro handed him two round-trip tickets from Livingston to Birmingham.

"Where is the other passenger?" the conductor asked.

"Dat's for my wife. She's layin', a corpse, in her box up ahead in de baggage car."

"But you didn't need a round-trip ticket for her."

"Yassuh, boss, I does. You see, my wife she got lots o' kinfolk up to Bummin'ham. I'se takin' her body up there for them to moan over her, an' then I'se goin' bring her back to Livingston to bury her. If I had 'a' let all them folks come down to Livingston to moan over her, dey'd 'a' et me out o' house an' home!"

Mrs. Tartt's maid asked for the week-end off, explaining:

"I'se gittin' married on Sat'day night, an' Sunday me an' my husband is goin' on a weddin' trip." Sunday morning, however, the maid was back on duty in the kitchen, arousing her mistress' curiosity.

"Why, what happened? I thought you were getting married last night?"

"Yas'm, I done got married."

"What about your wedding trip?"

"Well, you see, when I found out my husband wuz plannin' on takin' me to Bummin'ham—you see, I done been to Bummin'ham, so I jes' let my sister go in my place!"

A New York publisher asked me to secure for a Christmas book the words and music of a dozen cotton-picking songs. During the cotton-picking time, many Negroes leave their jobs in the cities to work in the cotton fields. It is a grand holiday for them. The actual labor is light, and the pickers can work in groups. Chatter and laughter and songs run along while hands snatch out the cotton and stuff it into sacks swung from their shoulders. And at night they sleep in the cotton pens or in the long rows, using their cotton sacks for pillows.

Out in the starved red hills where the white limestone bones poke their outlines up through northern Alabama, twelve miles from Livingston, Mrs. Tartt took us to see Aunt Harriet McClintock, who, according to rumor, knew a cotton-picking song. As we could not get the car up to Aunt Harriet's cabin, we parked it, and Miss Terrill set up the recording machine on the ground by the roadside. Aunt Harriet, seventy-nine, amiable and smiling, would sing for us. So down the hill came a procession including three great-grandsons, one of them bringing a rawhide-bottomed chair for Aunt Harriet to sit in.

The singing was most successful. When I played back her cornfield dances, lullabies and reels, Aunt Harriet shouted with delight: "Sing on, ol' lady! Don't you hear me? Yeah! Dat's me!" I sat on the ground beside her while the machine was running, holding the microphone ready to catch everything she said. At one point she seemed annoyed at the whirling disk and ordered me to "Stop dat ghost!" She sang a lot of songs, one a motion song about ginning cotton; as well as *Po' Little Johnny*, a quaint and tuneful melody. "Dey sang it in de cotton patch, jes' a-whoopin' an' a-hollerin'":

Way down in de bottom whar de cotton so rotten,
You won't git yo' hunderd today;
Po' little Johnny, he's a po' little feller,
He won't git his hunderd here today.

De boll is so rotten, de cotton so trashy,
I can't git my fingers out de boll.
Befo' I'll be beaten, befo' I'll be beaten,
I'll leave my fingers in de boll.

In a game-song Jacob pursues Rachel into the woods shouting, "Where you, Rachel?" and Rachel replies, "Here I, Jacob," though, of course, Rachel is never there when Jacob reaches the spot. And another song was about a "fo'-day creeper" who scratched late at night at the window of his lady love.

"Did you have many Jacobs when you were a girl, Aunt Harriet?" I asked.

"Only one after I wuz married," she replied.

"But before you were married?"

"Oh, three or fo' Jacobs then," she laughed.

"Did any of these Jacobs ever scratch at your window?"

"Whut wuz de use, chile? De big do' wuz standin' wide open!"

"Yassuh," she said, "I had plenty hard times, too; plenty sickness. My husband been gone, honey, 'bout forty years. I had three chillun; all daid but two. No, my chillun cain't giv' me much. Dey cain't hardly take care o' demselves. I gits he'p fum de Guv'nor. Dis money you gives me goes straight to de sto' for a new dress an' some meat. I ain't had a skin o' meat in de house fo' weeks."

In Livingston, I found a running mate for Professor Howard Odum's Left-Wing Gordon. In addition to his many talents he was a musician of parts. He played the harmonica, and despite his years and husky voice, he sang effectively. His name is Richard Amerson. If ever a person looked like an abandoned and hopeless vagrant, Richard Amerson was that person. His clothes were ragged, dirty and held together by garish safety pins. His shoes were slab-sided, most of his toes poking out. He had all the appearance of a tramp on his last legs. Yet he was no tramp. He belonged to one community. He lived close to home base. He was only a shiftless Negro who worked just enough to keep body and soul together. His wife, "Little Bit," had gone "too fur away fo' me to foller." Richard stayed around Livingston and dug wells at twenty-five cents a foot, where "never-failing" living water ran thirty feet below the surface.

He needed a "French harp" to give imitations of a train, a fox-hunt, a barnyard festival. I bought one and presented it to him. When he failed to appear at the appointed time, after a long search

I found him. He had loaned the harp to a friend who at that time was fifty miles away. Later I learned that he had converted the harp at half price into a pint of bootleg liquor. But he made me feel that I had done him a great wrong. Richard, as he insisted, was a paragon of virtue, unappreciated by his white friends. Yet, somewhere down in this raw collap of nature, lived a spark of genius. "I'se got a dancin' mind," said Richard. Liar by practice ("I wuz educated on hard work in de field an' graduated in lies"), a drunkard whenever and wherever possible, unkempt, a "no-'count black man," he was, at the same time, a most interesting man. "Nigger is jes' like a mule," he said. "White man like a hoss. You jes' tech de bridle an' de hoss goes. But you got tuh beat a mule to make him move outen his tracks." How much Richard Amerson was talking for effect, how much he really believed, I do not know.

The unforgettable Richard claimed to be a "double-j'inted" man—twice as strong and could eat twice as much as any man of equal weight. As a steamboat roustabout he had carried up and down the gangplanks bales of cotton and barrels of molasses, each weighing five hundred pounds. When I asked him if he were not exaggerating a little, he answered, "Maybe I is, but de Bible says you gotter lie sometime to keep de peace." Then he added: "I never does lie unless I am by myself or wid somebody." In addition to having been a roustabout, Richard had been a section hand on a railroad, well-digger, minstrel, mule-skinner on the levee, minister, farmer and voodoo doctor. He chanted a song which the men sang as they loaded cotton and molasses onto steamboats. First he would set the scene:

"All de way from Moffett to Selma on Mistuh Pickens' boat; my boss man wuz name' Mistuh Will, straw boss' name Jim. When we unloaded fert'lizer, we had to go down in de hull an' walk up a tall step. Ev'ry time we come up from de top an' th'owed it down, de feller 'd tell yo' an' commence callin'

Go git yo' sack!
Whoa back buddy, whoa back!
I gotta coat here to fit yo' back!

On and on till the boat was unloaded.

Next day, tired by his singing and dramatizing, Richard ended the session by remarking: "I done sung yo' all de propersitions in de premises."

"Dat's directly all right in de full," he declared when he heard one of his records played back to him. "You can't git after niggers for singin' blues, 'cause Job he sing de blues fust."

And this is Richard's Heaven:

If I had a heaven of my own,
You brown-skinned women 'ud be settin'
all 'roun' my throne.

Richard, vagabond, drunk when he can find alcohol, a no-account black man, sums up his attitude toward work in one trenchant sentence: "Pickin' up is better than totin', but puttin' down beats de world!"

"What I wants," he said, "is a job whar yo' can set an' eat an' sleep."

He called one time on "de release folks" in the early thirties, but when they suggested work on the public roads and pointed to some long-handled hoes and shovels leaning against the doors, Richard dismissed himself promptly, remarking safely: "I'se done had full 'quaintance wid dem things." "Den," he confided, "I 'splained to de release man 'bout lookin' fur a settin'-down job, an' he jes' sorta motioned to de do'."

One Christmas I sent the Livingston singers some money. Mrs. Tartt, asked to deliver the money, stopped Richard on the highway. "Richard, here's a dollar Mr. Lomax sent you for Christmas." His eyes opened wide and his lips twitched as he exclaimed, "White woman, shet yo' mouf!" On a recent visit, while talking to Richard with Mrs. Tartt present, I turned to him. "Did you get a Christmas present from me, Richard?" "Yassuh." "What was it?" "Money." "How much money?" Richard's lips twitched again as he cocked his head, glanced at Mrs. Tartt, and said thoughtfully, "Les' see. Two quarters make a half-a-dollar, don't hit?"

"I heard that you'd been in jail for stealing a ham," I ventured. "Yassuh, I wuz in jail for stealin' a ham, but I didn't steal hit. I done told 'em dat if de feller what did steal hit would jes' divide up, I wouldn't mind stayin' in jail a week for ha'f a ham. Jes' so's I can put my teeth in hit!"

He philosophized about the ministry: "No man kin preach empty. Never wuz a hungry man could preach directly right. Ef I had a pot o' greens an' 'leben dozen biscuits an' a gallon o' pot-licker, I could sho' preach." He explains: "Ev'ry man live by de sweat of his own eyebrow."

In his story of Hell, God struggled with "Lucifire" who had his "tail wrop 'round a third of Heaven." Lucifire tried to "straddle a deep gully but he couldn't quite make hit. His foot done slip an' down he fall, an' he ain't quit fallin' yit. An' he's grabbin' out an' tryin' to carry all de mens down with him." Again Richard explains: "De King's daughter wrop little Moses in a cowhide—dat's what de bull-rushes wuz."

He declares that the Bible tells how the City of "Rum" was saved by the cackling of geese and how Chicago was burned when a coal-oil lamp was kicked over by a cow that her mistress was trying to milk from the wrong side. I challenged him on these two stories. Back he countered: "I know for a fact dat de geese story is in de Bible an' de cow story go wid hit so good hit jes' nacherly belong wid hit. I cain't hardly tell one widout de other. Ef de cow story ain't in de Bible, hit's so close to hit dat you might say hit's jes' a step to Jesus an' de Bible."

He sang for us his version of the beautiful spiritual *Little David, Play on Your Harp*, interpolating the details of the story of "David an' Golijah" with dramatic gestures. David "th'owed de little rock clean thoo Golijah's head." He then ran up to examine and determine whether he had killed the giant. In his triumph Little David set his heel on his enemy's head, "th'owed his harp in his mouth an' begin to play." (The only kind of harp known to Richard is the French harp, or harmonica.)

"One day w'en Golijah an' his mens wuz takin' a walk, one of his mens says: 'Golijah, dey tells me dat dere's a feller on de other side o' de river what says he am a heap stronger man den you wuz. Does you know 'bout him? Name's Samson.'

"'Humph!' says ol' Golijah. 'Yas, I'se heard tell o' ol' Samson—he ain't nothin' 'side o' me. Le's ramble along up dis ravine an' le's find ol' Samson; I'se goin' play a prank on him.'

"So dey ramble on up de ravine till dey sees Samson 'cross de river playin' 'round wid his friends. Den Golijah says to his mens: 'Run me up some cows here—some big cows.' An' dey runs up de cows. 'Dat's good. Now run me up dat heaviest cow dere.' An' dey runs him up a cow what weighs 'bout two thousand pounds.

"Den big ol' Golijah he take an' cotch dat big ol' cow by de horns. An' he lif' him up an' sling him 'round his head an' th'owed dat cow plum' 'cross dat river right inter de middle o' Samson an' his crowd. Some of dem wuz purty bad hurt, an' de res' o' dem scattered out; but Samson, he jes' laugh; he warn't hurt a-tall, one hoof jes' graze de back o' his han' a little.

"But hit make Samson powerful mad. 'Who dat do dat?' he roared. Den he hear ol' Golijah an' his mens hollerin' an' laughin', an' he know. 'I'll show you who de stronges' man 'round here!'

"So nex' day he see Golijah an' his mens walkin' sof'-like th'oo de ravine 'cross de river, lookin' to see wuz Samson dere or wuz he scared off. An' nen ol' Samson look up at de sky like he wuz prayin', an' nen he reach down an' wrop his arms right down nex' de groun' 'round de biggest tree he could find—fo'teen feet acrost. An' nen he 'gun to pull; you could hear de roots creen an' crack.

"Ol' Samson didn't even have to grunt; he jes' keep pullin'. An' in a minute up come de tree by hits roots. Nen Samson he slide his arms up 'round de limbs an' lif' up de tree from de groun', an' shake out de roots—you knows, jes' like you shakes de dirt out f'um a bunch o' turnips. Nen Samson he lif' dat tree 'bove his head an' he swing hit 'round an' 'round, an' he pitch dat tree 'crost de river at Golijah an' his mens. An' he kill ev'ry one of Golijah's mens, an' he bad-hurt Golijah, too, till he had to rest up a long time."

When we thought his story finished, Richard added, with almost professorial condescension: "You see, ol' Samson couldn't kill Golijah dead, 'cause dey had to save Golijah for Little David to kill him."

Richard Amerson, explaining the silence of his friend, Enoch, told me; "No, suh, he don't talk much; he jes' formally transfers his jedgments by signs." On our first two meetings at Livingston, Enoch had spoken no word at all. He replied to questions with loud explosions of laughter; and he "hollered." His nervous laughter was not unusual but his hollering was unique. His powerful voice would carry for miles and miles. Alan and I, from the beginning of our travels through the South, sought for "hollerers," but we never found one who equaled Enoch.

In slavery days Negroes used calls or hollers to transfer messages to adjoining plantations. Only recently I talked with Uncle Bob Ledbetter, a relative of Lead Belly's, who still lives on a plantation near Shreveport, Louisiana:

"Yes-suh, we uster send word by hollerin'."

Then he tried to give the call. But Uncle Bob is now seventy-eight, and his voice cracked on the high notes. "I uster call my friend dataway," said Uncle Bob. "He live on de 'j'inin' plantation. I would holler: 'I ain't got nobody to wash my clothes,' an' he would holler back."

"What would he say?"

"Jes' what I said, 'Ain't got nobody to wash my clothes.' I knowed by dat he'd be over dat night an' he would run 'round wid me to de gals' house."

Enoch, finally yielding to my persistence, told me about his call, "You uses hit in de fiel' when you off by yo'sef."

"What do you say in your holler, Enoch?"

"Blues done gone!" And then he explained, "Song done carried de blues away." I had already caught other words in one of Enoch's lonesome hollers:

Jes' a few mo' days,
An' I won't be here no longer.

On our last visit to Livingston we stopped, as usual, with Mrs. Tartt. Just before daybreak the first morning, aroused by a noise, she saw a black face pressed flat against the windowpane. Startled, she cried out: "What do you want?"

Said Enoch, solemnly, "Is dey come?"

A little later the entire household was aroused by Enoch's call coming from a thicket close by—his greeting to the white visitors who had once sent him a Christmas card.

Mrs. Tartt had delivered our greeting to Enoch, along with a good breakfast, on Christmas morning. The next morning he called and asked for a possible second card. No card, but he got another breakfast. The next day, still another call and another breakfast. The schedule was kept up faithfully until Mrs. Tartt, harassed and amused, declared: "I believe Enoch thinks that Christmas card is a meal ticket." Another Christmas she handed him a present from me. He took it in silence. "But what shall I tell Mr. Lomax?" she inquired. After a long, pondering pause: "Tell him I got it."

I first heard Enoch's call one summer evening as I sat on the porch of the Tartt home. From far off in the darkness long, lonesome, full-voiced, brooding notes pierced the stillness of a perfect night, indescribable and unforgettable. Starting on a low note, the cry reached a crescendo in such pervasive volume and intensity that it seemed to fill the black void of darkness. The sound came from everywhere and nowhere. Then the cry shaded downward, with the lower notes thrice repeated. Suddenly silence.

"That's Enoch crossing the long bridge from Livingston," said Mrs. Tartt. "He always stops at night in the middle of the bridge and gives that call. I have asked him to come and see you, but he is very shy."

At about the same time the next night the cry rang out again, this time startlingly near. I found Enoch leaning against a big oak tree close by the house, a dim, shadowy figure. He answered me only by outbursts of nervous laughter. He shied away from my microphone. His call blasted the microphone even when it stood fifty feet away. A year or two afterward I tried again to make a satisfactory record of Enoch's hollers. On the third trip I had better success. There would be no further opportunity, for Enoch's voice was beginning to break.

One day, as he was going away, from far down the hill his voice came back singing:

Oh, de blood, oh, de blood,
Oh, de blood done sign my name.

The evening following I saw him standing in the shadows listening to a group of singers in Mrs. Tartt's back yard, where the recording machine was set up.

"Enoch, I want to record the song I heard you singing yesterday."

He doubled over, laughing uproariously, repeating over and over, "You didn't think I could sing, did you?" When the crowd had gone, I finally persuaded him to sing what he called "de blood" song. Afterward he added another, a "sinful" item: *Whoa, Mule, I can't put de saddle on.*

But it is Enoch's holler that puts him among the immortals of folk singers. Some day it ought to form the core of a symphony, just as the night bird, Enoch, might serve as a part for some actor in a great American play.

Vera Hall and Doc Reed, cousins, have sung together many years, mainly spirituals. They are perfect in "seconding," or "following after," as they call it. Having no book learning, they have stored in the back of their heads many tunes and stanzas. Vera Hall is especially quick to catch up a new tune. While she sings the old-time spirituals with as deep sincerity and feeling as Doc, yet she does not refuse to sing "worl'ly" songs, learned from her mother, her husband, Richard Amerson and, especially, Blind Jesse Harris. If Vera can hear a song through once or twice, it is hers and she can sing it herself.

"Vera, do you know [for instance] *Railroad Bill?*" I would ask.

"No, sir," Vera would reply, "I can't say I knows it. But I used to hear Blind Jesse sing it."

"How did it go, Vera?"

"Le's see. I don't know as I can put it together ezackly." But a gleam of remembrance would come into her eyes, she would shift her feet, throw back her head, open her mouth and throat, and out would come—

Railroad Bill is a mighty bad man,
I'se skeered o' Railroad Bill!

And away she would go for ten or twelve stanzas.

Play-party songs and other children's songs she sang, too, though "It's been a long time," she said. "We used to sing *'All Hid?'*" Looking about her as if she thought Mrs. Tartt's pretty garden would be a very good place for hiding, she started off her chant: "Is it all hid?— No, no." With this song her mind slipped back into its play groove, and Vera, at this one sitting, gave me five other children's songs.

At the close of another day's recording Vera sang a *Boll Weevil Blues*, which she had learned from Blind Jesse. I asked if she knew other Blues.

"No, sir, I b'lieve not. My husband sings a pretty one, at least I likes it, 'Another Man Done Gone.' No, sir, I ain't never sung it except to myself, but maybe I can catch it up."

And after a pause she straightened herself in her chair and sang:

Another man done gone
From de County Farm;
I didn't know his name;
He had a long chain on;
He killed another man;
I don't know where he's gone.

Each line by repetition becomes a stanza.

This song of Vera's was played in the Library of Congress on the seventy-fifth anniversary of the Emancipation Proclamation. And it has charmed friends who have heard the record played in my home, Carlton Smith, Jan Struther and Carl Sandburg among them.

We had picked up Doc Reed waiting for us on the roadside ten miles out of Livingston that Sunday morning. Doc, to his great embarrassment, could never get my name straight. Today, with his broad, vacant grin, he greeted me as "Mistuh Merrimack," laughing loudly at my feeble repartee as he crawled into the car. I asked him if he would be drafted for World War II. "Nossuh," he replied. "I wuz too old to register dis time. I had to sign up for de las' war, but dey adjourned befo' my number come up."

Doc's large expressionless eyes seemed to look at distant objects rather than those close by, as if he might be seeing "far-off, half-remembered things and battles long ago." But his speaking and singing voice—deep, vibrant, resonant, tremulous at times—always tore at my heartstrings, brought chilly sensations along my spine. Let the soul be what it may, Doc's soul must have had intimations of immortality not given to ordinary mortals. Or perhaps he, like Browning's Lazarus, brushed away, as one would buzzing flies, rumors of war, while the toss of a child's hand would drive him into an agony of fear.

Doc's Sunday dress was pathetic. The pink tip of a gay handkerchief peeped from the breast pocket of a cream-colored coat much too small for him. The vest and trousers were of different color, his shoes unpolished but brushed clean. He wore a tie and a collar that seemed to choke him. Dressed in his Sunday best was Doc, for we were all on our way to Sallie Ann's funeral at Brown's Chapel, a Negro church several miles down the road. There, cluttered about the building, stood many wagons, carts, buggies, a few automobiles, among the last an ornately plumed hearse. Negroes stood in groups outside. Inside the house every long, unpainted pine bench was packed tight, every window nailed down, as I found out later when I suggested more ventilation.

Although the services already had begun, Mrs. Tartt went forward to the pulpit and secured permission for us to record the sermon and the singing. While the audience sang, with Doc's help we quickly set up the recording machine in a far corner from the pulpit. Unscrewing the microphone from its stand, I hid it under my arm as I walked down the long aisle with the cable uncoiling behind me, and seated myself on an overstuffed sofa alongside the two officiating ministers.

Sallie Ann's body lay in a decorated white coffin underneath the high pulpit. The chief mourners, heavily veiled, sat on the front seats, which because of the overcrowding, were jammed close to the coffin. Only two doors of the building were left open. Even the windows back of the pulpit were fastened. The inside of the church became steaming hot, rank from the smell of crowded human bodies. I felt faint and sick.

Just who Sallie Ann was we never learned. Where she was born or when, we never found out. Did she have a family, husband or children? No information. What work she had done, what relatives she was leaving behind, remained unanswered. Only two incidents of her life were mentioned by the three speakers: Sallie Ann had joined the church; Sallie Ann had died at Electric Mills in Mississippi. Every person should join the church, for everyone must die, just as Sallie Ann had died.

Reverend Boyd, a visiting pastor, spoke first. Small in stature, thin-lipped, with shifty eyes, dramatic (soon he was springing from one side of the pulpit to the other, falling on his knees, gesticulating wildly, slapping the shoulder of his elderly co-preacher), his shouted exclamations failed to raise his hearers to a high pitch of fervor. He foamed at the mouth, spat wildly and frequently, held his right jaw with his right hand as if to prevent dislocation (Richard Amerson claimed he was "holdin' in de Ghost"), as he rasped out at the end of emphatic phrases the unintelligible, untranslatable "Ahuh!" At one point he said: "I cain't fool 'roun' wid Moses all day—I got tuh pass on to Jesus."

The older man, Reverend Cage, known to the people, heavy, deliberate, deep-voiced, solemnity dripping from his garments, followed the shrill-voiced visiting preacher.

First he complimented the young minister, who represented "one of our great congregations." Then he added: "We are glad to have with us today these friends of the superior race with their instruments in their hands. We owe them much. They have learned us everything we know—everything. They taught us how to steal; and they taught us how to lie and cuss. Yes, sir, but thank God, they taught us the way back to Jesus! When I see them sitting here I feel happy."

Scattered through the audience were newly uniformed Negro

soldiers. They carried registration cards, "tickets," so that "you can walk the roads, you can ride the train, without being uneasy." Suddenly Reverend Cage shouted in a dramatic crescendo, "Wait! Wait! Wait! Yonder in Electric Mills, Sallie Ann got her ticket, too" that calls for a room in Heaven.

"'Is this my room, Lord?' 'No, yours is a finer room than this one.'"

"You know," the Reverend added, "the kind of furnishings in your house in Heaven depends on the kind of good deeds you do in this world. Many of our boys have just got their registration cards for the United States Army, and Sallie Ann has got hers for the Heavenly Army." Then he broke into song:

Have you decided which way to go?
You got to leave here,
God knows you can't stay here;
Have you decided which way to go?

The audience joined in as the mourners writhed and sobbed:

My mother decided which way to go—
She decided on Sunday which way to go.

And all other members of the family likewise "decided." On and on, until the singing grew into a storm of shouting, of clapping hands and stamping feet.

The pastor stilled the tempest to introduce the undertaker, announcing: "This entertainment is being held under the auspices of the American Burial Society." The undertaker, dynamic and businesslike, mounted the pulpit and spoke:

"The Lord saw fit to fix me to fix dead folks and the preacher to fix their souls to go to Heaven. That's been my job for twenty-two years. You've all got to die like Sallie Ann has died. Make your arrangements now. You can hand in your application for membership in the American Burial Association with your first payment today."

Then came the climax. The undertaker opened Sallie Ann's coffin and invited the audience to come forward. Every person, including the "white visitors," complied. Meanwhile Reverend Cage had placed a collection table on the pulpit just over Sallie Ann's head. "There is always expenses connected with these sad occasions," he said. Often the line was held up by a member asking for change, the money passing forward and back again directly over the open coffin.

The congregation, meanwhile, had broken up into shouting groups and the singing had stopped. The chattering of some grew into explosions of laughter, mingling with the piteous cries of Sallie Ann's intimates, wringing their hands as they bent over the coffin. Just then my friends, Doc and Vera, sweet singers of many spirituals, standing near our recording machine, broke into song:

> It may be de las' time, I don' know;
> It may be de las' time I ever see my mother.

The shrieks about the coffin grew more piercing as the words of this song reached the ears of the mourners. I walked over to catch Doc's song. I noticed that his body quivered as he sang; Vera put an arm around him, patting his shoulder as if to steady him. Then his knees began to shake violently, his shoulders heaved, his entire body seemed racked by an electric shock.

When he turned his unseeing eyes on me Doc no longer saw "Mistuh Merrimack." What he saw no man could know, for Doc couldn't tell when I asked him afterward. He threw up his arms and began to shout:

"Oh, Lawdy, oh, Lawd! Bless de Lawd, my mother done got her ticket, too!"

He ran across the room, then back again. Backward and forward he went, twisting and writhing. Men tried to hold him. He broke away, crying out deep shouts of ecstasy. I feared he might hurt himself against the benches, but he avoided them, as he did everyone who stood in his path, while he shouted:

Bless Jesus! Dat's my bread!
My Lawd! Dat's my meat!
Oh, Marster! Dat's my clothes!
My Jesus! Dat's my food!
Oh, bless de Lawd! I'se happy! I'se happy!

Doc dashed out of doors, repeating over and over these exulting cries, as, winding through the crowd, he continued to shout. Finally two strong men led him away. Already for years Doc had been a devout Christian; so he was not "gittin' religion." Doc was only "happy."

Presently he sat alone with me in my car. He came to look for me as soon as the "seizure" was over. We talked quietly. He seemed entirely normal.

"Doc," I asked him, "what happened to you a while ago?" Doc laughed silently: "I jes' got happy, Mr. Merrimack." I had no heart to probe him further. I have great respect for Doc.

Far up the road, stirring up clouds of dust, "hacks all dead in line," rolled a gaudy hearse bearing the body of Sallie Ann.

9

BURIALS, BAPTIZINGS AND A PENITENTIARY SERMON

We had come to Murrell's Inlet, near Georgetown, South Carolina, through the invitation of Mrs. Genevieve W. Chandler, after a journey of a thousand miles, to hear the singing of primitive coast Negroes of the Negro Republic on Sandy Island. As if to provide a stirring theme for the singing, Ben Small was murdered the night we drove in. We heard the shot as we sat on Mrs. Chandler's porch. Ben was the leader of the Negro church choir that was to sing for us.

Ben Small suffered no heroic death, that is, according to the Anglo-Saxon code of morals. For Ben didn't get away with it. An angry husband, who had warned him in the presence of witnesses, shot persistent Ben dead, when he found Ben in a certain bedroom. When the facts were brought out, Ben's murderer was promptly set free.

"And over Ben they sang again" on and on all night long and the following night and throughout the next day for thirty-six consecutive hours. The wailing of Ben's wife and all her female kin only made them sing louder, either to drown the cries of grief or to spur them on—I could not tell. During the entire time I saw no sign of emotion from any male persons except, indeed, the half-dozen ministers who at different times spoke or prayed over the dead body. The little boys, tricked out in their Sunday best, looked indifferent, sometimes really bored, while by the time of the burial even the voices of the chief women mourners had become worn and husky. No longer could they scream in ear-splitting tones. Physically, too, they were so exhausted that their male "holders" had a fairly easy job of controlling their writhing bodies. Using a rolling log for a pillow, my next neighbor at the graveside, a young Negro man, slept throughout the burying.

It had been different that morning during the preliminary funeral services at lonely Jerusalem Church in the pines—out in the "free land" district several miles from the village. We found this church packed and running over, Ben's pastor, the Reverend Aaron Pinnacle, in the midst of his sermon, the core of which was the warning question, shouted again and again, "Who will go next?" "One day," he added, "Death is coming to our chamber. What are you doing to get ready to meet him? You can get around to paying the store kind of debt. You can say you haven't got the money. But when Death comes, you got to pay the debt principally! You can get used to anything except Death. Whenever he comes, you ain't acquainted with him. He is always new." The solidly built black minister kept his heavy voice at such a high pitch that it became more and more difficult to follow his words. As a climax he spoke in a trembling falsetto: "No more will we see Brother Ben in Sunday school; no more will Brother Ben lead the prayer on Wednesday night; no more will we hear Brother Ben's voice in the choir. Brother Ben is gone until the Resurrection morn. Some day Brother Ben will meet us, way somewhere in the noncomitant of an uncloudy day."

"Thank you, Lord," shouted the audience, while many feet tapped the floor in an ever-faster crescendo of grief. This tapping rose and died away in unison with the inarticulate moaning that swept the room, just as the moaning grew in volume and sharpness with the jumbled shouts of the preacher.

During the entire sermon, cries from the women mourners seated near the pulpit answered the minister's appeal to their emotions. Now the name of "Brother Ben" seemed to call for physical as well as vocal expression of grief. A dozen women sprang to their feet, waving their arms, stamping on the floor, bending double, first backward then forward, jerking their heads far back as if in the last gasps of death. Some gave sharp, short cries; some repeated the words of the preacher, "He's gone; he's gone"; others followed with long, wailing, ear-piercing screams, one after another, until the voices were broken into husky gasps, while women with busy palm leaf fans followed the struggling groups, fanning vigorously the tortured victims of grief. Meanwhile the preacher sat stolid and impassive behind the pulpit. His work was done. Most of the audience, too, were quiet, motionless, waiting. Only the chief women mourners and the big strapping "holders" were active. When the violent frenzy seized a mourner, one, sometimes two, official "holders" were always ready to catch the waving arms, put their arms about the heaving body so as—apparently—to prevent the grief-stricken persons from hurting themselves. I was startled to see a big black man turn a struggling woman over to his friend and come down the aisle with a message to me from the pastor asking if I wouldn't make a talk to the crowd! When I had politely confessed my inability, he retraced his steps and relieved his friend in his efforts to restrain the struggling woman.

"It's time to go to the graveyard," suddenly said the preacher. The cries stopped as if by magic. The "holders" shuffled away from their charges, who began to rearrange their disordered clothing. The congregation filed slowly out, chatting amiably.

The hearse, a small truck with the pine box coffin on a trailer, led a straggling line of cars over a dirt road past the Church of Heaven's Gate, through the forest to the graveyard nearly ten miles away. There in a virgin wood of pines and oaks on the banks of the river was the Negro burial ground, more than a hundred years old. The place was as quiet as the dead it harbored. One did not hear the note of a bird. Soft breezes waved the silver moss hanging from the trees like ghostly shrouds. The automobile tires slipped through the sandy road without a sound. The cars in twos and threes straggled furtively into Death's clearing.

Only a single gravestone marked the spot where hundreds, perhaps thousands, of bodies lay moldering. Later I found a few rotting stobs, driven into the ground about six feet apart, showing other last resting places. On the tops of many of the mounds lay cups, plates, glasses, spoons, half-filled medicine bottles, used in the last illness of the person that lay underneath. I was horrified to see the crowd tramp heedlessly on these mounds. The towering trees, some a hundred feet and more tall, stood sentinels, far more permanently than any graven marble headpiece. "These trees will all be gone befo' de Day of Judgment," said a Negro to me.

"Why so?" I asked.

"Because," he answered, "don't de Scriptures say dat de dead will rise free and wid no trouble. De Lord won't have these trees here to git in their way when they starts to fly away."

The grave was hardly begun when the funeral procession came up. The crowd quickly and quietly scattered through the woods, while the gravediggers, chatting cheerfully, without hurrying, scooped up with spades the golden sand that lay many feet in depth under a thin covering of soil. As I stood watching the men, one of the diggers threw up some short pieces of rotting plank from the bottom of the grave. "Here's another box, boys," he said. "We nearly always find one, sometimes two or three, when we dig a new grave," said a Negro at my side. And I stood aghast, unable to move, while the grave diggers uncovered a skeleton, cleaned the bones, laid them alongside the grave, to be placed under Ben Small's box when they let it down. "De las' one down de fus' one up," a man explained.

The digging was quickly finished, the crowd assembled, the nearest places being given to the female near kin whose tears flowed anew. But the three or four preachers who again led the singing or prayed or read from the Episcopal service, could get but a weak emotional response. A day and a half, including an all-night vigil, was too much for the tired and worn bodies of the women. Only when some one started a song the refrain of which repeated endlessly, "Goodbye, Ben! Goodbye, Ben!" did the mourners come alive. Again they struggled with their "holders," the group staggering away from the graveside out among the trees, the tortured mourners now feebly pulling the "holders" about, their cries barely audible; meanwhile the pine box was let down between the sandy walls, eager hands easing it to the bottom of the grave. A pinch of the same sand provided material for "Dust to dust." Soon the grave was filled by the younger men, who spelled each other at short intervals. The mourners rounded up the sand, smoothed it down, and drove two freshly cut stakes into the earth, one at the head and the other at the foot. The cook from our hotel had furnished the only flowers for the funeral. Now the dozen or more stems of the bouquet were stuck in scattered pattern into the sandy mound. Mom Hagar looking down said, "Ain't that purty now? That's just how I wants to be put away." "Amen," said the preachers in concert. The curtain had fallen on Ben Small.

The business of the moment being finished, the crowd broke into small groups greeting each other, renewing former acquaintances. Sandy Island folk do not come often to the mainland. Other remote communities were attached to Ben through intermarriage. People rushed about, howdying, exchanging gossip. Already Ben Small seemed forgotten.

I kept looking back at the fresh mound of golden sand with its pathetic array of wilted flowers. Some one else also seemed to be thinking of poor Ben. Suddenly Mom Hagar, the mother of Ben Small's wronged wife, left a group and came back swiftly to the grave. She waved her hands over it and stared up through the trees at the sky. What she was saying I could not understand. Perhaps it was Cherokee, for she was half Indian; perhaps Gullah speech, for she came from Sandy Island. "What were you saying, Aunt Hagar," I asked. She looked at me steadily out of her small, hard, black eyes. "Ben's soul's done wropped up in de care of de Lord, and nothin' mo' in dis world kin harm him." And she glided off into the woods muttering and mumbling.

One Sunday in the summer of 1940 I was told in Natchez, Miss., that Clara Musique had between three and four hundred Negro families living on her plantation and that we should probably find preaching services there, where we could hear some good spirituals and perhaps locate singers of work songs. Clara Musique is the widow of a well-known and wealthy Negro physician, from whom she inherited the plantation. When we stopped about ten miles out from Natchez to get explicit directions, we learned that the crowds of Negroes we saw on foot, in wagons, buggies, automobiles and trucks were bound for a baptizing. We followed the trail of dust through the fields.

There was plenty of time for howdys and exchange of news before we heard the chanted song that called our attention to the procession in white. First came the preacher, followed by the deacons and other assistants, and then the nine candidates, more women than men, as I recall. All were dressed in white, at least from the waist up, and all had white head coverings. The preacher wore white silk, a long coat and cap, but the deacons and the candidates, not frequently having need of such equipment, had used great ingenuity in assembling their costumes of white. On their heads they wore maids' caps, bakers', chefs', boudoir, painters', with somewhat less variety in jackets and robes.

"Let us go down to the Jordan" was the burden of the processional chant. On the sandy beach of the river the group halted and the throng of witnesses crowded around them. The preacher read sentences from a little book; some were scripture quotations, some were long, involved doctrinal declarations whose big words he found difficult to master. These quotations would give him a new text for a fresh ten minutes' discourse. As if to allow the preacher opportunity to catch his breath, a brother would interrupt with a prayer or a hymn. One lined off the hymn, "Heaven Is My Home," another raised "I'm on My Way to the City," with similar "turnings" to "I Started for the Kingdom and I Can't Turn Back"; another brother interrupted with "When I Gets on My Dying Bed" and "His Name Is on My Tongue." Perhaps these hymns and prayers and ejaculations (one sister kept insisting, "Take yo' time and *TELL* hit!") were rather interweavings than interruptions, for, without design, perhaps, they were timed to build the crowd up to the desired state of exaltation.

I can remember only disconnected fragments of the hour's sermon at the river's side:

"Too many preachers got de clo'se on but de man ain't in 'em."

"Heap of us waits to pray twell we'se swoll wid de asthmy, ["Right here," cried a sister], or whupped down by de fever." ("Dat's me!" exclaimed another.)

"When de court sets, ev'ybody gits pitiful."

"God has no respectable person."

The preacher used the not unusual pronunciations "mycles" for "miracles." His most surprising phrase, repeated several times during the services: "Borned of de Holy Spearmint!"

At last he moved forward into the water and took his position between the two upright stakes at the head of the line of shivering candidates. One sister raised the tune:

Wade in de water,
Wade in de water, chillun,
Wade in de water,
God's goin' trouble de water.

The deacons formed a lane from the preacher to the beach, and one by one the candidates came forward. Each candidate was assisted to his position beside the preacher. In most cases the ceremony for the men and boys was simple enough, a statement by the preacher, a "yes" or a nod from the candidate, the immersion—and then the candidate was guided back to the dry beach, where a friend threw a coat about him. When the women candidates came to the water's edge, I noticed that they all had cords wrapped around their legs from the knees down. At first I thought that this was contrived to keep the dress from floating, to save embarrassment. But I learned that it served another purpose; for every woman-person came up out of the water either writhing or helplessly inert, and the wrapping of her limbs made her body easier to carry and to control. To other members of her family, especially to mothers and sisters, "holders" were assigned, as to chief mourners at funerals, to prevent them from falling or doing other harm to themselves when they became over-joyed at sight of their kin "being resurrected from the death of sin," all this to the accompaniment of crescendos of moanings and sing-ing, punctuated by shouts of rejoicing from the sympathizing throng of witnesses. The preacher delayed long over three candidates—one who "had wandered far," another whose "father died in his sins and is already in Hell," the third an elderly woman over whom the church members evidently had prayed long. Her case merited a fifteen-minute talk. All that time she stood in water so cold that it must have chilled her through and through. Holders assigned to the family and special friends of this hard-won new child of God were clearing space and otherwise preparing for a great demonstration. At this point we left the crowd. As we walked away the preacher was immersing the last candidate "two feet under: we digs de mortal grave six feet deep; four feet for de box and two feet to kivver. So I buries de candidates two feet under de water to show dey is dead to sin."

Later I came on an open-air baptismal service near Austin, Texas. The scene was set in a rocky gorge, the banks of which were festooned with overhanging cedars; the sparkling pool of clear water surrounded by a shelving bank, so that the place formed a natural amphitheater. In this spot was assembled a large group of Negroes, the women and children dressed in bright colors. The gorge rang with their merry laughter and light-hearted chatter until the minister, a solemn-faced, deep-voiced, white-haired old man, lifted his hand for silence. Then the crowd sang, as only Negroes can sing, a spiritual in which the terrors of death and hell are described in a way to startle the imagination. Next a visiting preacher prayed, the audience joining in with vocal approval, from time to time repeating the words that impressed them most. As the candidates for baptism, ten or twelve in number, approached the waterside, they were led out one by one by two deacons to the preacher standing in the middle of the pool, while the crowd sang:

Let's go down to Jordan, let's go down to Jordan,
De clear river Jordan is mighty deep;
Let's go down to Jordan,
De old river Jordan is mighty deep,
But 'ligion is so sweet.

Then, beginning with the smallest girl, each candidate was baptized. Just before one was immersed the congregation would sing:

Missionary Baptist is my name, Missionary Baptist is my name,
Missionary Baptist is my name, 'ligion is so sweet.
De Lord said baptism it must be, for 'ligion is so sweet;
De Lord said baptism it must be, we are goin' to 'bey His will.
De Lord said baptism it must be, for 'ligion is so sweet.
What kind o' manner o' man is He? All things they obey his will.
What kind o' manner o' man is He? He spoke to de sea and de sea
was still.

De Lord said baptism it must be, de lil' Babe in de manger;
What kind o' manner o' man is He? He walk on de land an' he
walk on de sea,
An' all things here obey his will; He speaks to de sea an' de sea is
still,
An' 'ligion is so sweet.

Each candidate as he came up out of the water was seized with a queer sort of physical convulsion, which my yard man, Sam, afterward explained to me as "the working of the Holy Spirit." The final outbreak of the candidate when he was on terra firma was to stretch out his arms and wave them in a vain effort to fly. A large, fleshy woman was "seized with the Spirit" just before her baptism and had to be taken out of the water until she became calm. She was then baptized and again underwent a weird seizure. The last man baptized was a muscular ditchdigger who required four strong men to get him out of the pool. I heard the minister, who was being pushed out toward the deep water, mutter to his helpers: "Get him out o' here before he drowns us all." As each candidate was led out of the water the congregation sang with splendid effect:

New-bawn, new b-a-w-n,
New-bawn child, new-bawn child;

Like a lil' Babe in a manger.
De ole River Jordan was mighty deep,
But 'ligion was so sweet.

By the time the service was over the sun's rays no longer reached the bottom of the gorge. The quiet of evening fell, a breeze came up and stirred the branches of the fragrant cedars. The crowd seemed awed by the influence of a most sacred and solemn ceremony, the effect of which had been intensified, now and then, by the shrill voices of the women in shouts of religious ecstasy. The baptized persons stood around with the crowd grouped about them, as the old minister with hands outstretched to heaven pronounced a benediction. And then again they sang, in a minor key, wonderfully sweet and touching:

De old River Jordan was so deep,
An' now our brother in Christ we greet;
De old River Jordan was so deep,
But 'ligion was so sweet.
He said baptism it must be
If he from sin 'll set us free,
An' all things here obey His will,
Spoke to de sea an' de sea was still,
For 'ligion was so sweet.

Slowly the shadows darkened while with occasional shouts of joy the crowd trooped away, and the baptizing was over. Yet not quite, for from far down the gorge came floating back to me the song:

When my blood runs chilly an' cold, I'se got to go
'Way beyond the Sun.

Ef you cain't bear no crosses, you cain't wear no crowns,
'Way beyond the Sun.

I'se got a mother in the Beulah Land, she's callin' me,
'Way beyond the Sun.

Do, Lord, do, Lord, do remember me,
Oh, do, Lord, do, Lord, do remember me,

Oh, do, Lord, do, Lord, do remember me,
Oh, do, Lord, remember me.

The Reverend Sin-Killer Griffin, employed by the State as Chaplain to the Negro convicts of the Texas Penitentiary system, looked his part well. His gray hair and mutton-chop whiskers, his Prince Albert coat which almost touched his shoe tops, his dignified and courtly bearing, his deep and sonorous voice, were most impressive. This ministerial manner was heightened by a very slow walk, slow speech, and a long, long pause between questions as if he were consulting Higher Powers.

"Reverend," I said, "I hope you will preach your favorite sermon to the boys tonight. The Captain has agreed for me to record it, and I plan to deposit the records in the Folk Song Archive of the Library of Congress. A thousand years from now people can listen to the words you will preach."

"I'll preach my Calvary sermon," he assented gravely. "Today is my Easter service."

The two long wings of the dormitory of the Darrington Farm, near Houston, where the convicts slept, were separated by a wide hall. Alan and I set up the recording machine near where the Reverend Sin-Killer had arranged his pulpit and altar. He stood where his powerful voice could reach the three hundred convicts lounging on their beds in their pajamas or peering curiously through the bars at the strange doings. Some of the more devout worshippers—deacons and preachers, out in the free world—were seated in a circle near the Reverend. At a sign from him the penitentiary song-leader led them in a swinging spiritual:

    Lord, I want to love my enemies in my heart,
    Lord, I want to be more humble in my heart.

When the song was finished, the leader invited the "sinner friends" to come forward to the front seats. No one moved. "Those who mourn shall be comforted," he said. "Let us mourn, brethren."

Something swept through that crowd, something powerful and poignant. No words were uttered, only waves of sound, deep and pregnant, moans of unutterable woe. The silence grew deeper and deeper.

"Thousands and thousands and multiplied thousands are cast off from de golden opportunities," the leader said. "Let us sing." They sang a song, an impressive song, entitled, "Wasn't that a mighty storm that blew the people away," after which the leader led them in this prayer:

    This evening, our Father,
    We begin before death in early judgment,
    This evening, our Father,
    I come in the humblest manner I ever know'd,
    Or ever thought it,
    To bow.

    I'm thankin' Thee, O Lord,
    That my laying down last night
    Wasn't my cooling board,
    And my cover was not my winding sheet.

    O Lord, thanking Thee, this evening, my Father,
    That my dressing-room this morning was not my grave.

    O Lord, thanking Thee, this evening, my Father,
    That my slumber last night was not for eternity.

O Lord,
Just bless the widows and orphans in this land,
I pray Thee in Jesus' name;

Take care of them, my Father,
And guide them;
And, then, my Father,
When they all is standing in glory,
And Thou art satisfied at my staying here,
O meet me at the river, I ask in Thy name.
Amen!

After an impressive silence the leader, in a more casual tone, said: "You knows whether you are to eat the body and drink the blood of Christ. If you eat and drink the Lord's food unworthily, you eat and drink to your damnation."

He distributed white crumbs of bread such as the men had eaten for supper and grapefruit juice from the prison commissary for the "wine." When all who dared had participated, Sin-Killer Griffin stepped forward, dignified and solemn, and took charge of the services.

"My dear brothers and sisters"—the Captain's wife was the only woman present—"sinner friends and all," he began, and then, in poetic diction, impressively and hypnotically said:

The ears hear the voice
An' notify the eye where to look.
One day as I was walking along
I heard a little whisper but I saw no one;
Something was bringing about a disturbance—
That was the wind,
The water was jumpin' in the vessel.

The force of his voice, the intensity of his appeal, almost instantly brought from the audience exclamations: "Sho' nuff!" "Sure!" "Amen!" "Oh, yes!"

Next he took them into a song:

Dem little slippers dat my Lord give me
Goin' to outshine de sun,
Dat little harp-h dat my Lord give me,
Dat little robe dat my Lord give me.

On and on went this tawdry song, entirely different from the splendid, almost sublime, words of the speaker.

From the enthusiasm aroused by this song Sin-Killer quickly
plunged into his description of the Crucifixion:

Lightnin' played its limber gauze
When they nailed Jesus to the rugged Cross;
The mountain began to tremble
When the holy body began to drop blood down upon it.
Each little silver star leaped out of its little orbit;
The sun went down on Calvary's bloodied brow,
Lightnin' was playin' on the horse's bridle reins
As it leaped to the battlements of glory,
When the morning star was breaking its light
On the grave.

All at once Sin-Killer broke away from his poetic chanting and with a
voice that pointed like an outstretched finger, shouted:

"You keep foolin' with the Marster and he will shake the earth
again!"

From this brutal warning he went from one dramatic situation in
the Old Testament to another, skipped lightly to the New Testament,
and back again: Moses and the burning bush, Jacob's sacrificing
Isaac, the breaking of the seven seals and other scenes from Revela-
tion—all these set forth in dramatic intensity. When Sin-Killer had
to catch his breath, he started a song while he mopped his face, and
kept up the growing excitement of the congregation by a shouted
word which fitted perfectly into the tempo of the song. Then he went
back to his sermon:

Roman soldiers come riding in full speed on their horses,
And splunged Him in the side,
We seen the blood and water come out.
Oh, God A'mighty placed it in the minds of the people
Why water is for baptism
And the blood is for cleansin'.
I don't care how mean you've been,
God A'mighty's blood 'll cleanse you all from sin.

I seen, my dear friends, the time moved on,
Great God looked down,
He began to look down at the temple.
Jesus said to tear down the temple,
And in three days I'll rise up again in all sight.
They didn't know what He was talkin' about—
Jesus was talkin' about His temple, body.

I seen while he was hangin', the mounting begin to tremble
On which Jesus was hangin' on;
The blood was dropping on the mounting,
Holy blood, dropping on the mounting, my dear friends,
Corrupting the mounting;
I seen about that time while the blood was dropping down,
One drop after another,
I seen the sun that Jesus made in creation;
The sun rose, my dear friends,
And it recognized Jesus hanging on the Cross.
Just as soon as the sun recognized its Maker,
Why it closed itself and went down,
Went down in mournin',
"Look at my Maker hanging on the Cross."

And when the sun went down, we seen the moon;
He made the moon,
My dear friends, yes, both time and seasons—

We seen, my dear friends, when the moon recognized Jesus dying
    on the Cross,
I seen the moon, yes,
Took with a judgment hemorrhage and bleed away!

Good God looked down.
Oh, the dyin' thief on the cross
Seen the moon goin' down in blood.
I seen, my dear friends, about that time they looked at that,
And when the moon went down, it done bleed away,
I seen the little stars, great God, that was there
On the anvil of time,
And the little stars began to show their beautiful ray of light,
And the stars recognized their Maker dyin' on the cross.
Each little star leaped out of their silver orbit,
The torches of a unbenointed world.

It got so dark
Until the men who was puttin' Jesus to death
They said they could feel the darkness in their fingers.
Great God A'mighty, they was close to one another,
An' it was so dark they could feel one another and hear one
    another and talk,
But they couldn't see each other.
I heard one of the centurions say:
"Sholy, sholy, this must be the Son of God."

'Bout that time we seen, my dear friends, the prophet Isaiah,
Said the dead in the graves would hear his voice and come forward.
They saw the dead gettin' up out of their graves on the east side of
    Jerusalem;
Gettin' out of their graves,
Walkin' about, goin' down in town.
Oh!—'way over on Nebo's mounting [shouted]
I seen the great lawgiver get up out of his grave and begin to walk
    about,

My dear friends, walking, because Jesus said,
"It is finished."

I seen forty and four thousand in Heaven,
Just in the moment, the twinklin' of an eye.
Great God! Three and twenty elders,
Each one left their seats
Cryin', "Holy, holy";
And when the angels got near the earth, the earth began
To quake and tremble. The peoples began to say,
"What's the matter here?"
Good God A'mighty! First and second day, no harm, nothing
    happened.
But here on the third mornin', looky here!
The earth quaking!
Good God! The earth began to quake.

'Bout that time while they were watching the earth,
The angels darted down and a-seated right by the side of 'em,
Rolled back the stone,
Took a seat by the side of 'em,
Never said a word to 'em,
But just set there.
And when the angels took their seats,
Good God!
Jesus got up;
Yes, got up out of his grave,
Began pullin' off his grave clothes.
Great God! Taken the napkin from around his jaws,
Shook the girdles,
Then laid them in the grave.

We seen the angels watch old Mary and Marthy,
An' told 'em just about when the morning star would break,
Told the girls to go on down to the grave.

Every child of God, he had something to carry to Jesus.
"Oh—how you abused Me in this world! [singing]
An' how you caused Me to shed briny tears!
How you caused Me to stand with folded arms!"

Sin-Killer closed with a mighty invitation for sinners to come forward. None came. Perhaps they had become hardened to his pleas. Alan had been able to catch only fragments of the hour-long sermon. Every seven minutes a disk must be turned, every fourteen minutes a new one had to be inserted.

After Sin-Killer had bade farewell to the convicts he joined Alan and me. The loud-speaker was turned on so that the convicts could hear the play-back. Three hundred leaned forward to listen—more intently than they had listened to the preacher. Sin-Killer never once moved as his service came from the machine.

"Mr. Lomax," he said, when the last word had passed out of the loud-speaker, "for a long time I'se been hearing that I'se a good preacher. Now I knows it."

Late one Sunday afternoon I happened upon a small remote Negro church-house tucked away among the live-oaks and elms bordering a large cotton plantation in the Brazos River bottoms. Hearing singing, I parked my recording machine outside the church and went in. Only a small group of Negroes was present, mostly white-haired men and women with faces seamed by lines of age and toil. I was welcomed and given a seat near the pulpit.

The testimonies went on—for it was an experience meeting—each speaker attempting to find something in his restricted and uneventful life for which to utter thanks to an all-wise and overruling Providence. Over and over again they repeated the same phrases from the Bible, often using words high-sounding and musical. Now and then, however, a speaker would give utterance to forceful and vivid expressions:

Jordan's river am chilly an' cold;
It chills the body an' not the soul.

Usually he would work up his feelings as he spoke until, at the close, his voice would trail off into a musical chant to be joined in the refrain by the audience. The talk centered around the hard times of early life, the certainty of death:

De hammer keep a-ringin' on somebody's coffin;
'Way over in de new buryin' groun'.

Long grave an' short grave
Everywhere I go.

A more realistic man chanted:

Well, de grave mus' be an awful place;
Lay a man on his back, throw dirt in his face.

One fleshy, copper-colored Negro woman shouted as she sat down:

I am so glad God fixed it so
Dat de rich man mus' die as well as de po'.

Another, a tall, very black giant, followed and chanted at the close of his talk:

Sinner man lay sick in bed;
Death come a-knockin' at de do';
Says he, "Come in, doctor, go 'way, Death,
I ain't ready to go."

Now wasn't dem hard times?
Triberlations, Lord?

Now wasn't dem hard times?
I'se bound to leave dis world.

Christian man lay sick in bed;
Death come a-knockin' at de do';
Says he, "Come in, Death, go 'way, Doctor,
I'se ready to go, I'se ready to go."

Now wasn't dem hard times,
Triberlations, Lord?
Now wasn't dem hard times?
I'se bound to leave dis world.

The trials and tribulations of earth would find recompense in the joys
of Heaven:

One of dese mornin's, bright and fair,
Gwine to hitch my wings and try de air!

I'm gwine to tell my Jesus howdy,
I'm gwine to walk an' talk wid de angels;
I'm gwine to kneel 'round de Union table,
I'm gwine to ride on de whistlin' chariot,
Some o' dese days.

They would need the whistlin' chariot when "De Lord gwine to set
dis world on fire." But Heaven attained would prove to be a place of
physical rest. They could "set down":

Oh, Lord, you know what you promised me;
You promise me a golden waistband
When I get home.

Go, angel, and get that servant a golden waistband,
And set down, servant, you set down.

Dere's a long white robe in Heaven for me;
No more sunshine for to burn you,
No more rain for to wet you;
Every day will be Sunday in Heaven.

From other songs I jotted memorable phrases:

You may carry me away to de old bone-yard,
But you come for to carry me home,
But you come for to carry me home.

Heaven is a beautiful place, I know, I know.
Heaven is a peaceful place, I know.
Won't be no mournin' there, I know;
Won't be no sinnin' there, I know;
Won't be no sorrowin' there.

Oh, when I git to Heaven, gwine to set right down,
Ask my Lord for a starry crown,
Settin' down side o' de Holy Lamb.

Oh, when I git to Heaven, gwine to be at ease,
Me an' my Lord gwine to do as we please,
Settin' down side o' de Holy Lamb.

Two white horses side by side,
Me an' my Lord gwine take us an evenin' ride.

Near the close of the vesper service a Negro sang with exquisite
pathos several stanzas, one of which ran:

Lemme tell you, white man,
Lemme tell you, honey,
Nigger makes de cotton
But de white folks gits de money.

Ain't it hard, ain't it hard?
Ain't it hard to be a nigger, nigger, nigger?
Ain't it hard, ain't it hard?
For you cain't git yo' money when it's due.

As dusk deepened the congregation was dismissed and drifted away in groups down a winding, sandy road. Still they sang and I caught these fragments:

De Lord will shoe my lily-white foots
When I climbs de golden stairs.

🎜

Ef salvation was a thing money could buy,
Den de rich would live an' de po' would die.

🎜

Jes' so de tree fall, jes so it lie;
Jes' so de sinner live, jes so he die.
Befo' dis time another year I may be gone,
An' in some lonesome graveyard—
Oh, Lord, how long?

Sister Crockett, co-pastor of the Church of the Holy Ghost out in the West End District of San Antonio, welcomed me into the parlor of her home. She was a Negro woman of dignity and pose, dressed in a flowing black robe, cut in imitation of one of the Catholic orders. She had just driven home from her daily rounds of selling lye hominy from a rattletrap buggy drawn by a hungry-looking, emaciated pony. This hominy, made from white field corn, she cooked at night to supply a daily demand. Sister Crockett was tall, stately in manner, her voice resonant and deep from much public speaking. Deep-graven, firm and resolute lines etched an impressive face. Seventy years she had met the storms of life, more than fifty as a minister of the Gospel calling her people to repentance.

Around the room and over the doorway at which I entered placards shouted warnings: "Tomorrow you may die," "A sinner will burn in everlasting fire," "Come into the Kingdom before it is too late," "Be converted and be sanctified." (Sister Crockett explained carefully to me that when a sinner received pardon from on high he could go on and seek and obtain a Second Blessing, which would free him from the danger of backsliding. He could then sin no more. Sister Crockett claimed herself a sanctified person.)

"When I was sixteen years old and living near Nashville, Tennessee," said Sister Crockett, "conviction seized me. For two months I was a seeker before my heart found peace. I prayed all day and I prayed all night. I went to sleep praying. I woke up praying. My people lived close by a big woods. I went far out among the trees and found me a sunshiny spot. Every morning I went there for a grove meeting with the Lord, pleading with him to pardon my sins. I prayed so long and hard, wrestling with the Saviour on my knees, that I wore out the grass. Though I watered it with my tears the grass withered and died, leaving a bare round spot. But I couldn't find no relief.

"One night I was setting out before our house with my heart all heavy and burdened with sin, and I looked up at the stars. I picked me out a little, lonely-looking star and prayed to it. 'Little star,' I said, 'you is close up there to Jesus. Won't you step over and ask Him to help me in my suffering and to save me from my sins?' And when I was talking to the little star it shuttered and went out. Then I felt worser than ever.

"But another time I was 'seeking' in the little church on the top of the hill, and the members a-singing, 'I went down in the valley to pray and my soul got happy and I stayed all day.' The Lord broke up the Devil's nest in my heart and I got up from the mourners' bench and waved my arms and shouted. I wanted to tell everybody that my dungeon's been shuck and my chains is done fell off. But the next day the Devil come back—he was always a-coming—and told me that I wasn't saved. And I tried to fight him off. But I couldn't. My heart got set like it was in cement. And then I talked to the Lord a little bit, and the fire went to burning up again. And I was free to worship my Lord."

By this time Sister Crockett was on her feet, walking up and down the room. Her arms were upraised and waving. Tears coursed down her cheeks. I thanked her for her story and begged her to sing for me, so that her voice might go down for a thousand years persuading sinners to leave off their evil ways. And she did sing into my microphone in her rich, deep voice, all the more effective because it still was tremulous from the emotions aroused by her own life story.

I then put on records for the Library of Congress "Drive Old Satan Out of de Corner," "I'm Walkin' on Borrowed Land," "Steeped in Iniquity," "All my Sins Been Taken Away," "You Say You're a Christian," and "Flood in Omaha"—some of the songs partly her own composition.

"The last two," said Sister Crockett, "I made myself. Sometimes when the spirit comes I rise and sing these two songs. When I am preaching and can't find the lost word, I stop and sing these songs and, bless God, the mourners come tumbling over each other."

Said Sister Crockett: "I was thinking of the foolishness they carry on in religious worship for the benefit of the church, instead of having a heart to give God what he wanted or needed—foolishness, such as frolics and concerts and all such. And it was in my mind and I began to sing this song:

You say you are a Christian and your heart is clean,
If you give God a dime, why you want a saucer cream?

How is that? That is no Christian;
How is that? Oh, you don't love God.

On and on she sang tirelessly, setting forth in detail the sins and pretenses of the church member:

> The church ought to be God's pure bride,
> But you bring in godlessness on the inside.
>
> Oh, how is that? Can't you be a Christian?
> How is that? Oh, can't you love God?

Sister Crockett went on: "I was reading the newspapers about the Omaha storm, and I was stirred up. And one day I was walking the street of Lake Charles, Louisiana, and was thinking real seriously over the matter, and all at once I began to sing:

> Oh, just look at Omaha;
> Children there without Ma or Pa,
> Children there without Ma or Pa,
> For a tornado swept through Omaha.
>
> God was worried with their wicked ways,
> God was worried with their wicked ways,
> God was worried with their wicked ways,
> And God's getting worried with your wicked ways.
>
> There was a place in Omaha,
> They called a pool room, and I guess it was a bar;
> The tornado came and blew it down,
> And thirty-six bodies in there were found.
>
> God was worried with their wicked ways,
> And God's getting worried with your wicked ways.

And on she sang about Omaha through ten stanzas.

As I told Sister Crockett goodbye she raised her right hand and asked Divine favor for me. I walked out under the arched gateway of her home over which blazed an electric sign: "Prepare to meet thy God." Down the street stood her little tumbledown church with its bleak board benches, in sharp contrast to the somewhat elegant leather-clad furniture of Sister Crockett's parlor. Back of that parlor were rooms of eight young deaconesses, also clad in flowing black robes. I had heard their voices, the noise of doors opening and shutting, whisperings. Perhaps only the little star, so "close to Jesus and his throne," can tell all the story.

Professor George Lyman Kittredge was in Texas to lecture for the State Folklore Society. From his suggestion it was born, and it has since grown (being nurtured by Frank Dobie) to a goodly stature. On Sunday morning during his visit I asked him what he would like to do. He said he would fall in with my plans. I then proposed that we attend Negro church services where he could hear the congregation sing Negro spirituals. Over we went, to be met at the door by the Negro minister, a man of education and dignity. He conducted us to a front seat almost underneath the high pulpit. The presence and appearance of Professor Kittredge created unusual interest in the large audience. Picture a sea of somber black faces, many of them old and wizened, in contrast to the appearance of the Kittredge we knew, who sat erect, eyes to the front, clad in a gray suit—in effect almost white—with skin very fair, with white brow and a noble head crowned by hair of silvery sheen. The audience gazed at him with a mixture of awe and reverence.

The large choir sang some conventional hymns, the minister made his announcements. The collection was to be placed on a table near Professor Kittredge. On this table, presided over by two deacons, the contributors, walking forward, placed their offerings, some of them making several trips to the front, each time dropping more money. Some mild excitement was occasioned when Professor Kittredge reached over and slipped a crisp dollar-bill on the table. Then came the sermon, a thoughtful, sensible appeal for a better life. The minister led the audience in singing a number of Negro spirituals, without the accompaniment of the organ. The audience swung with fervor into these stirring melodies. As song followed song in rapid succession many of the singers were soon swaying their bodies, shuffling their feet and gently clapping their hands in unison with the rhythm of the music, the effect being greatly heightened by the shrill notes of several falsetto voices scattered throughout the audience.

Suddenly a woman screamed wildly, another followed and then another. They sprang to their feet, waved their arms, and threw back their heads as if seized by some uncontrollable emotion. Presently a group of these women stepped into the aisle of the church. All were old, with bodies bent by time. All were moved by powerful religious fervor; but they had not forgotten their impressive-looking guest. As the swaying line of singing and shouting marchers, following each other in rhythmic procession around the aisles, passed Professor Kittredge, each old woman leaned over and earnestly shook his hand. They passed me by without notice. Around the church swung the marchers for a second time; and again, for the second time, each seam-faced old saint leaned across me (still without seeing me) to shake the professor's hand. Perhaps they thought he was some modern Moses, come to honor their services. The excitement became so acute that the minister raised his hand and stilled the singing.

Then came another song of quieter tempo. The old women found their seats; the tension eased; the excitement died away. Coming down from the high pulpit, the pastor bent over me and asked me to speak to the congregation. I excused myself.

"Perhaps your friend will speak?"

"I will ask him," I answered. Professor Kittredge surprised me by saying:

"I should like to speak very much indeed."

Whereupon the minister climbed back to the platform and said to the audience: "My friends, we have with us today a very distinguished visitor from the North who has consented to speak to us. I now have the pleasure of introducing to you Professor George Lyman Kittredge of Yale University." Springing to his feet, Professor Kittredge pointed a long index finger at the minister and exclaimed:

"Harvard, if you please!"

Again Professor Kittredge surprised me. Instead of speaking from where he stood, he walked up onto the platform and into the tall pulpit and stood there, a dramatic and impressive figure. He gave one of the most inspiring ten-minute sermons I have ever heard. My Negro friends yet speak of that occasion.

On his last visit to Texas, when Professor Kittredge was having dinner in our Austin home, we introduced our Negro maid. The dignified, gray-haired Elnora greeted him cordially. "I'm so pleased to meet you. Mrs. Lomax has told me what a great poet you are." I laughed; whereupon Professor Kittredge protested vigorously: "Lomax, you needn't laugh. I *am* a poet. Ask my wife. She has poems that I have written to her."

10

CHANTEYS, BALLADS, WORK SONGS AND CALLS

You would hardly expect to find a singer of sea chanteys on top of a high mountain. That's where I came on J. M. Hunt. Everybody called him Sailor Dad.

When I asked him how he happened to be living far back in the Virginia mountains, he told me that when the highways were being built in that section there was a demand for a person skilled in the use of ropes, block and tackle and other equipment used in bridge building. Who would be better qualified for this job than an old sailor?

"Well," said Sailor Dad, "I fell in love with the mountains and I married a mountain woman. She claims she likes to hear me sing 'Haul Away My Rosey':

Talk about your harbor girls around the corner, Sally;
But they couldn't come to tea with the girls from Bible Alley.
I once loved a French girl, but she was fat and lazy.
With her "Parlez-vous, oui, oui francaise," she nearly drove me
  crazy.

We sailed from Liverpool, bound for the Gulf of Mexico;
We sailed into Galveston all loaded up with cotton-o.

Singing, he interspersed a lot of "Haul Away My Roseys" after every couplet. He sang "Sally Brown," and another with a swinging chorus about Texas and Santa Anna. When I asked Sailor Dad if he knew a good drinking song, he told me a story and sang me a song. I'll let him tell his own story of the song that brought him and his companions fourteen mugs of good Welsh beer.

"*When Jones's Ale Was New* is very historical; and, according to history, it was sung over three hundred years ago. And I learnt this song from a Welsh sailor out in San Francisco; and years—a few years—afterward when I went steam-boatin' after quittin' the old windjammers, I went to Glasgow. And the coal miners were on a strike in Glasgow and we couldn't get no coal; but we had enough coal in the bunkers to carry us down to Swansea, Wales, where we intended to coal up and then go back to Boston.

"In the meantime, three of my shipmates, who had been to Swansea before, knew all about Swansea. I didn't. And they said, 'Come on, let's go on up to Mother Sullivan's—that's a free-and-easy, about a mile and a half up toward Landors.' So we went up there, and when we went in there was men and women sittin' around drinkin'. And they had a stage there, with a piano-player and an announcer. And they said, 'Jack, go on up there and give 'em *When Jones's Ale Was New*. If you do, we'll have plenty of beer comin' to us.' So I got up there and announced myself, and the announcer introduced me to the audience, who I was, where I was from, and so forth. And I sang *When Jones's Ale Was New*. And I got a couple of encores, and when I come on down to where my shipmates was, we had fourteen mugs of beer on that table."

Then he sang for the record:

The first to come in was a soldier,
With his knapsack over his shoulder;
For none could be more bolder
And his long broadsword he drew.
He swore every man should spend a pound,
And they should treat all hands around—

And he jolly well drank their healths all round,
(bum! bum! bum! with the beer mug)
When Jones's ale was new, my boy,
When Jones's ale was new.

Then the landlord's daughter she came in
And we kissed those rosy lips again,
We all sat down and then we'd sing:
(bum! bum! bum! with the beer mug)
When Jones's ale was new, my boy,
When Jones's ale was new.

Several others "came in," including the weaver, the tinker and the candlestick-maker, a stanza for each newcomer and plenty of concerted noise from the beer mugs.

Sailor Dad, with his imaginary mug full of beer, his big, booming voice caroling the most noted of sea ditties, achieved high folksong fame—an invitation to sing to President and Mrs. Roosevelt in the White House. There he sang his beer-drinking song, making the fine chandeliers of the Crystal Room tremble with his bellows.

In the Autumn of 1936 I received a letter from a lady reporter in Akron, saying that a wonderful ballad-singer lived in that town. I packed my car and arrived in Akron the following week. The kind reporter brought to my room a big breezy, wholesome, smiling man.

"I'm the last of the Ohio Canal Captains," said Captain Pearl R. Nye. "You know I was born on a canalboat which ran from Akron to the Ohio River, down which we floated our cargoes to Louisville, Kentucky.

"My family was a singin' bunch. My great-grandmothers brought many folk songs from England, and we all picked up more songs in this country wherever we traveled. We knew hundreds. I'm fixin' them all up to send them to the Library of Congress."

Captain Nye had brought with him an armful of manuscripts rolled into scrolls, each scroll made up of twenty or thirty long yellow sheets pasted end to end together. Before he had finished his recordings, he was almost covered in a pile of manuscript. He first sang a long song about a trip on the Canal, *The Dark-Eyed Canaler*:

> It was a comely young lady fair
> Was walking out to take the air;
> She met a canaler upon the way,
> So I paid attention to hear what they did say.

"My mother used to sing it to me and the rest of us children when we were small, gathered around her knee on the deck of the canalboat, which was our home," he explained. "That was many years ago."

"How long were you on the canal, Captain Nye?"

"Forty years."

"Didn't you tell me that you were born on the canal?"

"Yes, sir, I was born and raised there, in Chillicothe, Ohio, the Upper Tenth Street Bridge, on the canalboat 'Reform.'"

"Tell me a little something about your family on the canal."

"They were a large family; there was eighteen of us—eleven boys, seven girls. I'm the fifteenth youngster, ninth boy. And we had one great old time, swimming, falling overboard, as you might expect from a large family. And music and song more or less controlled our home. We all had a good time. Take a trip on the canal if you want to have fun." He sang:

> So haul in the towline and take up the slack;
> Take a reef in your shirt-tail and straighten your back;
> Whatever you do, be sure don't forget
> To tap the mules gently while the cook is on deck.

"When I first started to write down the words of the old songs," Captain Nye went on, "I often found that I remembered the tune but not the words. I'd keep hummin' the tunes till all of a sudden the old words popped up. The way I love the songs of old England proves, I guess, that I'm a real Britisher. I guess *Barbara Allen* is my favorite of them all."

Captain Nye sang through their entire lengths at least a dozen of the standard English ballads. The Library of Congress has eighty-three versions of *Barbara Allen*, but none more beautiful than the tune Captain Nye sang for us:

All in the merry month of May,
When green buds were a-swelling,
Sweet William came from Western States
And courted Barb'ry Allen.

Captain Nye declared: "I was blessed with comical parents. My father's songs especially were nothing but nonsense, We all liked to sing *Daddy Be Gay* when other folks would gather on our stern deck where we had a sure enough jollification." This song turned out to be an amusing version of the scolding wife who, when sent to Hell, whipped the Devil, beat out the brains of one little Devil and sent the rest "scrambling up the walls."

After I spent two happy days with the jolly old bachelor, he said to me, gravely, as we parted: "These songs are sacred to me. They bring back memories of the silver ribbon, the Ohio Canal. That was the best life a man ever had. Perhaps, though, you can't see things just as I do. I'm not supposed to see as you do—for my mind is Canal."

Many years ago while I was on a folksong lecture tour among the colleges of the United States, I spent one night in the home of Professor E. E. Hale, a member of the English faculty of Union College at Schenectady, New York, whose father wrote the classic short story, *The Man Without a Country*. My host, himself a folksong lover, gave me one stanza of a ballad which he said was popular among the boatmen and mule-drivers on the Erie Canal.

Later a ranchman from Montana sent me another stanza of the same song. Some time afterward I found a third stanza at a ranch on the Rio Grande in Texas. A few years later W. D. Totten, a lawyer in Seattle, Washington, sent me three additional stanzas, the refrain, and also the music of the song which he had learned while working as a towpath boy on the Canal during the years from 1871 to 1877.

Again Dr. J. V. Denny, professor of English in the University of Ohio, added another stanza. Yet another came from Chicago, and in the library of Allegheny College at Meadville, Pennsylvania, I found still another. Walter D. Edmonds, needing a stanza for one of his stories, made one up on the spot, and got away with it.

This group of stanzas I put together without changes as one song, *The Ballad of the Erie Canal*, in the form of a continuous narrative. Perhaps these words were never sung together, and time and travel have certainly brought changes in the original composition and music. Doubtless the original song was the result of growth, no one person being its author. Maybe the ballad was much longer before it got broken up and scattered. Who knows?

Here are sample stanzas. It's a grand song—full of vivid and exaggerated descriptions, rough humor and frank satire:

I am all the way from Buffalo, upon the good boat "Danger,"
A long, long trip we had, my boys, I feel just like a stranger.
Petty fogs, artful storms, forget them I never shall;
I am every inch a sailor, boys, on the Erie Canal.

Chorus:
So haul in yer bowlines, stand by the saddle-mule;
Low bridge, boys, dodge yer head, don't stand up like a fool;
For the Erie is a-risin', an' the whiskey's gittin' low;
I hardly think we'll git a drink till we git to Buffalo.

We left Albany harbor about the break of day;
If rightly I remember, 'twas the second day of May.
We trusted to our driver, although he was but small,
Yet he knew all the windings of that ragin' Canawl.

Early every morning ye can hear the flunkies call,
Come aft and git yer lime-juice, come aft one and all;
Come aft and git yer lime-juice, and don't bring any back,
Before you git to Syracuse ye'r goin' to git the sack.

Three days out from Albany a pirate we did spy,
The black flag with the skull and bones was a-wavin' up on high.
We signaled to the driver to h'ist the flag o' truce,
When we found it was the *Mary Jane* just out of Syracuse.

Two days out from Syracuse the vessel struck a shoal,
And we like to all been foundered on a chunk of Lackawanna coal.
We hollered to the captain on the towpath treadin' dirt;
He jumped on board and stopped the leak with his old red flannel
    shirt.

The cook she was a kind soul, she had a ragged dress;
We h'isted her upon a pole as a signal of distress.
The winds began to whistle and the waves began to roll,
And we had to reef our royal on the ragin' Canawl.

When we got to Syracuse, the off mule he was dead,
The nigh mule got blind staggers and we cracked him on the head;
The captain he got married, the cook he went to jail,
And I'm the only son-of-a-bitch that's left to tell the tale.

Four long days we sailed the Hudson, Sal and I and Hank;
We greased ourselves with tallow fat and slid out on a plank;
The crew are in the poorhouse, the captain he's in jail,
And I'm the sole survivin' man that's left to tell the tale.

That the Erie Canal men did sing is proved from an old law that
I found in the Library of Albany, New York, assessing a penalty
against passing night boats, the singing of whose crews disturbed the
sleep-loving burghers of that city with some such raucous refrain as:

Drop a tear for Bigfoot Sal,
The best damn cook on the Erie Canal.
She aimed at Heaven but she went to Hell,
Fifteen years on the Erie Canal.

Up and down the Canal I went one summer, hoping to find more folksong treasures. Alas! the pioneer boatmen had died or drifted West. Only fragments fell into my ballad net. One again speaks touchingly of the perennial red-headed canalboat cook:

> Our cook, she's daisy and dead stuck on me,
> Has fiery red hair and she's sweet sixty-three;
> Though sunburned and freckled, a daisy you bet,
> And we use her at night for a headlight on deck.

The Music Professor stopped his car after we had gone a couple of miles on the rawhide road.

"I don't believe we can go any further—too many stumps and rocks. We can't afford to tear up the automobile out in these wilds and be forced to walk back to Mena." We had driven out from this Arkansas town in the southern Ozarks early that morning, and had turned off from a fourth-class highway at a mailbox marked "Mrs. Emma Dusenberry." Some wagon tracks marked a dim trail through the woods. Ours was perhaps the first automobile the startled squirrels had ever seen.

"Let me go ahead on foot and see if we can make it around this bend." (The day was growing hot and I didn't fancy a long tramp in the sultry heat.) On came the careful professor and his car, until I was again able to mount and ride with him. Suddenly we came on an open space of two acres or more. On the far side stood a log cabin. The doorway framed a woman aroused by the rumble of our car. She had the serene face one finds in the pictures of saints and martyrs. She greeted us as we came up, saying:

"I'm Emma Dusenberry. I'm 79 years old. I've been blind for forty years. My daughter in the kitchen is fifty-one and she has never been married yet. Come in, won't you? I can't get around much—only to feed my chickens and ducks."

Two rooms made up the cabin. No glass was in the windows—only slabs of rough pine boards, at night let up and down on rawhide hinges and fastened on the inside. The patch of ground was not cultivated. They had no horse; but two milch cows grazed near by, and the yard swarmed with ducks and chickens. To them the long arm of the national government reached down at the rate of $6 a month pension for the elder woman.

For two days Emma Dusenberry sang almost continuously into a microphone from which records were made of eighty-two songs for the Library of Congress. Singing of knights in golden armor riding curvetting steeds, and ladies dressed in damask and royal purple, she seemed to forget her sordid surroundings, the remote poorly furnished cabin of the Arkansas Ozarks:

Lord Ronald he lifted his lady fair
To a snow-white palfrey standing there.

Among her songs was the greatest number of the "Child Ballads" ever recorded from one person, so far as I know.

"I learned them in the mountains of Georgia when I was a young girl," she said, "and have remembered all that I've heard since. You see I'm blind and never could read, so I think about lords and ladies, the lady fair and the gallant knight, dressed in gold and purple. I forget the wooden shutters in the place of windows, and wish for the days when I was a girl dancing to the tune of 'Shoot the Buffalo.'"

With the professor to aid, the work of recording went forward with unusual rapidity, and the singer's voice seemed never to tire. On the second day, while we were busy in the middle of a long ballad, a hen flew up on one of the windowsills and announced her astonishment at what she saw. Mrs. Dusenberry stopped her song and spoiled a record: "That's Blackie," she said; "it's her time to lay. Her nest is in the corner over there. She can't wait no longer. We'll have to stop."

So we retreated to the kitchen, where dinner was cooking. After a time, no further word from Blackie. So back we came to the sacred precincts where she was hid in a box in the corner of the room. The recording went on. Presently, while Mrs. Dusenberry was singing, Blackie perched on the rim of her nest and shrilly made an announcement. Her loud cackles of triumph cut across the sound-lines of the tragedy of "The Brown Girl," announcing a unique musical record where the cackle of an Arkansas hen serves as an accompaniment to an old English ballad theme. For while Blackie cackled, Mrs. Dusenberry sang serenely on.

Engagements forced me to drive alone all the following night—a journey of five hundred miles. About 3:00 A.M., when sleep and weariness combined to overcome me, time after time I roused myself from stupor by laughing aloud as I recalled how four people waited for Blackie to lay an egg.

Down in the piney woods of North Florida, gaunt, 72-year-old Mrs. Georgy A. Griffin sat on her front porch and rocked gently back and forth, as I recorded the ballads that she knew. Between songs, as the old lady rested, she talked as she might have talked to Mrs. Dusenberry:

"My father was a fiddler. I learnt most of my songs from him. Still got his fiddle. All the children bid for it, and I bid it in for $92."

Professor Alton Morris of the University of Florida, who had introduced me to Mrs. Griffin, asked her about Lord Derwentwater (Child 208). The song is a standard English ballad not previously recovered from any singer in North America. She called it, "The King Wrote a Love Letter." She said, "Why, yes, I learnt that from my father, too. I remember him standin' on top of the barn and singin' 'The King Wrote a Love Letter' so loud that the neighbors three miles away said they heered him. They was a creek there, and I guess his voice went down the creek."

Mrs. Griffin calls herself a Georgy Cracker. When she was yet a young girl, she and her family walked 178 miles from their home in Georgia, to Newberry, Florida. "And we was all barefooted," she said. "Nights we slept out in the open fields."

"How did you happen to leave Georgia, Mrs. Griffin?"

"Well, my Ma had a sister down there she wanted to see, so her an' five of us kids jes' come. We lef' Pa home, an' he come later."

"How did you come?"

"Walked hit, ever' step of hit. Tuck us three weeks. But when we wuz bigger, me an' my brother walked hit agin in seven days an' nights." She had twelve children, all brought to maturity, eleven of them still living. "My children all had the same father. I hain't never been that way except fer one man, an' as the Lord's my witness I hain't never knowed but two men in all my life, an' them two wuz my husbands. An' I've been th'owed with men in every way. I've worked in the fields with 'em, rid horse races with 'em—why, I run a horse race right over thar, ridin' bar'back, made some money, too—not bettin', but jest the prize money; an' I've built a house with my own hands, an' when I married Mr. Griffin I wuz runnin' a sawmill of my own, an' had twelve men a-workin' for me."

Explaining that she was not on good terms with one of her daughters who probably could remember some of the song words that she had forgotten, Mrs. Griffin said: "Will Brown, he's my daughter's husband, told me he'd kick me off the place if I ever come near his house. An' d'ye know why? Well, I told 'em plain out that Nellie, that's their daughter an' my own grandchild, too (I hain't a-denyin' that); but I told 'em she wuz goin' to burn in hellfire for breakin' up another man's home. She went an' got a man to fall in love with her, then she tuck an' divorced her own husband an' made this other man divorce his wife, an' then they wuz married. Twarn't nothin' but plain adultery, an' nothin' cain't save her from hell, an' I told 'em so, an' they don't like hit.

"Anyhow my daughter cain't sing any better than I can, fer she's snaggle-toothed too. I used to work a large farm; once had $22,000 in bank. Lost most of it in bank failure." Mrs. Griffin calls a spade a spade. She can't write; "Never went to school a day in my life." This came out when she complained that she had difficulty in shopping: "I have to send my grandson here, an' he cain't remember but one thing at a time; so I have to send him fer meat, an' then when he gits home with the meat, I have to send him back for beans."

"Why don't you write out a list for the grocer?" Then came the explanation. But Mrs. Griffin is wise in many ways beyond "book larnin'."

I traveled from Texas to her home a second time, and got a brave list of songs to supplement seventy that she already had sung for me, twenty being included in the Child Collection. When Professor

Child died, not a dozen of the standard English ballads were then known to be current in the United States. Of one, she said: "I hadn't thought of that one since the last time I milked the cows in the old cowpen."

She claims to be a relative of Mary Hart of Revolutionary fame, and says that her father bore the astounding name of John Milton Moses Bradley James Madison Daniel Spangoe Moses Springfield Lawrence R. R. Hart. I brought her a box of chocolates to bribe her to tell me more about her early life.

First, she hid the candy above her head on a half-finished quilt swinging high up in its frame. "I've got too many grandchildren around here to git any for myself," she apologized. Then she added for the record:

"I've done everything in the world a woman could do, except lying and stealing. Ain't done nothin' like that, but anything else in the world. I've sawed, I've hoed, I've made potatoes, I've made sorghum, I've made corn. I've made vinegar, I've raised hogs, I've run cows, I've run horses, I've run horse races; I've done everything in the world a woman could do that was honest. Yes, I've been on the stage, too, me 'n' the old man. (Do you want me to talk that and you catch it on that thing?) I've split rails, I've plowed, I've hoed, I've built a house—the house standing over yonder now, built when this young girl here was a baby. I had a big sawmill, I ran a BIG sawmill. I had thirty head o' mules and two head o' horses—I had 'em to a buggy, double buggy. I had five wagons and four horsecarts, and four mules to every one o' them horsecarts, and 275 head o' milk cows, cattle, you know, scrub cattle."

"You made your Negroes work, didn't you?"

"Yes, I did. They was all willin' to work; they wanted to work; never had a bit o' trouble in the world with 'em, not one bit."

She broke off and would go no farther.

"Come back next spring, and I'll go fishing with you. I cain't sing and talk no more for that thing," pointing at the recording machine. "My lips get sucked in the holes ertween my teeth." She gave me an exhibit as proof.

I met only one of her eleven children, a daughter, not long out of college. She sat silent when her mother wished to talk.

"I could sing more'n two hundred songs in my young days," said Mrs. Griffin. Eighty titles bearing her name are on deposit in the Folk Song Archive, as a result of our afternoons.

Five hundred miles to the West, deep in the piney woods of Texas, I had found another great singer very different from Mrs. Griffin, but equally interesting and productive of songs and rich tales:

"Yes, sir, Boss, I got your letter all right, but I didn't see no use to answer it, 'cause ev'rything done changed. I'se turned preacher, an' I can't sing those songs you wrote about." Besides Henry Truvillion was tired. "Please 'scuse my seat [he was sitting down]; we've jes' got back from my wife's brother's wife's fun'ral. She lef' a month-old baby girl behind, an' my wife's in the house tendin' to her now."

"Are those your children?" I asked as several pairs of bright eyes peeped around the corner of the house. "Yes, sir, five head; at least my wife says they're mine."

In 1934 Alan and I had followed Henry into the East Texas timberlands where the Wier Brothers were cutting lumber. He was the boss of the track-lining gang, and his calls and songs had made interesting and beautiful records. I was still eager to save for the Folksong Archive all that Henry Truvillion had stored away in his "remembrance." Henry would talk of nothing but spirituals, "When the Roll Be's Called in Heaven, I'll Answer to My Name" and "The Mighty Rider": "We sings short meter, common meter and long meter, mostly long meter." "The Lord's secretary keeps a list," he explained, "an' God's goin' to call all our names some time or other, an' we got to answer to 'em. 'Sfor me, I don't keer how far down the list my name comes, an' when they gits to it they can jest' skip it if they wants to."

For nearly twenty years he had been head tracklayer for the lumber company at Wiergate, which in that time had denuded of pine trees many square miles of that section. Henry's gang goes into the woods at daybreak, but they come out at three in the afternoon. Henry's

Ford each morning bounces him eight miles down the highway in time "for me to do a good half-day's work. Sundays I preaches." The previous Sunday they had collected seven dollars, Henry told me.

"How much went to you and how much to the Lord," I asked irreverently.

"I takes all. The Lawd done had plenty; he don't need it."

"What kind of sermon do you preach?"

"That depends. Sometimes my congregation's paralyzed, then I has to revise 'em."

Henry grew up on a farm in Mississippi. He has been quite a traveler, and speaks familiarly of New York, Boston and Chicago, San Francisco. "Them wuz my ridin'-th'-rod days," he chuckles.

In his early childhood Henry followed the plow, cut and hauled wood, chopped and picked cotton. But for forty years, since he was thirteen, he has worked mainly on railroads, the first that he worked for "regular" being the "Illinois Central main line." "I couldn't hardly count the years I stayed bent down with a white man over me."

He has done all kinds of railroad work in his time, and he can tell them off on his fingers: "First, gradin' in th' levee camp, now called 'gradin' camp'; then up and down the river on a cotton boat, cuttin' willow an' makin' mats for holes in the levee, an' placin' 'em. Made a dollar a day cuttin' willow—a mean, tedious job." After that he did "river work—a little too killin'," he said. "Spent twelve years with the shevil [shovel]." For the past twenty-four years, he estimated, "or a little wusser," he has worked in eastern Texas and western Louisiana. For over nineteen years with the Wier Lumber Company, 'track-layin', steel-layin' [spiking], track-linin' [straightening].'"

Henry's wife served as a second line of defense for his conscience in the matter of singing "worl'ly songs." But after she heard the spirituals played back, she made no objections to his recording his everyday work songs. Then she could see no harm in his singing inoffensive children's songs, especially when he took Ruby Lee into his lap to help with *Mary Had a Red Dress*. Hadn't he sung her to sleep with it many a night? "From then out," Henry relaxed and let his mind slip back—"way back yander"—to his childhood days in Mississippi and on through his varied experiences of work and amusement.

Originally Wiergate, on the Sabine River, was a Texas sawmill community in the midst of a great dark forest of pine that stretched through what was No-man's Land between Texas and Louisiana. There Henry Truvillion, as foreman of the railroad gang, followed the lumberjack crew through the forest with new spurs of track, laid and moved by his crew as needed. Out along these spurs thundered cars loaded with yellow pine logs. The cars rolled on Henry Truvillion's rails. He was the boss, and all day long—the year round—he kept the men moving by his songs and calls. Railways must be built to drag the big logs to sawmills miles away; the work must go on. In the early morning hours, Henry's holler serves to rouse his men:

Raise up, boys, raise up and look,
Four o'clock done come at last;
Raise up and get your four o'clock coffee,
Raise up, boys, raise up!
Big bell call you, little bell warn you,
If you don't come out now, I'm gonna break in on you.
This ain't no place to collar no nod,
White folks want you in the lumber yard.
White man calls you, you come all right,
Nigger man calls you, you want to fight.
Ain't you gwine? Ain't you gwine? Ain't you gwine?

In listening to the track-lining and tie-tamping songs of George Clark and Jeff Horton and Richard Amerson at Livingston, Alabama, I was reminded of the close kinship, both in the words and the tune, of all railroad building work songs. Lightning and his crew in Texas and Henry Truvillion at Wiergate had first sung them to Alan and me; then Allen Prothero and others in the penitentiary at Nashville, Tennessee. Afterward we found almost the same identical tunes and words in Mississippi, Alabama, Florida, Georgia, North and South Carolina and Virginia. In every State when the men tamped the clay and gravel around and under the wooden ties they sang, almost caressingly:

Oh tamp 'em solid,
Tamp 'em sound,
Tamp 'em up solid, solid, bully,
So dey wont come down,
So dey wont come down,
So dey wont come down.

They were making that new track safe for the "Midnight Mail" and "Red Ball Flyer" and the "Sunshine Special." Over and over the words were repeated as the tamping went on.

"Tie-shuffling" is the lining, or straightening out of a newly built railroad track and, in this Henry Truvillion in the swamps of East Texas—Henry Truvillion, who for so many years has headed gangs as they built the South's railways—is at his best. Henry stoops over and squints off down the shining rail; then stands up and bawls out directions to his gang in the impossible technical language of track-lining crew. The men, with heavy wooden bars on their shoulders, trot off down the track, jam their lining-bars under the rail on the inner side and brace against them. One of their number, a handsome yellow man, when he is sure they are ready to heave, throws back his head and sings as though for all the world to hear.

On the first and the next to the last beat of every verse, each man throws his weight against his bar; the refrain is repeated until Henry, who meanwhile has kept his eye to the rail, shouts his directions about the next "johnny-head" (the next joint ahead, thirty-three feet away). At that signal the song breaks off, the gang stops heaving and then the whole scene is repeated a few yards down the track. Let Henry further explain: "When the steel gets tight with the sun shinin' right warm on it, the track bucks, an' it look jes' somethin' like an ol' slavery-time stake-an'-rider fence row, in an' out. Well, this day the sun wuz shinin', the track wuz buckin', an' I'se walkin' an' talkin'. The passenger train's due now, an' I got to git out down there an' line that track up straight—jes' like a knittin'-needle—befo' th' train gits there. I holler an' call some of my best men by name. Chances are I'll call Hank Stevens, Sonny Watkins, Sam Justice, Jim Williams, to git their linin' bars an' go down there. I have to tell 'em where to git it."

So Henry stands thirty or forty feet away, chanting themes to keep their timing perfect:

Run down yonder to the third Johnny-head an' touch it easy.
Quick, make haste, I heard the train a-comin'!
All right now, boys, let me tell you what I had for breakfast now.

Leader and gang sing:

Little *rice*, little *beans*,
No *meat* to be *seen*.

Hard *work* ain't *easy*,
Dry *bread* ain't *greasy*.

Oh, *Joe*, Joe *Lily* Butt,
Oh, *Joe*, cain't you *pick* it up?

Henry Truvillion chants:

Now, wait a minute, you stop right there,
Now put yo' guns on yo' shoulders
An' come walkin' back.
Go on to the nex' one now an' jes' barely move it.
I want you to jes' barely touch it.
Touch it jes' a little bit,
Jes' somethin' or 'nother like a fraction.

And so on until Henry Truvillion chants:

Now you'll have to put yo' guns on yo' shoulders an' come by me,
An' come in a hurry,
Come trottin',
Come laughin',
Come like you goin' to git paid for it.
Git a move on you! [shouting]

An' go by the water-tank an' git yo' some water,
Git you' linin' bars an' git yo' back-breakin' holts,
Th'ow it North! Th'ow it North!

Leader and gang sing:

Yeah—
In the *mornin'* when you *rise,*
Pick an' *shevil* by yo *side.*

In the *mornin'* when you *rise,*
Got a *pain* in yo' *side.*

Henry Truvillion talking:

Now, boys, put yo' guns on yo' shoulders an' git back in the shade.

But the men who drive the spikes that fasten the long, steel rails to the wooden ties sing the most thrilling tune of all—the hammer song, the song of the long, ten-pound hammer with its two heads, scarcely more than a couple of inches in diameter, that is swung free from the shoulder in a complete circle about the head (the rainbow round the shoulder was a full arc—a John Henry hammer in rapid motion), that song with its own vibrant and stirring tune:

Oh, ring, ol' hammer,
Hammer ring!
Ringin' on the buildin',
Hammer ring!
This ringin' like jedgement,
Hammer ring!
Doncha hear dat hammer?
Hammer ring! (etc. etc.)

One spike, with two strikers, would be driven home long before these verses were sung.

Another kindred railroad song grew out of directions chanted by the foreman of a gang lifting the heavy steel rails from a flat-car to the ground, or lifting the rails from the ground back on the car, or placing them in two parallel lines of track.

Again Henry Truvillion is ready with graphic directions. His voice ringing like steel, never repeating himself, his collected calls would make a grand opera. Hear him as he deals ton-and-a-half, thirty-three foot rails, in the language of a card shark, the men, meantime, lifting to their shoulders the heavy bars of steel, walking to a flat-car and dumping them in:

> We got a carload of steel to load here now.
> Now, this is ninety-pound steel, thirty-three foot rails,
> An' we don't want to lose nary finger.
> (Course they's plenty mo' in the market down yander,
> But they don't fit like these.)
> This here's a good way to git a laig broke,
> A good way to git somebody killed,
> If you don't pay 'tention to what I tells you.
> The first man to let go contrary to what I says,
> I'm gonna run him away from here.
> You understan' that, now, don't you?
> You all pay strict 'tention to me.
> Now, now, come on now, all of you git in [His voice goes louder]
> Git up and down there.
> You see this here rail right here?
> Now git yo' han's on it.
> Git right ready now.
> Now when this man right here kneels, you all grab it,
> Jes' like a cat will a hot hoe-cake,
> Jes' grab it like you were goin' to grab somethin' what wuz good to
>   eat.

[Shouting]
Catch my deal!
Break off in the quarter down there.
Take up all along.
Now walk up to the car, boys,
Steady yo'self,
Th'ow it away!
That's good iron—
I heard it ring!

Come on back a-walkin',
Now come a-trottin',
Come a-lopin',
It's gittin' away over toward dinner-time.
Look at that crazy nigger over there,
Puttin' his foot on it—git up in there!
Pick it up! Th'ow it over!

De—al! [shouting]
Break off in the quarter down there,
E—asy! Lawd!
My wife's scared of thunder!
Th'ow it away!
'Twuz good iron—
I heard it ring!

Go on back an' git another,
Come on—boys,
The Capting's settin' down yander with his book an' his pencil
Checkin' on them rails as they hits the groun'.
Jes' let a rail bit the groun' [Now Henry is unloading a car]
'Bout once every minute

[Shouting]
Break off in the quarter down there,

Turn an' walk.
Come on all the way over here,
Come on, Stonewall, I'm lookin' at you.
Git yo' hands on it, boys,
Bear-hug it.

Put one hand over it
An' put yo' other under it.
Now pick it up.
That's what I'm talkin' about.
Now walk up to the car,
Th'ow it away!
That's good steel—
I heard it ring!

From the Negro have also come songs of labor as he loaded and unloaded steamboats, built the levees or delved in the mines, cut the canals, dug a path for the railroad, or transformed a wilderness into cultivated fields. That all these results of human endeavor have been effected with rhythmic accompaniment, that the sweat and grime and toil and heave have been canopied by music, that this music, part of it touchingly tender, has been the product of this labor, should inspire some poet to create a mighty epic as a tribute to the men of toil who helped to build America.

In our ballad books, Alan Lomax and I have attempted, by words, music and spoken directions, to translate what we saw and heard of Negro work songs. From Henry Truvillion we secured a most complete group of railroad songs. His authentic and artistic mastery of this medium has been long recognized by his employers for its economic value; though he does no manual labor, his pay check is greater than that of his companions.

I first met Henry Zweifel when I walked into his office in the Aviation Building in Fort Worth to volunteer my services in support of his effort to elect Orville Bullington Governor of Texas. During a month's close association in that campaign he often invited me to spend a week-end at his country home at Fort Spunky. "It's in Abby Bend, north of George's Creek," he explained, "just across the Brazos River from Comanche Peak." But I never could spare the time to go. As we later discovered, the political job we had on hand was too much, even for the energy and resources of Henry Zweifel. It's a hard task to elect a Republican Governor in Texas, although Bullington did get over 300,000 votes.

More than two years after that busy summer, I drove out the highway leading from Glenrose to Cleburne until I reached a certain filling station. There I turned north over a bumpy country road which dipped down every little while into the beds of numerous creeks running out of the hills into the Brazos River. Finally the "fork hand" side roads grew so numerous that I stopped and inquired of a lady who sat on the back porch of a house blackened by age. "Keep straight ahead fur about a quarter," she called back; "then turn to the left fur a mile and a half; then take the right hand and keep on goin' as fur as you kin." I drove on across two creeks with "living water" into a sandy country, through post-oak woods, next a gate, two more square turns, then past an unfinished driveway on by a white stone house. High up above the second story on the side of this house next to the road glowed a large crimson neon light sign, "Bar Z," the ranch cattle brand. I knew this was the end of my journey; I had at last reached Henry Zweifel's ranch headquarters.

Henry was not at home. Instead I was met by Will, the white-jacketed, former Pullman car Negro cook and house-boy, who greeted me with faultless manners and with words of welcome phrased in English almost as faultless. The big high-ceilinged living room into which he ushered me, with five-foot oak logs crackling in the wide fireplace, made me realize why Henry Zweifel loved his country home. For a time it became for me a sort of second home. From the windows of my room upstairs I could see the lights shining from numerous log dwellings of his men and their families set back in the trees. I caught the gleam of white curtains in some of the windows in contrast to the dark post-oak logs chinked with straight white lines of cement. And just outside of these windows tall flowering cosmos swayed in the wind. To me that night Fort Spunky seemed near to fairyland.

Henry came in for supper, after which he sent for his people to sing for the Library of Congress collection of folk tunes. Some few of his visitors were descendants of old residents of the Brazos Bend country, though many more belonged to the drifting tenant farmer class caught in the eddy of Abby Bend. The big comfortable living room was filled with the men and their families. Henry Zweifel presided as a cordial and genial host. He was good enough to start off the evening by consenting to be the first performer before the microphone. He also introduced the singers. All that was said went down on the records, so that they would give the whole effect of the evening's entertainment. Henry began in his deep voice, as if lecturing his crowd:

"'Way on in the wee hours of the morning, after you have lost three dollars in a poker game, here's the way you feel:

[Henry sings]

"I went up on the mountain
And I give my horn a blow
I told 'em I was comin' back
But I was comin' slow.

"After the game breaks you get your old horse and buggy and start home; you go drivin' up to the water trough—an' here's what happens:

[Henry sings]

"I drove my horse to the water trough
And he wouldn't drink and he wouldn't back off,
That worries me
Oh, that worries me.

"Then in the morning you go up on the hillside to do a little huntin; and you sing:

[Henry sings]

"My old fiddle, tuned up good,
Is the best old fiddle in the neighborhood.

"That was rotten," said Henry, as the crowd laughed and agreed with him. But the ice was broken as I played back his talk and singing. All became eager to help.

We began by making records of calling dogs, hog calling, and cattle calling, Henry acting as interlocutor and introducer.

"You get outside the cowlot gate and start calling like this:

"Sook calf, sook calf, sook calfie,
Sook calf, sook calf!

"And then the little calf comes running out of the brush down to the barn.

"Then when you want to call the old cow up late in the evening just before dark you say, to call her a short distance: 'Soo-ok, soo-ok, soo-ok, cow.' If she's off a little further way from the barn, you'll say: 'Whoo-oh, whoo-oh, whoo-oh.'

"Then if she's clear out of sight, or off in the meadow somewhere, you'll get your voice a little higher." Here Henry let his voice out on the "whoo-oh" call until the dogs outside began to bark.

Then came the others, ambitious to excel their boss.

"All right, David, you belch up something. You call the cows up for salt." And David came through in fine style, repeating the last call with variations.

"Now, Dan, you call them cows up like you do when you go to feed 'em that cake early in the mornin'." And Dan did his part.

"All right now, Jess, you call the cows like you call them when you go down into the pecan orchard or the Bermuda patch and want to call them up for salt, to find out if there is any worms among them, or find out if there's anything needed to be done to take care of the range cattle." Jess Wylie is ranch foreman, and Jess showed off his longer experience.

"All right, Mr. Roberts, call up the hogs." (On the Zweifel ranch there are about three hundred pigs who get fat in the fall on pecans and acorns.)

Shouted Mr. Roberts in a voice to admit no rival:

"Pig-oo, pig-oo, pig-oo, who-oo,
Pig-oo, oo-oh, pig-oo-oo-oh,
Pig, pig!!"

Henry again led off in the dog calling contest by talking to his shy pup, Spot, calling him the finest little dog in the Abby Bend country.

"Now, Mr. Roberts, I want you to call your dogs up from a distance and tell the folks how you get 'em to you and how you get 'em ready to go hunting." Mr. Roberts responded with: "He-ah, he-ah, he-ah, heah-heah," repeated and ending in a long "he-oh-ah."

"Now, Mr. Jonathan, you just call your dogs from under the floor like you're going to get ready to go off in the woods squirrel hunting, and tell the folks how you get 'em out from under the house and how you start 'em off."

Mr. Jonathan added to the regular "he-ah" some cajoling admonitions, "Git to 'em over there! Go on! Git to 'em."

"Mr. Wylie, you call your dogs from under the floor and send 'em down to the potato patch and get them hogs out."

Sharper and more urgent calls; calls that would move the laziest hound pup.

"All right, now," said Henry to me, "we'll give you an imitation of the dogs goin' out into the woods and strikin' a coon's trail."

Pandemonium, each man and boy imitating the cries of a pack of hounds in a hot chase. I afterward recorded from this company a group of folk songs, including the American versions of two long old English ballads. This is the full list:

The Gol-darn Wheel—Natural Born Rancher—
Cotton Picking Song—Billy Barlow—
The Brown Girl—Mollie—The Drunkard's Dream—
The Blackbirds on the Rush—That's the Way

With the Texians—Hog Drovers—Pretty Little Pink—
If One Won't Another Will—Old Man Bugger—
Old Blue—High Loping Cowboy—Truthful Bill—
Green Corn—The Rambling Boy—Zebra Dun—
Cole Younger—Strawberry Roan—Dead Man's Walk.

Bud Wylie, the foreman, in concluding this delightful evening, sang a song for children that I never before had heard. With its pretty tune, it deserves wide circulation:

"Let's go huntin'," says Risky Rob,
"Let's go huntin'," says Robin-de-Bob,
"Let's go huntin'," says Dan'l and Joe,
"Let's go huntin'," says Billy Barlow.

"What shall we hunt?" says Risky Rob,
"What shall we hunt?" says Robin-de-Bob,
"What shall we hunt?" says Dan'l and Joe,
"What shall we hunt?" says Billy Barlow.

"Go hunt rats," says Risky Rob,
"Go hunt rats," says Robin-de-Bob,
"Go hunt rats," says Dan'l and Joe,
"Go hunt rats," says Billy Barlow.

"How shall we kill 'em?" says Risky Rob,
"How shall we kill 'em?" says Robin-de-Bob,
"How shall we kill 'em?" says Dan'l and Joe,
"How shall we kill 'em?" says Billy Barlow.

"Go borry a gun," says Risky Rob,
"Go borry a gun," says Robin-de-Bob,
"Go borry a gun," says Dan'l and Joe,
"Go borry a gun," says Billy Barlow.

"How shall we haul 'em?" says Risky Rob,
"How shall we haul 'em?" says Robin-de-Bob,
"How shall we haul 'em?" says Dan'l and Joe,
"How shall we haul 'em?" says Billy Barlow.

"Go borry a cart," says Risky Rob,
"Go borry a cart," says Robin-de-Bob,
"Go borry a cart," says Dan'l and Joe,
"Go borry a cart," says Billy Barlow.

"How shall we divide 'em?" says Risky Rob,
"How shall we divide 'em?" says Robin-de-Bob,
"How shall we divide 'em?" says Dan'l and Joe,
"How shall we divide 'em?" says Billy Barlow.

"I'll take shoulder," says Risky Rob,
"I'll take side," says Robin-de-Bob,
"I'll take ham," says Dan'l and Joe,
"Tail bone mine," says Billy Barlow.

"How shall we cook 'em?" says Risky Rob,
"How shall we cook 'em?" says Robin-de-Bob,
"How shall we cook 'em?" says Dan'l and Joe,
"How shall we cook 'em?" says Billy Barlow.

"I'll boil shoulder," says Risky Rob,
"I'll fry side," says Robin-de-Bob,
"I'll bake ham," said Dan'l and Joe,
"Tail bone suck," said Billy Barlow.

But the song which has caught the ear of the American public, of those that I found that evening, is the song about a dog, *Old Blue*, who "Died so hard he shook the ground."

"Blue, what makes your eyes so red?"
"I've run them possums till I'm almost dead."

Old Blue died, I laid him in the shade,
I dug his grave with a silver spade.

I let him down with a golden chain,
Link by link slipped through my hand.

There is only one thing that bothers my mind,
Blue went to heaven, left me behind.

When I get there, first thing I'll do,
Grab me a horn and blow for old Blue.

Chorus: (Varied in wording to fit the stanza.)
Saying, "Come on, Blue, boo-hoo."

11

SOME INTERESTING PEOPLE

At the A. & M. College of Texas, where I first began active folksong collecting, I came to know Uncle Dan, who drove a span of big gray mules hitched to a dray. Uncle Dan and his mules did all the campus hauling, and once a week called for garbage. He was a grizzled, kindly Negro, and I enjoyed talking with him. We became good friends.

When Christmas came around I made eggnog with no one to drink with me. Uncle Dan grew more sweet potatoes than he could use. He liked eggnog as I liked sweet potatoes. So Christmas morning regularly brought us together on my back porch with a foaming bowl of wonderful nectar between us, a sack of sweet potatoes lying under the table. Uncle Dan always insisted on doing his part.

One Christmas day after I had filled Uncle Dan's glass for the third or fourth time, he became talkative. Only one daughter was left at his home. His "passel" of boys had scattered.

"Do you know where they are?" I asked.

"I know where one is," cautiously replied Uncle Dan.

"Where is he?"

"Up at Mumford in the chain gang."

Silence, and another round of drinks.

"Uncle Dan, I know that you are a useful person around the College. You and your gray mules for many years have been doing favors for everybody. All the folks like you. But how do they show it? Have they given you a title when there are so many titles floating around? Now we have the President of the College, Professors, Assistant Professors, Instructors, Student Assistants, the Commandant, Colonels, Captains, Lieutenants, Sergeants, Corporals, Privates, Chaplains, Farm Superintendents, Steward of the Mess Hall, and so on and so on. Everybody seems to have a title but you."

"But I has a title," interrupted Uncle Dan, a bit woozily, perhaps.

"And what is your title, I'd like to know?"

"I'se de Filter of de College," declared Uncle Dan. "I thought it up myself."

"How did you figure that out?"

"Don't I haul off all de filth?" said Uncle Dan.

A few miles away from College Station runs the Brazos River. The broad bottomlands of that river were covered with large cotton plantations. There one day in 1908 behind lowered curtains in the home of a bachelor overseer I first saw jazz danced between the sexes. Even this rough man was unwilling to allow the public to know that he permitted young Negroes to dance in the postures now accepted as a matter of course in barrel-houses and honkytonks in cities of the South. I discovered at this time the "Ballet of the Boll Weevil," Dink's "Fare You Well, Oh Honey," and many "blues." Carl Sandburg, whom I place first among all present amateur folk singers, uses regularly the first two songs on his programs. He says that Dink's song reminds him of Sappho.

I found Dink washing her man's clothes outside their tent on the bank of the Brazos River in Texas. Many other similar tents stood around. The black men and women they sheltered belonged to a levee-building outfit from the Mississippi River Delta, the women having been shipped from Memphis along with the mules and the iron scrapers, while the men, all skillful levee-builders, came from Vicksburg. A white foreman volunteered: "Without women of their own these levee Negroes would have been all over the bottoms every night hunting for women. That would mean trouble, serious trouble. Negroes can't work when sliced up with razors."

The two groups of men and women had never seen each other until they met on the river bank in Texas where the white levee contractor gave them the opportunity presented to Adam and Eve—they were left alone to mate after looking each other over. While her man built the levee, each woman kept his tent, toted the water, cut the firewood, cooked, washed his clothes and warmed his bed. Down on the dumps nearer the river clouds of drifting dust swirled from the feet of moving mules and from piles of shifted earth, while the shouts of the muleskinners sometimes grouped themselves into long-drawn-out couplets with a semi-tune—levee camp hollers:

> I looked all over the corral,
> Lawd, I couldn't find a mule with his shoulder well.
> Lawd, they won't 'low me to beat 'em,
> Got to beg 'em along.

But Dink, reputedly the best singer in the camp, would give me no songs. "Today ain't my singin' day," she would reply to my urging. Finally a bottle of gin, bought at a nearby plantation commissary, loosed her muse. The bottle of liquor soon disappeared. She sang, as she scrubbed her man's dirty clothes, the pathetic story of a woman deserted by her lover when she needs him most—a very old story. Dink ended the refrain with a subdued cry of despair and longing— the sobbing of a woman deserted by her man:

> One o' dese days, an' it won't be long,
> You call my name an' I'll be gone.
> Fare-you-well, O honey, fare-you-well!

> 'Member one night, a-drizzlin' rain,
> 'Round my heart I felt a pain,
> Fare-you-well, O honey, fare-you-well!

I got a man an' he's long an' tall,
Moves his body like a cannon ball,
Fare-you-well, O honey, fare-you-well!

When I wore my apron low,
Couldn't keep you from my do'.
Fare-you-well, O honey, fare-you-well!

Now I wears my apron high,
Sca'cely ever see you passin' by.
Fare-you-well, O honey, fare-you-well!

Now my apron's up to my chin,
You pass my do' an' you won't come in.
Fare-you-well, O honey, fare-you-well!

If I'd 'a' listened to what Mamma said,
I'd 'a' been sleepin' in my Mamma's bed.
Fare-you-well, O honey, fare-you-well!

If I had wings like Norah's dove,
I'd fly up de river to de man I love.
Fare-you-well, O honey, fare-you-well!

And while Dink sang this song in the Brazos bottoms of Texas, as she washed her temporary man's clothes, her little two-year-old nameless son played in the sand at her feet. "He ain't got no daddy, an' I ain't had no time to hunt up a name for him," she explained.

"Do you love this new man of yours, Dink?" I asked. She scrubbed a garment vigorously on the wooden washboard as she answered: "Some o' dese days I'm a-goin' to take all dat man's clothes an' put 'em in dis washtub an' get 'em good an' soakin' wet. Den I'm goin' to roll up dese wet clothes in a gob an' cover de pile up right nice in de middle o' de bed—smooth down de covers, an' stick 'em all in 'round de edges. Den I'm goin' on off up de river."

And Dink sang again:

De worry blues ain't bad, some folks say;
Take a long freight train wid a red caboose to carry my worry blues
    away.
When my heart struck sorrow, de tears come a-rollin' down.

Suddenly she threw back her head and laughed a joyous, carefree laugh, and added in different motif and tone (by this time the gin was taking effect):

All you long-lived skinners better learn how to skin,
For de Louisiana skinners is on de road agin'.
Git on de road, git on de road,
Ev'y big nigger got to git on de road.

And then she added: "Takes a long, tall, teasin' brown to satisfy my soul."

A few months ago I inquired about Dink at Yazoo City, Mississippi, her home, she had told me. "Done planted up there," said a Negro woman, pointing to a nearby tree-clad hill. I could see a few slabs of marble shining through the low green foliage. Dink had sung me a spiritual about a lonesome graveyard, with the refrain: "I wouldn't mind dyin' if dyin' was all!"

My friend, the banker at Jasper, Texas took me to see Uncle Billy Macree, who claimed to be 117 years old. First, we opened a gate at the end of a lane, went down a path with sweet-potato vines growing on either side, then through another gate to the big house. Although he owned the land about the big house, Uncle Billy lived in a little log cabin in the back yard, shaded by persimmon and chestnut trees. We found him seated in a split-bottom chair in front of his cabin. I could see at once that Uncle Billy was impressed by a visitor introduced by the President of the First National Bank. My friend went away, and Uncle Billy and I talked long after the sun was hidden behind the big trees that shaded his home.

"How many children have you, Uncle Billy?"
"Thirty-five."

"How many boys?"

"Eighteen."

"How many girls?"

"Oh, I never could count up them girls," said Uncle Billy.

Only "the twins," middle-aged men, were at home. The others were "jes' scattered."

"I was a singer and dancer and patter when I was a boy, and I'm a good footman right now. I can do ev'y kind of dancing on my head and on my toes. I was a boy . . . that was long ago, in slavery times. But songs, no, I can't remember none but short ones."

Jaybird pullin' the turning plow;
"Sparrow, where was you?"
"Legs so little and awful small
'Fraid they'd break in two."

Later he spent two evenings in my hotel room and sang in his thin piping voice some "play tunes" from slavery days. He spoiled a record by jumping to his feet and beginning to dance in the most dramatic moment of a song. Even his patting feet on a shaky floor injured the quality of other records. He was a bit timid of the microphone, and talked and sang most freely when we were seated under the shade in front of his cabin. A hundred feet away stood a massive oak with an umbrella-shaped top.

"One evening I shot a big turkey gobbler out of that tree—a wild turkey at that," Uncle Billy said. "He brought his flock in from the woods to roost. Out from the settlement they was many wildcats and pant'ers to bother Mr. Turkey. He knowed that too," Uncle Billy chuckled, "I was a great hunter. In my time, I have killed 550 deer with a rifle while they were runnin'." Uncle Billy seemed proud of the fact that he kept three beds for himself, all of which he insisted that I inspect. They were clean and comfortable. "I goes from one to the other when I feels restless," he said. "But the little cabin bed I likes best. I always starts off in it."

Despite his claim to great age there seemed to be plenty of life in the old fellow. He was small—though in his youth he had been a "log roller"—springy like a cricket, alert intelligence in his keen black eyes. Before his cabin door as we sat smoking and talking often passed young Negro women, roomers in the "big house," perhaps, or simply callers curious about the persistent white visitor.

"Uncle Billy," I said, "the wise men of old tell us of a time in all our lives when the grinders cease because they are few! I notice you can't talk very well because all your 'grinders' are gone except two tusks. But the almond tree does not flourish with you, for I see you have few gray hairs; nor has the grasshopper become a burden, for you yet cultivate your own patch of ground and grow collards and tomatoes and sweet potatoes and goobers. But, Uncle Billy, when you look at these blooming young Hebes around here, what I want to know is, as the Good Book says, has 'desire failed'?"

"Of course not," said Uncle Billy firmly.

"But you are more than a hundred years old. I—"

He interrupted me with a story: "When I was seventeen years old my master one winter sent me up into the Indian Territory to look after a herd of cattle. An Indian Medicine Man told me that when I got old he had a remedy for me. I'se 'membered what the Indian said, and I'se had no trouble a-tall. I'se got some of that medicine now. It's just a few feet from where you are settin'."

"Lead me to it, Uncle Billy."

Inside the shed room to his sleeping quarters stood a large icebox. From this icebox Uncle Billy took a half-gallon fruit jar full of a dark liquid covering a dozen or more white objects reaching from bottom to top of the jar.

"What's in the jar, Uncle Billy?"

"Good rye whiskey," he said.

"But what have you got in the whiskey?"

"Bull-nettle roots!" he answered proudly. "Two drinks of this tonic ev'y week keeps me in fine condition."

As a barefoot boy I had been stung by bull-nettles many times, and I often had plowed up the white roots that Uncle Billy showed me in his magic tonic.

Just across the street from the Funeral Home in Columbia, South Carolina, stands a saloon and dance hall for Negroes; over the front of it is a large painted red apple. Below a sign reads "The Big Apple" underneath a rhyme: "Ale and beer, full of good cheer."

"We get a good deal of business from that place," said the assistant Funeral Director to me as we sat and chatted on the steps of the Funeral Home, a structure completely covered with ivy. He recalled that the dance hall not always had been known by its present name.

"Several years ago," he explained, "a Negro in the dance hall was showing his girl a new dance step. Soon their dancing attracted attention. One of the boys went over and asked him what he and his friend called the dance.

"We call it the Big Apple," was his reply.

"Quickly all the dancers were practicing the new step. Then the students of South Carolina University took it up, and the dance spread all over the country. So the owner of the dance hall gave his establishment its new name."

D. W. White, a Negro laborer, worked two days to bring his group of singers together in the chapel of the Funeral Home, where they were accustomed to sing for any funeral managed by the Home. Here their singing was spontaneously unaffected.

"What will you sing first tonight?" I asked the leader. "I never knows till I stand up," he explained.

"Don't forget that I want another record of 'Honey in the Rock,'" I told him. "I'll git to that," he said; but it took him a long time.

More than two years before Miss Terrill and I had recorded several spirituals sung by the Funeral Choir. It was a stifling hot night in August. The machine was in need of repair, the singers listless. But I had not forgotten the thrill of "Honey in the Rock."

The singers, twelve women and seven men, remained seated while they sang. Suddenly the leader stood up and raised his hand. Silence instantly followed. Without announcing the song, he blared forth on "Gonna Be a Time," with the choir following close behind. Nowhere in my experience have I found so powerful a voice as D. W. White's. He led twelve songs at its tip-top. I returned to the far corner of the room with my microphone, yet still the needle slammed crazily about. Nor were matters helped much when I turned the face of the microphone away from him. Naturally the choir followed him and sang out too loud for my small microphone.

Yet I have always found that suggestions to folksingers, changes in their manner of rendition, are unfortunate—sometimes disastrous. It is better to turn them loose. At least you capture the spirit of their singing. In this instance, my patience was rewarded. Finally, after ten new spirituals, the choir leader gave me "Honey in the Rock." D. W. White said that his choir could sing more than a hundred spirituals. In this regard, it is noteworthy that this unique group comes entirely from working people, including several Negro washerwomen, and they use no books.

"I'm nearly ninety-four. That's getting pretty old. I had some heart trouble last winter—smothering spells. When one would come on, I would take just enough raw whiskey to reach my windpipe. It would make me feel better." The old man peered at me as if he were anxious to read my mind. We were sitting on his front porch as twilight fell. My car was parked out in front where I had left it when I came in to ask him for a night's lodging. Behind in the kitchen I could hear sounds that suggested fried chicken for supper.

"During the war I was a courier for Jeb Stuart," the old man rambled on. "Early one morning after riding all night I brought him some dispatches from General Lee. I was tired and sleepy as I stood there, waiting for orders after General Stuart had read the dispatches. He looked up presently and said, 'Wait, young fellow, you look all tuckered out; I've got something that will do you good!' Then he brought me a long, stiff toddy. As I drank it, the General was busy over the fire. Presently he handed me a plate with two fried eggs on it, and a big, sizzling slab of ham. Maybe I'm the only private that Jeb Stuart ever cooked breakfast for.

"Anyhow, I fought on through the war. When General Lee surrendered, me and my partner swam the river and got away on our horses into the mountains and headed for Texas. There's a song about

The Unreconstructed Rebel. That's me. I never have surrendered and I never will."

Then the old man chanted:

I fought with old Bob Lee for three years thereabout,
Got wounded in six places and starved at Point Lookout,
I caught the rheumatism a-fightin' in the snow,
But I killed a chance of Yankees and I wish I'd killed some mo'.

Three hundred thousand Yankees is dead in Southern dust,
We got three hundred thousand before they conquered us;
They died of Southern fever, of Southern steel and shot—
I wish there wuz three millions instead of what we got!

I don't ax any pardon for what I was or am;
I won't be reconstructed and I don't give a damn!

Suddenly he broke off: "I don't like the way your car is parked. Come and we'll put it back."

"It's locked," I said, "besides, there is nothing of value in it."

But he insisted. So I drove the car after him as he guided me around the house. As he walked ahead of me, I noticed he leaned far forward as he walked. Age and farm work had so stiffened his back, the vertebrae seemed grown together.

But his step was alert and vigorous. With his help my car was safely lodged for the night. When I looked up from locking it, he gave me a significant wink, crooked his index finger over his shoulder, motioning me to follow him. The path led by the kitchen, into the window of which, where his wife was cooking supper, he glanced nervously as we slipped along toward the springhouse. I was not certain where I was going, but I was willing to be a side partner to an ex-courier for Jeb Stuart, especially one who remained unreconstructed. The "springhouse" was full of worn-out farm machinery. I followed my companion down a long alley around two corners and finally we came to a big box with a swinging top. This top the nonagenarian threw back, revealing at the rear of the box an empty five-gallon kerosene oil container, the kind that Standard Oil sold in earlier years, from which were filled the lamps of farmers and ranchmen. My guide reached into the open mouth of this can and drew out a quart bottle full of clear fluid.

"That's rye," he said, "good, safe bootleg. I've been drinking it for ten years, and it hasn't hurt me. You didn't say anything when I was talking to you on the gallery, but from the way you looked I thought you would enjoy a drink."

I took a swig. He followed suit. A pause; then another round. "No more," I said, as he insisted in the hearty style of a Virginia gentleman. "In the morning," he adventured, "I get up early and milk eight cows. Before I start I come by and take a little nip. After I get through milking, I take another nip. You can join me either or both times. Or, since you know the way, you can refresh yourself at any time you wish."

He lowered his voice, looked toward the kitchen and added apologetically, "Because of certain domestic reasons, which I am sure you and every gentleman will understand, I am compelled to be a little quiet with my drams. You see, although I'm ninety-four and have lived with my wife for sixty years, she keeps on being afraid that I'm going to fill a drunkard's grave. Let's have one drink more to the sunny slopes of long ago."

"My mother taught me the tune to 'The Romish Lady' long before I knew all the words," said Mrs. Emma Floyd of Murrels Inlet, South Carolina. "I caught up tunes easy when I was a little thing. But I couldn't find anybody could tell me all the words straight through until I was a big girl, about grown.

"Way years ago, a lady got bad burnt. She lived in the woods way up the road from us. She was burnt awful bad, the worst I ever saw. And her husband, he was so old, and so bad crippled that he wasn't any good to help her; in fact, he was laid up in bed most of the time himself. Mother said one day we ought to go up there, and Pappy said we ought to go up there, too. We didn't have no money, nor nothing much to eat, except just enough to keep skin and bones together for all of us children. Well, Mother looked around, and she said she guessed anybody that was bad burnt could use some clean rags. So she got a big bundle of clean rags together. And I took 'em up there.

"Well, when I got there, it was the awfullest pitiful sight I ever saw. I was ashamed I didn't have no money nor even anything to eat with me. But as soon as the lady saw me, she said, 'The Lord sent you.'

"'No,' says I. 'Just my mother and daddy sent you some old clean rags.'

"'If they'd sent a ten dollar bill, it couldn't be better,' she said like she meant it.

"Well, I stayed on that day to sort o' clean up and cook 'em a little something to eat. Then they seemed to need somebody to nurse 'em so bad that I just stayed on for a spell. I was going to be married the next week, but I just put that off; and I stayed on there twelve weeks, all time putting off the wedding that much longer. And I guess it'd 'a' been just as well if I had put it off for always.

"The lady had a lot of books, most of 'em religious books and hymn books. One of 'em was called *Christian Harmony Note Book*, as I recollect the name. It had 'The Romish Lady' in it. And that's where I learned the rest of the words. I had plenty of time to learn 'em and sing in the evenings. I don't know what I would have done without my tune-singing, and the burnt lady said she didn't know what they would have done neither without me a-singing. I sure was glad to learn the rest of 'The Romish Lady.'"

Charlie Cason and I had planned a foolish undertaking. We were walking from the rim of the Grand Canyon in Arizona to the Colorado River and back by way of Bright Angel Trail. When we started, the river they said was a mile below us, straight down. The winding, dusty trail we took meandered, as I recall, ten miles to the river, with the same distance—only farther—back up the steep way. The clouds of dust from the shuffling feet of mule trains traveling the same trail added at least fifty per cent to the distance. In the late afternoon we heard groans from the miserable riders—old maid school teachers, sore, shaken, faces begrimed with dust which they were too tired to wipe away—pictures of absolute wretchedness. Two fainted and fell from their patient mules the day we went down, and were carried back to the top on stretchers. The August sun did not prevent Cason and me from skipping down the first two or three miles like a couple of young boys out for a morning lark. Then gradually came the heat and the pull of muscles doing an unaccustomed task with wearying repetition. Down, down, down, never a restful step upward or on the level. The thermometer rose a degree with each hundred feet descent. About halfway to the river we came to a ranch house. The door to the kitchen stood invitingly open. "May we have a drink of water?" said Cason to the man, busy over a crowded cookstove.

"Nothin' doin'," the cowboy returned cheerfully. "I haul all my water five miles from the creek. Run on down and help yourself. It's free and plentiful; it's just got in from the snow-covered peaks of the Rocky Mountains."

He grinned and then turned to stir a bubbling pot of beans.

"It's 120 degrees in the shade and I'm all tuckered out," muttered Cason. Then to the cowboy: "May we rest in the shade of your house?"

"Until the centipedes and the tarantulas and the vinegarroons come out to flirt with the Evening Star, recline on my shaded sward and be damned to you. I'll be out to see you presently while my beans are doing the slow-bubble jazz." Again our friend grinned happily as he waved us from his doorway.

Presently out he came to where two tired, disillusioned hikers, stretched flat on the ground, were deciding that the Colorado River could run safely along without further exertion on their part. We yearned only for the comfortable inn just up the hill, at least ten thousand miles distant if traveled then on our tired feet and strained tendons.

The cowboy squatted on the ground, resting his weight on the high heels of his Mexican boots. Balancing himself neatly and delicately on this precarious perch, he reached over, plucked a blade of grass, drew it between his teeth, and pulled out his stopper. That we

were in no humor to "arger" made no difference. "Where you from?"
"Nashville, Tennessee," growled Cason. (No show of interest.)
"Austin, Texas," said I. (For an instant the blade of grass stopped in
its see-saw journey.)

"Never have been to Texas. Always traveled some other direction. Want to get out that way sometime. You never heard of a fellow
named Lomax down there, have you?"

"John Lomax in persona," Cason pointed at me.

The gentle rocking motion of the cowboy ceased. He flung away
the blade of grass, fixed me with his eye for a moment. Then he rose
abruptly and went into the house. Presently he came back and thrust
a book into my hands, the yellow-backed first edition of my *Cowboy
Songs*.

"Did you do that?" he demanded.

"He's guilty," Cason interrupted. (Maybe Cason was hoping that
he would get off after I was shot.)

But—

"Fellers, my humblest apologies. Your servant now and forever.
Come in and partake of my homely fare." He bowed low and swept
the ground with his hat. Then twinkling humorously, he chanted the
Western chuck call, similar in meter to Browning's—

The hillside's dew-pearled,
God's in his Heaven,
All's right with the world.

The cowboy's chant was less poetic but momentarily fuller of meaning:

The coffee's on the fire,
The bacon's in the pan,
The beans are in the pot,
Come and git 'em while they're hot.

And did we? Our friend lived alone at the headquarters of a small
cattle ranch in this romantic spot.

The sun was low when we, watered and fed and rested and entertained, plodded on our upward, weary way, leaving that cheerful philosopher standing in the one doorway that faces Bright Angel Trail. I had said finally:

Whiskey is whiskey any way you mix it,
Texas is Texas any way you fix it;
When other good people have gone to bed,
The devil keeps a-workin' in a Texian's head.

"You're damn tootin'," retorted the cowboy.

On my last collecting trip, Alan Lomax sent me a batch of leads which had come to him from his broadcasts for Columbia's American School of the Air. Had I followed all of them, my two-months trip would have run a year or more.

In the midst of the mass of cards one attracted my particular attention. It came from Lottie, Louisiana, a small river-bottom swamp town about fifty miles west of Baton Rouge. Willie George King had written Alan as follows:

"While listening to your Program over my raider i thought i would sent you in a song:

"There is nothing in the jungle is any bader than me.
I am the badest woman ever come out Tenisee;
I sleep with a panther till the break of day;
I caught a tiger-cat in the collar and i ask him what he had to say;
And i wore a rattlesnake for my chain,
And a Negro man for my fob,
And i made a flee catch a train and a seetick grab the mail,
Their is nothing in the jungle any bader than me.
And i shave a gorelor tell he change his nitty, nitty name,
Then i got in my little boat and drifted on down the sea;
And i made a grisly gray lion shake glad hand with me;
Their is nothing in the jungle any bader than me,
I am the badest woman ever come out Tenisee."

"Willie George King" might be the name either of a man or a woman. Lottie, a wide place in the road, fortunately was on a main highway. Beguiled by that unusual letter, down the long, straight Huey Long strip of concrete we drove all the way from Shreveport to Lottie. I was bound to see the person those words described.

Twenty loafers about the two Lottie filling stations had never heard of Willie George King, post office box 115. As the post office was closed for the night, I went to the postmaster's home.

"Yes," said the kind old gentleman, "I know the holder of box 115. She lives near here and runs a sort of boarding house for Negroes [though he didn't say "Negroes."] I'll go along with you and show you the way to her home. But her name isn't Willie George King."

We left my car miles up on the highway, crossed a slough on a swinging, teetering, single-plank bridge walk, poked our way through a thicket of pine shrubs and tall swamp grass and came on a group of cabins. Soon we stood before the landlady, who rented box 115. She peered at me through eyes that needed glasses.

"Are you a detecative man?"

We reassured her.

"I think my stepdaughter's husband who lives up the creek a way, knows where Willie George King is at. She ain't here no mo'."

Then I knew for the first time that Willie George King was a woman.

"Up the creek," after more inquiries about "detecatives," we at last discovered the possible whereabouts of Willie George: "I ain't know exactly, but my husban' done got a letter from her de pas' week. It say she is workin' on de release in Winfield, North Louisiana."

The next day, after driving 150 miles north from Lottie, the first Negro I met in Winfield answered my inquiry:

"Yes, sir, 'bout an hour ago I met Willie George goin' to work." He crawled into my car and we drove down almost impassably rutty streets until finally we came to Willie George's door. None of her neighbors knew where she was "cleaning house for the white ladies." They did know that she lived with her "gentleman friend" in the two-room cabin. An hour later when she walked into the room, after Relief Headquarters had located her, I wondered—as I still wonder—if a six-hundred-mile journey on account of one sentence had been worthwhile.

Pointing to a scar on her neck, Willie George said:

"I had a goiter operation and hurt my vocus so I can't sing good any more."

Her furtive eyes brightening one instant and then suddenly becoming inexpressibly dull, her restless hands, her dignified posture—I could not quite make her out. She told fortunes, sold charms, practiced the voodoo arts.

"When I was eight years old," she said, "my mother hit me so hard with a stick that I ran away up the big road. I never went back home. I walked and walked until I got so hungry I stopped and asked a white woman for something to eat. 'I'll give you this piece of bread for Christ sake,' the woman said. 'Yessum, please put some butter on the bread for God's sake!'"

She could dance and she could sing. A group of dance-hall entertainers gave her board and keep as the child member of the company. She went to "Cuby" and sang in the low honky-tonks until her "vocus" got out of order. All her life she had been a drifter. Her power of throwing herself into a semi-cataleptic state and reciting gibberish stood her in stead both in low dives and in religious meetings. Either strong drink or religious emotion would bring on the fits.

Willie George had had four children, two boys and two girls, all born dead. She claimed to be 101 years old. She sang for us another song:

> Borned by a p'ickly pear,
> Suckled by a grizzly bear,
> Rocked in a cradle with butcher knives,
> Rocked many a man's baby
> (Thought were rockin' their own);
> But I has no father (you know
> I was borned in a p'ickly pear).

"I'se important," she said after she heard her records played.

Father Silva, after helping me to make records of Los Pastores, urged me to be in the back courtyard of the Church of Our Lady of Guadalupe in San Antonio by three o'clock the Sunday following to see him bless the animals. Father Silva, a sub-junior pastor of this church, was an exile from Guadalajara, Mexico, where he had been a professor of mathematics in a Catholic college. Father Tranchese, his superior, did not favor this survival of Indian Paganism. "Superstition, superstition," he whispered to me. But I was curious and interested, and I drove a hundred miles to join the nondescript crowd that filled the courtyard back of the church. Within the same enclosure lived the three priests who directed the worship of 10,000 Mexicans in the slum district of a city where the majority of its citizens come from across the Rio Grande River.

A few well-dressed San Antonians mingled with a motley crowd, many of whom were children. The greater number belonged to the Mexican poorer classes, most of the women and children either carrying household pets in their arms or leading them by strings or ropes. Some of the animals were necessarily in cages. Here and there families of guinea pigs nosed and frittered their time away. From the cages of shivering, subdued-looking canaries came no joyful welcome of the ceremony. Pigeons abounded, various in breed and color. One dear old lady, very small and looking lonely, toothless, with shiny black eyes, had stuffed her pigeon, tail downward, into a brown paper bag. To hold it securely, she had poked its head out of the open end of the bag and then firmly tied a soiled twine string closely about the bag and the neck of the pigeon. A fluted neckband of pink tissue paper partly hid the soiled string. The little old lady held this queer bundle clasped in her arms. Now and then she would glance down at her charge, and once I saw her lean over and whisper to it, as though she were encouraging it to be brave for the approaching ordeal. The pigeon occasionally nodded its head, while its eyes blinked solemnly.

Chickens of every variety, color and size were present. Tiny little girls bore the tiny little biddies that run about the kitchens of many houses. One happy tot held two brown twin chickens, a bit larger than a quail, also decorated with pink tissue neckbands with fluted edges. There were hens galore and a single stately red rooster—as though the masculine members of the barnyard had no special need of priestly mediation. Two tawny ducks, mates, frightened into solemnity, stretched and flapped their wings as if they would like to fly away from the confusion.

Dogs and cats by the hundred could not be induced even by the religious pageantry to bury their hereditary enmity, and fought among themselves; some of the cats, while the strife was fiercest, breaking away and scaling the high board enclosure, outward bound for freedom and safety. Little Mexican boys dangled baby puppies, one in each hand. Usually the small girls carried kittens, all adorned with blue or pink paper necklaces. A handsome, huge wolfhound dashed about, unruly and barking loudly, to the terror of the cat tribe and smaller dogs. Poodles were abundant, some tiny and hairless; according to vague rumors, the basic constituent of Mexican hot dogs. One Boston pug, hugged closely by his boy owner, wore a face so ugly and evil that no amount of holy water could possibly affect it.

The goats came usually in pairs, twisting and butting through the closely massed people. Two drew carts, a driver for each goat riding proudly behind. A venerable Billy stood in dignified quiet, solemnly chewing his undigested breakfast. Running around freely in the crowd, following closely the master of ceremonies was a lovely lamb, half grown in size, its neck banded with a broad green ribbon. The man called her Pacolita. He was busy arranging for the animals and their masters to pass single file in procession for the priest's blessing. Wherever he went, the lamb ran close behind, frisky, enjoying the excitement, sometimes even playfully butting her master in the rear as he stopped to straighten out a tangle in the long line.

The crowd milled about the bleak courtyard, and a cold wind blew from the north. The people kept coming, bringing more and more animals until the sun was low and the wintry day near its end. At last, through this surging mass of men, women, children, dogs, cats, burros, goats, sheep, chickens, ducks, pigeons, guinea pigs, canaries, and other animals, strode tall, lank Father Silva in his long flowing black robes, followed by his aides, two white-robed lads, one carrying a glass bowl of holy water. In his right hand Father Silva held a silver wand, its end a porous sphere perforated with fine holes. When dipped into the bowl this sphere would fill with water which, when the wand was waved vigorously, would fly out in fine spray. He and his attendants stopped near the head of the long, straggling procession, which at once began to move forward. I stood very close to Father Silva.

First came the master of ceremonies with his beautiful lamb. As it passed, Father Silva snapped his wand and dashed some of the holy water in its face, at the same moment chanting his blessing. The lamb dodged and flirted its long tail. (Its master had told me that he had never had the heart to cut the tail off.) Then followed the little old woman with her pink-necked pigeon imprisoned in a paper sack. It took the water without batting one of its starry eyes, while the old woman was muttering prayers over toothless gums through her wrinkled lips. She seemed to hold it dearer as she moved away. Next came miscellaneous groups as ordered by the busy master of ceremonies and busier lamb. The cats pointedly did not like the water. One dog barked as it hit its nose. The solemn and sedate billy goat appeared oblivious of the ablution. I think, also, that Father Silva missed a shot as the big wolfhound dashed by; and the face of the Boston pug, wrinkling its ugly nose at the cold shower, I am sure took on a more sinister expression. But the chickens, the ducks, the guinea pigs and the canaries behaved beautifully. They were attentive, quiet and most respectful. I thought I saw one of the guinea pigs twist its face into a smile, but perhaps I was mistaken. As for the two goldfish in a big glass bowl, I fear for them. They were deep down under when Father Silva sprinkled the bowl. One brown wrinkled old lady near the end of the procession suddenly drew an egg from her bosom and held it out for baptism. Father Silva looked a bit surprised, though he quickly recovered and blessed it, adding the due quota of holy water.

The last animal was sprinkled, and the ceremony ended abruptly. No prayer, benediction or song followed. The crowd drifted away.

"I could not catch the Spanish words of your blessing," I said to Father Silva. "I saw you glance at your ritual. Does the Church officially recognize this custom?"

"Oh, yes," he answered. "And the words I repeated are a prayer to the Lord to bless each animal, to the end that it may fulfill the purpose for which it was created."

"I understand," said I. "The hens should lay more eggs; the canaries sing more sweetly; the goats be more tractable to their drivers; the roosters! . . ." But Father Silva raised his hand, smiled a friendly protest and walked away.

12

MELODIES AND MEMORIES

As I look back on the years of my folksong collecting I do so with mixed emotions. It has been hard work, at times full of disappointment and discouragement, and at other times richly rewarding.

Alan Lomax joined me in 1933, when he was seventeen and had just completed his junior year at the University of Texas. For two years we traveled together, part of the time with Lead Belly. Alan reentered college in 1935, and I took up Iron Head as a traveling companion, Governor Allred of Texas having paroled him to me for six months. Both Lead Belly and Iron Head sang for me when I met groups of Negroes in or out of the penitentiary to show the people what kind of songs I was looking for. Otherwise I could not easily make my hearers understand. Furthermore, the singing of these Negroes always aroused the competitive instinct of the listeners, who would then freely give me their songs to show me how far they could excel those "niggers from Texas."

Lead Belly left me, and Iron Head again found permanent lodging in the penitentiary because of his lifelong disposition to steal. I went on the road again for a year while I served as adviser to the Writers Project on American folk songs.

I married Miss Ruby Terrill July 21, 1934. Nearly three years later she resigned the position as Dean of Women and Associate Professor of Classical Languages at the University of Texas, which she had held for eleven years, and came with me on my journeyings through the South and Southwest. Within a month after she ceased her work teaching Latin and looking after the special interests of three thousand young women at the University of Texas, she was running my recording machine, the sole white woman present in the midst of the clamor of four hundred Negro convicts in the dining room of the Mississippi penitentiary at Parchman. In Florida the superintendent would not permit her inside the prison walls for fear some of the desperate men might seize her and use her as a shield to break out of prison. She traveled with me to make recordings in the mountains of North Carolina, Kentucky and Virginia, along the coasts of South Carolina; to Captain Nye in Akron, Ohio, in Alabama and Mississippi, and very widely in Texas, from Texline in the Panhandle to the Gulf country at Brownsville and Port Arthur. A bookish ballad lover, she soon became an enthusiastic and competent collector whose quiet, unobtrusive manner softened the heart of many a recalcitrant singer.

Early in 1938 I left with my wife and my daughter Bess Brown Lomax for an eight-month stay in Europe. Just before leaving I completely revised my early *Cowboy Songs and Other Frontier Ballads*. The music in this new edition was edited by Mr. Edward N. Waters, Assistant Chief of the Division of Music of the Library of Congress, who also undertook the arduous task of seeing the book through the press in my absence.

I am now able, after thirty-six years, to hold in my hand a copy of the first edition of *Cowboy Songs* recently given to me by my children. Long ago I had given away all the first edition copies that had come to me. Some, perhaps, had been "borrowed" by friends and visitors. A Cleveland, Ohio librarian once told me that she had had to purchase forty copies of *Cowboy Songs* one at a time. Young boys, hurried by the closing of the library, slipped the book under their jackets and forgot to bring it back. This may explain why my royalty check for *Cowboy Songs* has not decreased much through the years.

I have been able to contribute, along with Alan Lomax, to the Archive of American Folk Song of the Library of Congress, more than ten thousand songs on records as we took them down in the field. As I look back on our hasty work I realize that, while we may have got some of the good songs recorded, we have barely touched the stores of folk songs which yet flourish among the people. We have hit only the high places, the plainly apparent source spots. The work is just begun. Many riches have been left untouched, which can be claimed only after systematic and thorough search.

In 1941, seven years after Alan Lomax and I brought out *American Ballads and Folk Songs*, we collaborated on a second volume of general content which we called *Our Singing Country*, with music carefully translated from records by Ruth Crawford Seeger of Washington, D. C. She worked in close co-operation with her husband, Charles Seeger, a distinguished musicologist. Mrs. Seeger in some instances played a record hundreds of times in an effort to attain perfection in her translation of the tune.

After *Our Singing Country* was published we returned to our former home in Dallas, "The House in the Woods," where I have been working on this book and have done much other writing and editorial work. My four children, Shirley, John Jr., Alan and Bess Brown are all scattered and married, with families of their own. Miss Terrill is the housekeeper in my quiet home six miles from Dallas, near the shore of White Rock Lake.

Had space permitted I should have liked to include in this book a chapter on Negro Blues, the old-fashioned Blues in which the singer repeats the first line three times as he sings to his guitar and then finishes with a sort of tour-de-force for the concluding line. Some day, I know, his power of phrasing truisms about his people, his trenchant economy of speech, his final outstanding ability to put into short expressive words his deepest emotions, we shall all recognize as a contribution to literature. Of the world of Blues material extant I have collected a large amount from the South, and I have recorded the music of many of the Negro Blues songs. Nobody has made a thorough study of these songs which Alan calls, by folk definition, simply "a good man feelin' bad" or "trouble on a po' gal's mind" or "the achin' heart disease."

The Negro says, for example, of his woman:

Got a yaller woman, got a brown-skin, Lawd, got a black one too;
My yaller woman don't love me, Lawd, but my black one do.
A dollar's made round, Lawd, goes from hand to hand—
Jes de way dese womens goes from man to man.

She done caught de Rock Island train an' gone;
I don't mind her leavin' me, honey, but she gone so doggone long.

Let me be your sidetrack till your mainline lover comes;
I can do mo' switchin' than yo' main line ever done.

And then he goes repeating, improvising, creating. How much he takes to heart, how deeply his own feelings are involved, no one knows. But he does reach the hearts of his listeners. You see it in their soft faces, you hear it in their muttered comment or in their exclamations of approval.

Then I should have liked to write a chapter about Mrs. Genevieve Chandler of Murells Inlet, whose back door opens on a bay in South Carolina near Sandy Island. On our many visits her cook, Lilly, sang many beautiful spirituals, "Heaven is a Beautiful Place" being one of our favorites. Mom Hagar was there, and the Reverend Aaron Pinnacle, and many another interesting Negro. They sang for me because they love Mrs. Chandler, who is now director of Brookgreen Gardens. She has five children and her "De Wind and de Tide," published several years ago in *Scribner's*, is an incomparable Negro story.

Up at Galax, Virginia, where the Blue Ridge mountains pile up on a corner of that lovely country, we found the Ballard Branch Bogtrotters, a group of natives who, under the leadership of Dr. W. P. Davis, spend their spare hours in preserving the native balladry of that region. They are all musicians. Organized in 1933, the Bogtrotters is composed, actively, of Dr. Davis, Uncle Alex Dunford, Crockett Ward, Fields Ward and Wade Ward. They play and sing three hundred pieces, a lot of them mountain ballads, using the violin, guitar and autoharp. They declare in their constitution that the purpose of the organization is "to collect and help preserve the oldtime folk music and stories." Rendering a program that would play to standing room only in New York, these men with their band visit only mountain towns with their program of "oldtime music, folk songs, folk stories, humorous recitations and clog and flatfoot dances. Old folks come and revive the memories of their youth. Young folks come and learn to love the music of their forefathers, the pioneer songs of a great pioneer race."

For several years Dr. Davis and his Bogtrotters promoted a two-day contest, attended by thousands of mountain singers with music played on homemade zithers, dulcimers, the violin and the guitar. Alan Lomax once took the Bogtrotters to Roanoke, Virginia, where they broadcast an entire program of mountain melodies. This program was a feature of the biweekly folksong program of the American School of the Air of the Columbia Broadcasting System. It would almost require a book rather than a mere chapter to say what should be said about these people.

I wish, too, that I might write chapters on the Gant family as I heard them sing in Austin, Texas, of Aunt Mollie and Uncle Joe McDonald, Mrs. Minta Morgan, Mrs. Louise Henson, Aunt Molly Jackson, Alex Moore, Roscoe Williams, Wee Willie Williams (nearly seven feet tall and big as a mountain), Track Horse, Big Nig, Miss Mary Elizabeth Barnacle, Senator W. J. Bryan, Owen Wister, Stewart Edward White, Black Sampson, Lightnin' (who could think faster than any of his keepers), and hundreds and hundreds of others, both white and black, with whom we had pleasant contacts—and most of our contacts were pleasant.

I'd like to protest again to the educated and the semi-educated Negroes of the South. Almost universally they opposed my project of collecting the folklore and folk songs on the ground that "we have got beyond that." Howard Odum Johnson, reviewing in the *New York Times* our *Negro Songs as Sung by Lead Belly*, praised my work but Tuskegee and other Negro colleges politely refused to allow me to talk to their students.

From the beginning the cowboys who gave me songs met me with frank disbelief in my undertaking and with little respect for the intelligence of a man undertaking the work of collecting such material. But my presence created a diversion in their busy lives. They endured me without having much respect for me. The mountain singers, on the other hand, were always cordial and shared their store of songs with glad abandon. I had no trouble with them. In Louisiana I recall the enthusiasm, especially of the young Creole singers. They soon forgot the clumsy machine and microphone in the sweep of their songs. I think it could be said with equal truth of all the many Mexicans who gave me their songs. Usually uneducated, they sang freely and enthusiastically whenever I called on them.

But the Negro stands quite apart in his relation to folk songs. He is more instinctively musical; he has a larger body of folk material than any or all others of the folk music singers. The lonely field worker, the gangs building levees and railroads, the cook, the housemaid, all sing as they work. They create new songs, new forms of expression while they cheerfully labor. They go singing, singing, all the day even where you would not expect to find music—in the penitentiaries.

I remember Roscoe McLean in the Florida penitentiary. He led all the singing there. For two days he brought the men who could sing to my microphone. We printed two of his work songs in *Our Singing Country*. When I went away he wrote and asked me to get him free, saying that he would travel with me and help me in my search for folk songs. I wrote to the authorities for his record. He was in for sixteen years for armed highway robbery. After serving for only two years he was on a bread and water diet for creating a riot in the dining room. "I'll sit and smoke if you don't help me," he wrote. I could do nothing for him. He had always been what the Southern man calls a "bad nigger." I wrote him that he must wait. Afterward came letters saying that Roscoe was sick with tuberculosis. I went back to Florida to see him. Inside the great high walls surrounding the penitentiary they had built a tall woven-wire fence about a neat cottage where the segregated sick men slept and took sunbaths. Roscoe, dressed in pajamas, came out to the wire fence and whispered to me. His voice was gone. When I had to say goodbye he broke into tears and turned into his quarters without looking back, clutching the money I had given him. Later the warden wrote me that my friend had died. I sent the prison library a copy of *Our Singing Country*, calling attention to Roscoe's two songs and saying that the gift of the book was due to him and his beautiful voice. His voice rang true, like a silver bugle note, as did that of Allen Prothero, the sweet singer of the Nashville penitentiary, who also went the tuberculosis route.

I think also of Doc Reed, of Livingston, Alabama, about whom I have already written and, who, with his cousin, Vera Hall, furnished me with some beautiful spirituals not found in any other community. I promised Doc ten dollars every year at Christmas. He and his wife, having no children of their own, are raising two orphaned children of Doc's dead sister. How he gets food for them Heaven only knows, for the farms in his section produce little of value. And Doc wears proudly a cork leg which he got while working for the WPA.

Doc Reed out in the free world, Roscoe McLean in the penitentiary, are typical of the singers whom I call my friends.

Roscoe McLean is gone now, but only a few weeks ago I saw Doc. He came stumping from his cabin, where he keeps one of my letters nailed over his bed, stood by my car in the road and sang to me in wonderful, tremulous tones:

Angel flew from the bottom of the pit,
Gathered the sun all in her fist;
Gathered the moon all 'round her waist;
Gathered the stars all under her feet;
Gathered the wind all 'round her waist,
Cryin', "Holy Lord,"
Cryin', "Holy Lord,"
Cryin', "Holy my Lord,"
Cryin', "Holy!"

Weep like a willow, moan like a dove,
You can't get to Heaven 'thout you go by love.

INDEX